THE ANHEUSER-BUSCH COOKBOOK

GREAT FOOD GREAT BEER

THE ANHEUSER-BUSCH COOKBOOK

GREAT FOOD GREAT BEER

185 Flavorful Recipes for Pairing Beer with Food

Foreword by
AUGUST A. BUSCH IV

Photography by
NOEL BARNHURST

Sunset

CONTENTS

ANHEUSER-BUSCH HAS A LONG TRADITION of making excellent beer. Our brewing methods have been shaped by a firm and time-honored commitment to quality in everything we do. We take great pride in our craft—and as a result, we provide some of the finest and most popular beers in the world.

Beer is a unique beverage. There's nothing quite as satisfying and refreshing as an ice-cold Budweiser on a hot summer day. At the same time, beer goes just as well when paired with the right food and enjoyed over a leisurely meal with good friends and family. In the pages of this book, the brewmasters of Anheuser-Busch have worked with master chefs to explore some exceptional ways to combine great beer with great food. With this collection of more than 180 flavorful and inventive recipes, they have taken into account the aroma, bouquet, taste, and body of a variety of beer styles—to help you find just the right style to create the perfect dining experience.

At Anheuser-Busch, we believe that beer is part of the good life...and we always say that "making friends is our business." I can't think of a better way to enjoy life than sharing great food and great beer with great friends.

With *The Anheuser-Busch Cookbook—Great Food, Great Beer,* I'm pleased to welcome you to our table. Enjoy.

August A. Busch IV
President and Chief Executive Officer
Anheuser-Busch Companies, Inc.

A PROUD HISTORY

Since 1852, Anheuser-Busch has had a rock-solid commitment to brewing innovation and quality. From the introduction of Budweiser, the first truly national beer, through the difficult years of Prohibition and the booming growth that characterized the last half of the twentieth century, the company never failed to find new ways to innovate.

Anheuser-Busch Brewing Association, St. Louis.

St. Louis, 1852

Anheuser-Busch traces its origins back to 1852 St. Louis, then the gateway to America's frontier, with the founding of the Bavarian Brewery—one of many breweries that satisfied the bustling young city's thirst for beer. Eberhard Anheuser, a German immigrant with a flair for chemistry, acquired and renamed the company in 1860; his son-in-law, Adolphus Busch, joined him in 1864. With these two men at the helm, the company grew quickly, adopting the name Anheuser-Busch Brewing Association in 1879. The company's success sprang from its willingness to try new things, including pasteurization and mechanical refrigeration. These developments enabled superior quality and national distribution. Busch also pioneered fresh marketing ideas—such as giving away pocketknives (then necessary for opening beer bottles) with the "A & Eagle" logo—and brewed a variety of beers, from dark bock to pilsners, hop ale, and light lagers, including, of course, Budweiser. These traditions of diverse brewing and commitment to quality continue today.

1861—Adolphus and Lilly
A beer dynasty is born when young, energetic German immigrant Adolphus Busch marries Lilly Anheuser, the daughter of a St. Louis brewery owner.

1872—The A & Eagle
The company, then E. Anheuser & Co., adopts its famous "A & Eagle" logo, showing America's national bird entwined in an elegant letter A.

1876—Budweiser
Budweiser Lager Beer debuts as the United States' first national beer; the "King of Beers" became Anheuser-Busch's flagship brand in the 1890s.

Surviving Prohibition

Innovation was also the key as Anheuser-Busch faced its greatest challenge: Prohibition, which was made law by the 18th Amendment in 1920. Beer production had already stopped during World War I, when President Wilson issued wartime orders to cease brewing in order to conserve grain. Surviving Prohibition, however, required both new ideas and economizing. Company president August A. Busch, Sr., even waived his own salary. In a bid to diversify, Anheuser-Busch expanded into new businesses, making and selling everything from root beer to yeast, ice cream, and even truck bodies and refrigerators. The tough times ended in 1933 with Prohibition's repeal. Beer became legal in April, and by December Budweiser was again available nationwide. To celebrate, Anheuser-Busch introduced its famous Clydesdales—an instantly recognizable symbol of the company's strength.

The First 100 Years

By 1952, when Anheuser-Busch marked its centennial, Budweiser was known as the "King of Beers." But the company was not content to rest on its laurels. The innovations begun in the nineteenth century continued after Prohibition, as the company began selling Budweiser in cans in 1936 and "Bud Jr." bottles in the 1950s. New breweries were opened around the country, and Budweiser sponsored a show in the exciting new medium of television. As Anheuser-Busch headed into its second century, its expansion—and commitment to brewing great-tasting beer—would continue.

Top: Introduced in 1916, Bevo, a nonalcoholic "near beer," enjoyed great success during Prohibition. *Bottom:* A hitch of Clydesdales on Capitol Hill, 1933.

1896—Michelob
Anheuser-Busch brings out Michelob, "a draught beer for connoisseurs," served at the finest retail establishments and brewed with premium ingredients.

1936—Bud in Cans
Anheuser-Busch begins selling Budweiser in cans, adopting the latest in packaging technology for a generation of post-Prohibition beer drinkers.

1952—Bud Jr.
The seven-ounce Bud Jr. bottle goes on sale, coinciding with the 100th anniversary of Anheuser-Busch's founding.

specialty beers, and Anheuser-Busch is leading the way, offering such new products as Michelob Ultra Amber, a low-calorie amber lager. And beer aficionados across the country have been able to vote for new regional beers in Anheuser-Busch's Original Beers program, in which the company's regional brewmasters invent craft beers to reflect local tastes, leading to such exciting new brews as New England's Demon's Hop Yard IPA and Missouri's Mule Kick Oatmeal Stout.

An American Taste for Beer

Americans are drinking all kinds of lager and ale these days, with a seemingly limitless selection of styles to choose from. For Anheuser-Busch—America's leading brewing company—the new flowering of American brewing is a return to the company's roots. From brewing a wide range of beers in its early days in St. Louis to introducing Budweiser—the first truly national beer—to participating in the recent renaissance of specialty brews, Anheuser-Busch has been instrumental in shaping Americans' taste for beer. As the American palate becomes even more adventurous, different styles offer new opportunities for appreciating beer, especially in its most natural role: paired with great food, plain and fancy. Whether light or full bodied, crisp or rich, hoppy or malty, all of Anheuser-Busch's brews share the insistence on quality and adherence to precise brewing practices that ensure dining pleasure from appetizers to desserts and a great beer-drinking experience every time.

What's Brewing

In the twenty-first century, Anheuser-Busch—led by fifth-generation brewer August A. Busch IV—continues the traditions of quality and originality that have distinguished it from the beginning. The crisp, smooth character of Budweiser and Bud Light continue to make them popular favorites not only nationwide but around the globe. At the same time, Americans are discovering the unique flavors of

1956—Bud "Bow-tie"
The Budweiser label begins to sport its instantly recognizable red bow-tie logo. Memorabilia with this logo are highly collectible today.

1963—Pull Tabs
Keeping up with packaging innovations, and making it ever easier for beer lovers to enjoy a cold one, Anheuser-Busch introduces cans with pull-tab openings.

1976—Bud Turns 100
Anheuser-Busch marks the centennial of Budweiser, far and away America's most popular beer, outselling all other domestic premium beers combined.

THE BEER-MAKING PROCESS

For more than 100 years, Anheuser-Busch has used the same traditional brewing method for Budweiser, its flagship premium lager. To ensure that quality remains high, a trained brewmaster tastes the beer at each stage by which barley, yeast, hops, and water are turned into beer.

1

MILLING

Different types of malted barley (two-row and six-row) and any adjunct grains, such as rice, are separately milled to break up the kernels and then carefully weighed.

2

MASHING

Malt and water are cooked in a large pot, called a mash tun, to release the grain's enzymes, converting its starches into sugars. The liquid, called wort, is strained.

3

BOILING

The wort is boiled in a brewkettle and hops are added, imparting their distinctive flavors; the brewmasters choose and blend up to fifteen varieties of hops to yield the desired qualities. The strained wort is cooled by evaporation and is allowed to settle and clarify.

4

PRIMARY FERMENTATION

Yeast and sterile air are added to the wort; the yeast converts the sugars created in mashing into alcohol, carbon dioxide, and flavor compounds.

5

SECONDARY FERMENTATION

The beer is placed in an aging, or "lagering," tank and freshly yeasted wort is added for kraeusening (a secondary fermentation, see box on page 82), which fully carbonates the beer and matures its flavor.

6

FINISHING

The finished beer is cooled to 29°F and "chillproofed" in tanks to ensure its clarity and stability. Finally, the beer is filtered, tasted one last time by a brewmaster, and packaged.

1982—Bud Light
Clean, crisp Bud Light makes its national debut, offering Budweiser flavor and quality, with fewer calories, to a new generation of beer drinkers.

1996—"Born-On" Dating
Anheuser-Busch introduces "born-on" dating on its product labels, guaranteeing that customers get a fresh, great-tasting beer every time.

2006—Michelob Ultra Amber
In keeping with its longtime emphasis on quality, Anheuser-Busch premieres a full-flavored amber lager that is low in calories and carbohydrates.

PAIRING BEER WITH FOOD

Whether you're grilling in the backyard or dining with guests, beer fits with the way Americans cook and entertain today. It partners naturally with food and its varied flavors can be matched to any menu, as long as you keep the principle of balance in mind.

To understand why a particular beer pairs well with a range of food flavors, take the time to taste the beer carefully and appreciate the nuances. A process for savoring beer flavors is described below. You'll then use this deeper understanding of the beer to seek the right balance with the food. Anheuser-Busch's brewmasters and chefs find balance by looking for either contrasting or complementing flavors in the food, as explained on page 13. They've given you a handy shortcut, however, as you use the recipes in this book. *Find the Icon, Make the Match* on pages 14 and 15 provides a key to beer-pairing symbols that accompany every recipe.

Tasting Beer

Tasting beer isn't fussy or formal. It's just a matter of paying attention to three basic components: the beer's scent, or "nose"; its taste; and its body or weight. Start with perfectly clean glasses, matched to the type of beer (see pages 18–19), and begin sniffing and sipping. You may want to jot down notes.

SNIFF!

The first step in tasting is to use your nose. Beer's scent has two components: *aroma* derives from ingredients, such as malt's toastiness, while *bouquet* describes scents caused by fermentation, such as the banana-like scent of some wheat beers.

Floral—Floral aromas frequently derive from hops, which impart a complex range of scents, and are especially common in pilsners.

Fruity—Fruity bouquets stem from esters created in fermentation and are common in ales, stouts, and doppelbock; fruity aromas, as in citrusy pale ales, derive from hops.

Grassy—As well as contributing fruity and floral notes, hops contribute grassy aromas to beer, characterized by a fresh, "green" scent or an herbal quality.

Toasty—Malt, especially if darkly roasted, contributes this rounded, rich aroma, found most prominently in brown ales, stouts, and dark lagers.

Yeasty—A complex, sometimes bready aroma that may accompany hints of fruitiness; yeastiness is more predominant in ales than in most lagers.

SIP!

The next step is to take a sip. Roll the beer in your mouth, so that it hits all your taste buds, and consider what sensations you perceive.

Fruity—Fruit flavors in beer convey a light tartness; examples include the lemony, citrusy taste of wheat beers or the cidery notes of lambics.

Roasted/malty—These flavors come from beer's main ingredient, malted barley, and may range from bready to deeply chocolaty. They leave a sweet impression.

Spicy/hoppy—The characteristic note contributed by hops is a spicy edge, found particularly in heavily hopped beers, such as pale ales, bitters, and porters.

Sweet—Although most beers are fermented until dry, some, like barley wine, have residual sugars. In other beers, such as cream stouts, sugar may be added.

SWALLOW!

As you swallow beer, assess its body or weight, textural qualities linked to its alcohol level, carbonation, and density. Is the beer rich and mouth-filling, clean and refreshing, or in between?

Light bodied—Light-bodied beers, such as German pilsners, some wheat beers, many American lagers, and ordinary bitter, leave a clean finish after swallowing.

Medium bodied—Weightier on the palate, medium-bodied beers include pale and brown ales, porters, American premium lagers, and amber lagers.

Full bodied—Rounded, mouth-filling, and sometimes creamy-textured, full-bodied beers may be higher in alcohol. Examples include stouts, extra-special bitter, dark lagers, and some bocks.

A Balanced Pairing

Beer and food pairings aim to create a balance of flavors, so that a single flavor never dominates but all the elements of the beer and the food work together. In some cases, more than one beer could make the perfect match. Balanced matches are created by applying either of the following two pairing principles: contrast or complement.

CONTRAST

Opposites attract and some foods pair perfectly with beers that have very different flavors and textures. Applying the principle of contrast to pairing means selecting a beer and a food with distinct, often opposite flavors. Think about the dominant flavor in either the food or the beer, and then choose a brew or dish that highlights an opposing characteristic. An example of such a pairing might be Pasta with Sausage and Broccoli Rabe (photo top right)—an assertively flavored dish with some spice—paired with a richly malty amber lager to mellow the spice and round out the sharper edges.

COMPLEMENT

A complementary pairing of beer and food melds together similar flavors in each to form a single, harmonious taste. For instance, one might match Scallops with Black Bean Sauce (photo bottom right) to a rich porter, resulting in an overall impression of medium-bodied spiciness; or, pair dark chocolate's creamy cocoa flavors with a toasty, malty stout for a sweet, rich flavor overall.

FINDING PERFECT MATCHES

The pairings our chefs and brewmasters offer throughout this book all create balanced, delicious matches between beer and food—pairings you can serve with confidence. For a key to these perfect pairings, simply turn the page.

FIND THE ICON, MAKE THE MATCH

Nobody knows the distinctive flavors of beer like the brewmasters at Anheuser-Busch. A team of these experts, along with our chefs, put their palates to work throughout this book to come up with perfect pairing recommendations for the recipes that follow—pairings that enhance the flavors of both beer and food. Ensuring the perfect balance between the food you cook and the beer you drink is as simple as looking at the top of each recipe for one of the icons shown here.

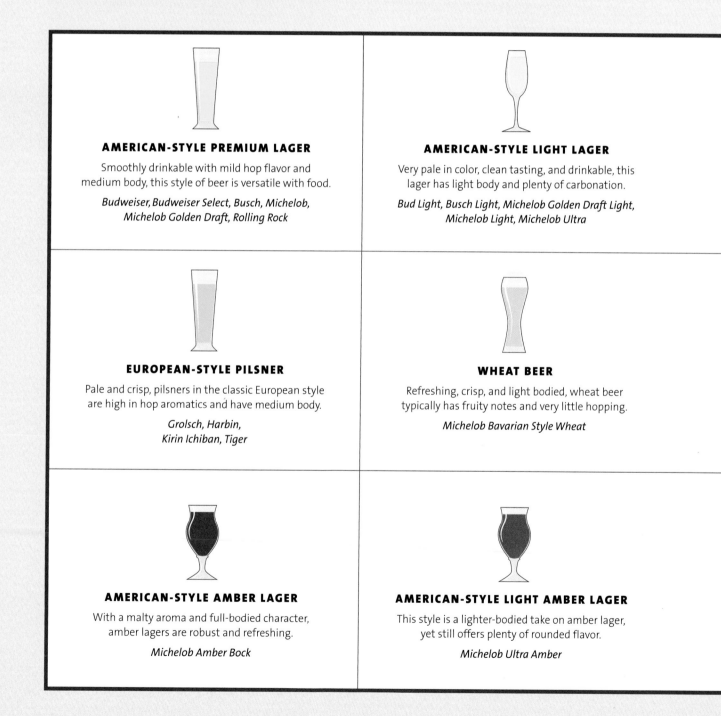

AMERICAN-STYLE PREMIUM LAGER

Smoothly drinkable with mild hop flavor and medium body, this style of beer is versatile with food.

Budweiser, Budweiser Select, Busch, Michelob, Michelob Golden Draft, Rolling Rock

AMERICAN-STYLE LIGHT LAGER

Very pale in color, clean tasting, and drinkable, this lager has light body and plenty of carbonation.

Bud Light, Busch Light, Michelob Golden Draft Light, Michelob Light, Michelob Ultra

EUROPEAN-STYLE PILSNER

Pale and crisp, pilsners in the classic European style are high in hop aromatics and have medium body.

Grolsch, Harbin, Kirin Ichiban, Tiger

WHEAT BEER

Refreshing, crisp, and light bodied, wheat beer typically has fruity notes and very little hopping.

Michelob Bavarian Style Wheat

AMERICAN-STYLE AMBER LAGER

With a malty aroma and full-bodied character, amber lagers are robust and refreshing.

Michelob Amber Bock

AMERICAN-STYLE LIGHT AMBER LAGER

This style is a lighter-bodied take on amber lager, yet still offers plenty of rounded flavor.

Michelob Ultra Amber

ENGLISH-STYLE PALE ALE

Medium-bodied, spicy English-style pale ale features higher hopping than the American style.

Michelob Pale Ale

MAERZEN AND OKTOBERFEST

Medium-bodied, golden brown Maerzen and Oktoberfest beers balance maltiness and hoppiness.

Michelob Marzen

DOPPELBOCK

Dark, robust, and slightly sweet, doppelbock offers malty flavor and full-bodied character.

Brewmaster's Private Reserve

SPECIALTY BEER

Enhanced with ingredients such as chocolate, specialty beers have varied aromas, flavors, and body.

*Michelob Celebrate Chocolate,
Michelob Honey Lager*

PORTER

Dark and malty, porters nevertheless offer a crisp finish and medium body.

Michelob Porter

DRY STOUT

Full-bodied, malty, and low in hops, stout is very dark, with caramel flavors.

Bare Knuckle Stout

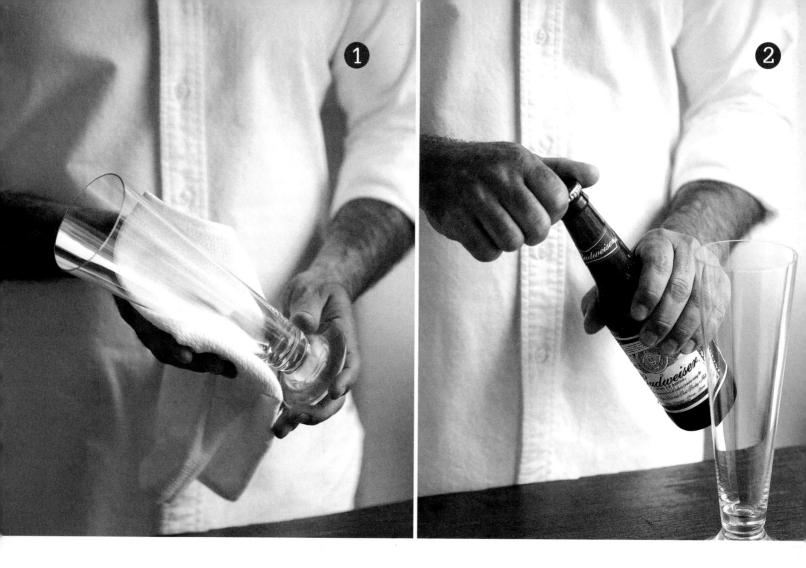

THE POUR

Pouring beer properly allows the carbonation trapped in the bottle after fermentation to escape, carrying the beer's aroma up to your nose. It produces a tight and proper head of foam and enhances the beer's flavor. Here's how:

1. Start with a beer-ready glass. Clean the glass with mild soap and rinse well with warm water. Dry the glass with a clean, lint-free towel. Pouring beer into an improperly cleaned glass can create flat beer or a false head that dissipates rapidly and can cause bubbles to stick to the side of the glass or an off taste.

2. Remove the cap from the bottle.

3. Place the glass on a flat surface. Begin pouring the beer by placing the neck of the bottle or the lip of the can over the edge of the clean glass.

4. Quickly raise the bottom of the bottle or can to a high angle, causing the beer to agitate into the glass.

5. Lower the bottom of the bottle or can to reduce the flow until the head rises to the rim of the glass.

6. Wipe away any of the head that might run over the rim of the glass with a cotton towel.

THE GLASS

Selecting the right glass for the various beers is a matter of flavor, tradition, and enjoyment. Certain glasses enhance the tastes of particular beers or simply came to be used by tradition—though any glass that accommodates a 12-ounce beer is better than none! Here's a primer.

Flute
AMERICAN-STYLE
LIGHT LAGER

Goblet
DOPPELBOCK,
SPECIALTY

Mug
MAERZEN,
OKTOBERFEST

Tulip
AMERICAN-STYLE AMBER LAGER,
AMERICAN-STYLE LIGHT AMBER LAGE

Pilsner

AMERICAN-STYLE PREMIUM LAGER,
EUROPEAN-STYLE PILSNER

Tumbler

ENGLISH-STYLE PALE ALE

Weiss

WHEAT BEER

Pub

PORTER,
DRY STOUT

A COOK'S GUIDE TO BEER

What's the difference between an ale and a lager? Why was beer served at Oktoberfest traditionally made in March? Sharpen your beer savvy by reading the glossary entries listed below.

Ale—Beer produced using warm (65°F) top fermentation, in which the yeast rises to the surface. Many ales use roasted malts, lending them dark color and full flavor, as well as plenty of hops. Types include malty British ale and English brown ale, hoppy American ale, pale ale, and Belgian ales such as Trappist and Abbey ales.

Amber—Describes a copper-brown or reddish tone found in certain lagers and ales. Amber beers are typically malty in aroma and may have a hint of sweetness.

American ale—Ales made in America come in a range of styles, including American brown ale, which is generally hoppier than its English counterpart; pale ale, which is quite hoppy and may have a fruity aroma; and amber ales.

American lager—Clean, crisp, and more carbonated than European lagers, American lagers and premium lagers are mild, with low hopping, and are known for smooth drinkability. Premium lagers are distinguished by their more flavorful, full-bodied character and often have a deeper color than other American lagers. Still deeper in color are American amber lagers, which also have a slightly maltier aroma, and dark lagers. American lagers may use adjunct grains, such as corn or rice, in addition to barley.

Barley—The basic grain used in brewing, barley is malted before use. Brewers use two types, defined by the number of kernels on the stalk: two-row barley, which results in a smooth, sweet brew, and six-row barley, which contributes crispness.

Barley wine—A sweet, high-alcohol specialty beer that uses wine or champagne yeast and offers a fruity, malty flavor profile. Barley wines may range in color from copper to dark brown.

Beer—The first known alcoholic beverage, beer is brewed from malted barley (and sometimes other grains), fermented with yeast, and flavored with hops. Beers fall two main categories: lagers and ales.

Bitter—This traditional English ale is made with low carbonation and is typically highly hopped. Usually served at room temperature, bitter comes in three styles: ordinary; the hoppier special; and full-bodied, malty extra-special bitter.

Bock—A sweet, often dark lager that originated in Germany as a seasonal beer served in spring. Types include malty traditional bock; paler, hoppier Helles bock; and sweet, strong, deeply colored doppelbock.

Golden ale—Also sometimes called cream ale, this crisp, floral, light-golden style of ale, commonly brewed in Canada, shares many flavor characteristics with lagers.

Hops—The flowering hop vine produces cone-shaped blossoms that add a unique aroma and spice to beer—a character known as "hoppy." Used for centuries as a preservative and flavoring, hops are grown in Germany and in the American Northwest. Brewers blend different varieties of hops to attain the desired flavor and aroma profile for their beers.

Ice beer—Crisp, clean-tasting ice beers are made using a distinctive process in which ice crystals are formed in the beer and then removed, resulting in a smoother taste.

India pale ale—Originally developed with a high alcohol content and heavy hopping to survive the sea voyage from Britain to colonial India, India pale ale is now brewed the world over.

Lager—Beer produced using cold (45°F) bottom fermentation, in which the yeast settles at the bottom after fermentation. There are many styles of lagers, but the best known are pale in color and crisp in flavor, with mild hops character. "Lager" means "to store" in German, and lager beers are aged for a period of time in lager tanks at cold temperatures. Many lagers are pale in color and crisp in flavor, but their color and flavor can range from the snappy, crisp qualities of American lagers to hoppy European pilsners to rounder dark lagers and bocks.

Lambic—A Belgian style of beer, often fermented with fruit, lambics are distinguished by using open-tank fermentation and wild yeasts, resulting in a sharp, tart, fruity flavor profile. They use both malted barley and unmalted wheat in brewing; fruit lambics typically feature cherries or raspberries.

Light lager—An American style of low-calorie beer that is extremely pale, with light body, high carbonation, and mild, smooth flavor.

Maerzen/Oktoberfest—Before the advent of refrigeration, beers were necessarily made seasonally; originally, lager served at Oktoberfest had been made in March ("Märzen") from new malt and aged until October, to be served at harvest festivals. Traditional Maerzen is golden brown in color, with a balanced maltiness and hoppiness. Today, Oktoberfest lagers range from golden to red-brown.

Malt—Barley that has been soaked in water, germinated, and then kiln-dried is known as malt. It contributes a characteristic sweet, "malty" flavor to beer. Malt may be roasted to varying degrees; the darker the malt, the darker the beer.

Pale ale—A light-colored, hoppy ale with medium body and little maltiness. English pale ales are typically very hoppy and spicy, whereas the pale to light copper American pale ales feature American-style hopping and a fruity bouquet. Similar but slightly darker and maltier in character are American amber ales. (See also India pale ale.)

Pilsner—A classic European type of pale lager. German pilsners tend to be very pale and hoppy, serving as a model for pale lagers worldwide. Bohemian pilsners, which take their name from the town of Plzen, are slightly darker and balance hoppy and malty character.

Porter—An extremely dark ale made from heavily roasted malt, porter may range from sweet to very hoppy. This style of beer originated in London and is medium bodied, with a crisp finish.

Specialty beers—Also called flavored beers; many brewers add fruit, vegetable, or spice flavors, ranging from pumpkin to chile peppers, to their brews. Some of these, such as fruits, may be added as an adjunct in fermentation; others may be added after brewing. A traditional German beer, *Rauchbier*, is smoke flavored by smoking some of the malt.

Steam beer—A style originating in nineteenth-century California. Because ice was unavailable, lager yeasts were fermented at the warmer temperatures typically used for ales, resulting in a beer with both ale- and lager-like flavors.

Stout—Distinguished by the use of unmalted, darkly roasted barley among its grains, stout tends to be low in hops, with malty and caramel aromas. Styles include dry Irish stout, sweet or cream stout, and oatmeal stout.

Strong beer—Beers with greater than 6 percent alcohol by volume are generally referred to as strong beers. Any type of ale or lager can be brewed to this higher strength; some of the most common types of strong beers include doppelbocks, pale ales, stouts, and porters.

Wheat beer—Found under several names—*weizen, weissbier,* or the popular *hefeweizen*—these beers are made using wheat as part of the grain profile. They tend to be refreshing, pale in color, and highly carbonated, with fruity flavors and little hoppiness.

SPECIAL PAIRINGS

Enjoying beer with appetizers and with dinner is a given, but you might be surprised to find that beer can move beyond the main course: it pairs perfectly with a cheese course and even sweets and desserts.

PAIRING BEER WITH CHEESE

Beer and cheese are a superb match. Look for complementary and contrasting characteristics in matching beer to these styles of cheese:

Creamy—Rich, soft cow's-milk cheeses, such as Brie, go nicely with light lagers that cut through their creaminess; nutty aged cheeses, like Gruyère, are good with stouts, mild porters, and ales.

Sharp—Tart fresh cheese such as chèvre goes well with delicate wheat beer; strong, hoppy beers such as pale ale pair nicely with sharp aged Cheddar, as does full-flavored lager.

Blue—Try mild, creamy blues, like Stilton, with barley wine or sweet stout, or sharper blues with rounded, mellow ales. Robust, full-bodied blues can stand up to an equally big bock.

PAIRING BEER WITH DESSERT

Sweets and beer go together remarkably—indeed surprisingly—well. In general, choose beers with a little sweetness or a rich texture to harmonize with the following dessert categories:

Fruit—Light, fruity desserts call for lighter beers such as premium lagers and light premium lagers; you can also serve fruity desserts with wheat beers.

Chocolate—Stout and chocolate is a classic, delicious pairing; chocolate-flavored beers, amber bocks, and doppelbocks are also a good bet with rich chocolate desserts.

Cream—Rich, creamy sweets like cheesecake call for equally rounded beers, such as stouts, amber bocks, or doppelbocks, while pale ales can balance creamy-tart desserts, such as a fruit-flavored crème brûlée.

MENUS FOR ENTERTAINING

The best way to pair beer and food, ultimately, is with family and friends. Use these menus to put together an easy party the whole gang will enjoy, or for inspiration in devising your own lineup of dishes.

FRESH BACKYARD BARBECUE

Seared Chicken with Tomatillo Salsa, *page 105*

Gorgonzola Burgers, *page 177*

Corn and Tomato Salad, *page 55*

Warm Potato Salad, *page 254*

Mixed Berry Shortcakes, *page 285*

SKI WEEKEND SUPPER

Warm Artichoke and Amber Bock Dip, *page 47*

Mushroom-Potato Soup with Paprika, *page 48*

Warm Spinach Salad with Apples and Bacon, *page 56*

Gingerbread Cake, *page 278*

AUTUMN TAILGATE LUNCH

Cheesy Pigs-in-a-Blanket, *page 40*

Maerzen-Braised Short Ribs, *page 190*

Roasted Fall Vegetables, *page 246*

Black-and-White Cookies, *page 289*

WINTER HOLIDAY MENU

Oysters on the Half Shell, *page 36*

Roasted Beet and Citrus Salad, *page 60*

Beef Rib Roast with Rosemary, *page 198*

Brussels Sprouts with Parmesan, *page 241*

Scalloped Vidalia Onions, *page 249*

Raspberry Cheesecake, *page 274*

BEER-TASTING MENU

From lively, light-bodied beers to dark, rich, full-bodied brews, this menu focuses on what's in the glass, serving a different beer with each course.

Spicy Shrimp Cakes with Corn Salsa, *page 28*
American-Style Light Lager

Mushroom-Stuffed Filet of Beef, *page 197*
English-Style Pale Ale

Roasted Asparagus with Lemon, *page 238*
Creamy Cumin Potato Gratin, *page 253*

Walnut-Caramel Tart, *page 281*
Porter

STARTERS, SOUPS & SALADS

Chef's Specialty

SPICY SHRIMP CAKES with CORN SALSA

Serve with an American-Style Light Lager, such as Bud Light

SHRIMP CAKES

1 pound medium shrimp, peeled and deveined

4 teaspoons olive oil, or as needed

1 small red bell pepper, stemmed, seeded, and finely chopped

1 garlic clove, minced

1/4 cup thinly sliced green onions, white and tender green parts

3 tablespoons mayonnaise

1 tablespoon fresh lime juice

1 1/2 teaspoons hot-pepper sauce

1/2 teaspoon sugar

1/4 teaspoon salt

1 large egg

1/4 cup finely chopped fresh cilantro

3/4 cup *panko* (Japanese bread crumbs; see Cook's Tip page 44), or plain dried bread crumbs

SALSA

1 cup frozen white corn kernels, thawed

3/4 cup diced peeled avocado

1/4 cup chopped fresh cilantro

3 tablespoons finely chopped red onion

2 tablespoons finely chopped seeded poblano chile

1 tablespoon fresh lime juice

1/4 teaspoon salt

1. To prepare the shrimp cakes, in a food processor, pulse the shrimp until finely chopped. Set aside.

2. In a large skillet, heat 2 teaspoons of the olive oil over medium heat. Add the bell pepper and sauté for 3 minutes. Add the garlic and sauté for 1 minute. Remove from the heat and transfer the bell pepper mixture to a large bowl. Add the shrimp, green onions, mayonnaise, lime juice, hot-pepper sauce, sugar, salt, and egg, stirring well. Stir in the cilantro and 1/4 cup of the *panko*.

3. Divide the shrimp mixture into 8 equal portions, shaping each portion into a patty 1/2 inch thick. Dredge both sides of the patties in the remaining 1/2 cup *panko*. Refrigerate for at least 1 hour.

4. In a large skillet, heat the remaining 2 teaspoons olive oil over medium-high heat. Add 4 shrimp cakes to the pan and cook until browned on the bottom, about 2 minutes. Turn and cook until browned on the second side, about 2 minutes longer. Remove from the pan, cover, and keep warm. Repeat with the remaining shrimp cakes, adding a little more olive oil to the pan if needed.

5. To prepare the salsa, in a bowl, combine the corn, avocado, cilantro, onion, chile, lime juice, and salt, stirring gently. Serve immediately with the shrimp cakes.

Cook's Tip: These shrimp cakes can be prepared a day in advance. Garnish with lime wedges, if desired.

Makes 8 first-course or 4 main-course servings

SHRIMP WRAPS with LIME DIPPING SAUCE

Serve with a Wheat Beer, such as Michelob Bavarian Style Wheat

1 pound large shrimp, peeled and deveined

¼ teaspoon salt

¼ teaspoon freshly ground black pepper

1 package (3 ¾ ounces) cellophane noodles (see Cook's Tip)

2 tablespoons rice vinegar

½ to 1 teaspoon red pepper flakes

2 tablespoons fresh lime juice

2 garlic cloves, minced

1 tablespoon sugar

¼ cup fish sauce

2 heads Boston or butter lettuce, cores trimmed and leaves separated, rinsed, and dried

1 large carrot, peeled and grated lengthwise into ribbons

¼ cup fresh basil leaves

¼ cup fresh cilantro leaves

¼ cup fresh mint leaves

¼ cup dry-roasted peanuts, finely chopped

1 Put the shrimp in a saucepan, sprinkle with the salt and pepper, and add cold water to just cover. Bring to a boil over high heat, then lower the heat to low and simmer until the shrimp are bright pink and the tails are curled, about 1 minute. Using a slotted spoon, transfer the shrimp to a colander and let cool.

2 Put the cellophane noodles in another saucepan and add hot water to cover the noodles. Cover the pan and set aside until the noodles are softened, at least 15 minutes, then drain. Using kitchen scissors, cut the noodles into pieces 2 to 3 inches long. Return the noodles to the pan, drizzle with the vinegar, and toss. Cover and set aside.

3 In a small bowl, combine the red pepper flakes and lime juice and let stand for 5 minutes. Add the garlic, sugar, and fish sauce, whisking until the sugar is dissolved. Transfer the sauce to a serving dish.

4 To assemble the wraps, arrange some noodles in the center of each lettuce leaf and top each with 1 shrimp. Garnish with the carrot, basil, cilantro, mint, and peanuts. Tuck up the bottom of each leaf, fold the sides inward, and roll to form a log. Serve with the sauce for dipping.

Cook's Tip: Cellophane noodles—also called bean thread or glass noodles—are available at Asian grocery stores and most large supermarkets, as are the other Asian ingredients used here.

Makes 8 to 10 servings

Bevo—Even though Prohibition was not enacted until 1920, the handwriting was on the wall when, in 1916, Anheuser-Busch introduced Bevo, a nonalcoholic barley brew that tasted somewhat like beer. It sold briskly enough to merit its own bottling plant by 1918, but the wide availability of bootleg alcohol in the 1920s caused the drink to be discontinued almost four years before Prohibition's repeal in 1933. To this day, four stone Bevo Foxes still adorn the corners of the original 1918 structure, one of the largest beer-bottling facilities in the country.

CORN PANCAKES with SMOKED SALMON

Serve with an American-Style Amber Lager, such as Michelob Amber Bock

½ cup sour cream

1 tablespoon minced fresh chives

1 ear sweet corn

⅓ cup all-purpose flour

2 tablespoons fine-ground yellow cornmeal

½ cup milk

1 large egg, separated

¼ teaspoon salt

¼ teaspoon freshly ground black pepper

1 tablespoon vegetable oil, or as needed

4 ounces cold-smoked salmon, cut into 24 strips 2 inches long

Snipped fresh chives (optional)

1 In a small bowl, combine the sour cream and minced chives, stirring with a whisk. Cover and refrigerate.

2 Over a small bowl, cut the kernels from the ear of corn. Scrape the remaining pulp from the cob using the dull side of the knife blade, then discard the cob. Set the corn aside.

3 In a bowl, combine the flour and cornmeal, stirring with a whisk. Make a well in the center of the mixture.

4 In a small bowl, combine the milk and egg yolk, whisking until blended. Add the milk mixture to the flour mixture, stirring with the whisk just until moist. Stir in the corn, salt, and pepper.

5 In another small bowl, beat the egg white with an electric mixer set on high speed until soft peaks form. Gently fold the egg white into the corn mixture.

6 In a large skillet, heat the oil over medium heat. Spoon about 1 tablespoon batter per pancake onto the pan, spreading to about 2 inches in diameter. Cook until the tops are covered with bubbles and the edges begin to set, about 2 minutes. Carefully turn over and cook for 1 minute longer. Transfer to a serving platter, arrange in a single layer, and keep warm. Repeat the process with the remaining batter, adding more oil to the pan if needed. You should have 24 pancakes.

7 Top each pancake with a strip of salmon and 1 teaspoon sour cream mixture. Garnish with the snipped chives, if you like, and serve.

Makes 8 servings

MUSSELS and OVEN FRIES

Serve with a European-Style Pilsner, such as Grolsch

3 large russet potatoes (about 1½ pounds total), peeled

4 tablespoons vegetable oil or melted coconut oil

½ teaspoon salt

¾ teaspoon freshly ground black pepper

1 very large yellow onion, chopped

4 garlic cloves, chopped

1 can (15 ounces) diced tomatoes

1 bottle (12 ounces) Grolsch

3 pounds mussels, scrubbed and debearded

⅓ cup chopped fresh flat-leaf parsley

1 Preheat the oven to 475°F. Cut the potatoes lengthwise into quarters and then cut each quarter lengthwise into 3 wedges. Place in a bowl with hot water to cover and let soak for 10 minutes.

2 Drain the potatoes and pat dry thoroughly with paper towels. Toss with 2 tablespoons of the oil, the salt, and ¼ teaspoon of the pepper. Pour the remaining 2 tablespoons oil into a large, heavy-duty rimmed baking sheet and spread evenly. Arrange the potatoes in a single layer on the pan and cover with aluminum foil. Bake for 5 minutes. Remove the foil and bake for 25 minutes longer. Turn the wedges, scraping up any browned bits from the bottom of the pan, and bake until browned and crisp, about 10 minutes longer.

3 Meanwhile, in a large (5- to 6-quart) nonreactive Dutch oven, combine the onion, garlic, tomatoes, and beer and bring to a boil over high heat. Stir in the mussels, discarding any that do not close to the touch. Cover and cook just until the mussels open, 5 to 8 minutes. Discard any mussels that failed to open. Stir in the remaining ½ teaspoon pepper and the parsley. Serve immediately in bowls with the sauce and pass the oven fries at the table.

Makes 6 servings

TUNA CEVICHE with CUMIN and CHILE

Serve with an American-Style Light Lager, such as Bud Light

1 bottle (12 ounces) Bud Light

⅔ cup *each* fresh lemon juice and fresh lime juice

1 teaspoon salt

½ teaspoon fresh thyme leaves

1 pound sushi-grade tuna such as yellowfin or ahi, cut into ⅓-inch dice

1 tablespoon olive oil

6 garlic cloves, minced (about 2 tablespoons)

¼ teaspoon white pepper

¼ teaspoon ground cumin

1 tomato, seeded and cut into ¼-inch dice

½ onion, cut into ¼-inch dice

½ green bell pepper, seeded and cut into ¼-inch dice

1 jalapeño chile (with seeds), minced

1 tablespoon finely chopped fresh cilantro

1 teaspoon raspberry or rice wine vinegar

Tortilla chips

1 In a bowl, combine the beer, ⅓ cup of the lemon juice, ⅓ cup of the lime juice, ½ teaspoon of the salt, and the thyme. Add the tuna and toss gently to coat. Cover and marinate in the refrigerator for 2 hours.

2 Drain the juices from the tuna in a colander and transfer to a serving bowl. In a small bowl, combine the remaining ⅓ cup lemon juice and ⅓ cup lime juice, the olive oil, the garlic, the remaining ½ teaspoon salt, the white pepper, and the cumin, stirring well. Add the citrus-juice mixture to the bowl with the tuna along with the tomato, onion, bell pepper, jalapeño, cilantro, and vinegar. Stir to mix well. Cover and refrigerate for 8 hours or up to overnight. Serve cold with the tortilla chips.

Cook's Tip: Easy to make and full of flavor, this is one of Chef Brent Wertz's signature dishes.

Makes 8 servings

OYSTERS
on the HALF SHELL

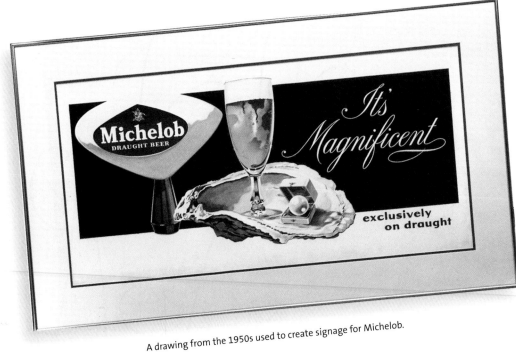

*Serve with a Dry Stout, such as
Bare Knuckle Stout*

OYSTERS WITH MIGNONETTE

¹/₄ cup champagne vinegar

¹/₄ cup fresh lemon juice

2 tablespoons freshly grated horseradish

2 tablespoons minced shallots

¹/₂ teaspoon sugar

Salt and freshly ground black pepper

1 dozen oysters on the half shell

1 In a small bowl, combine the vinegar, lemon juice, horseradish, shallots, and sugar, whisking until blended. Season to taste with salt and pepper. Serve as a topping for the oysters.

Makes 2 servings

OYSTERS WITH SPICY GRANITA

³/₄ cup fresh lime juice

1 or 2 fresh jalapeño chiles, minced

1 tablespoon sugar

1 teaspoon salt

¹/₄ teaspoon grated lime zest

1 dozen oysters on the half shell

1 In a small bowl, combine the lime juice, chile(s), sugar, salt, and lime zest, stirring well. Pour the mixture into a metal baking pan and freeze.

2 Using a fork, scrape the frozen mixture into an icy mound. Serve as a topping for the oysters.

Cook's Tip: Cold water makes good oysters, and in winter, they're at their plump and luscious best. West Coast varieties, such as Kumamotos and Olympias, have a creamy sweetness and are delicious served raw. Omit the chile seeds for a milder topping, if you like.

Makes 2 servings

A drawing from the 1950s used to create signage for Michelob.

SPANISH-STYLE SHRIMP with GARLIC

Serve with an American-Style Premium Lager, such as Budweiser Select

3 tablespoons extra-virgin olive oil

1/8 teaspoon cayenne pepper

6 garlic cloves, thinly sliced

1 bay leaf

1 pound large shrimp, peeled and deveined

1/4 teaspoon salt

2 tablespoons chopped fresh flat-leaf parsley

4 lemon wedges

1 In a large skillet, heat the olive oil over medium heat. Add the cayenne, garlic, and bay leaf and cook, stirring constantly, for 2 minutes. Raise the heat to medium-high. Add the shrimp and sauté until bright pink and opaque but still moist-looking in the center of the thickest part (cut to test), about 4 minutes.

2 Remove from the heat and discard the bay leaf. Sprinkle with the salt and parsley. Serve the shrimp with the lemon wedges.

Cook's Tip: Serve this tapas-style dish with grilled bread brushed with olive oil and sprinkled with a bit of salt.

Makes 4 servings

TERIYAKI CHICKEN WINGS

Serve with a European-Style Pilsner, such as Tiger

4 pounds chicken wings, tips cut off and discarded, wings split into 2 pieces through the joint

2 tablespoons extra-virgin olive oil

1/2 teaspoon salt

1/2 teaspoon freshly ground black pepper

1/4 cup soy sauce

3 tablespoons Tiger

1 1/2 tablespoons light brown sugar

1 Preheat the oven to 500°F. Line 2 baking sheets with aluminum foil.

2 In a large bowl, toss the wing pieces with the olive oil, salt, and pepper. Spread in a single layer on the prepared baking sheets. Bake until crispy and browned, about 35 minutes.

3 While the wings are baking, in a small saucepan, combine the soy sauce, beer, and sugar over medium-high heat. Bring to a simmer and cook until slightly reduced, about 3 minutes. Set aside.

4 When the wings are done, remove from the oven and let rest for 1 minute. Transfer the wings to a clean, dry bowl and pour the soy mixture over. Toss to coat, let stand for 5 minutes, toss again, and serve.

Cook's Tip: Making your own teriyaki sauce takes only a few minutes (you can do it while the wings cook) and it has a much fuller flavor than store-bought.

Makes 6 to 8 servings

GINGER BEEF MINI SKEWERS

Serve with a European-Style Pilsner, such as Harbin

³/₄ **pound beef tenderloin**

1 tablespoon peeled and thinly sliced fresh ginger, plus 1 tablespoon peeled and finely grated fresh ginger

¹/₂ **head garlic, cloves peeled and thinly sliced, plus 1 tablespoon finely grated garlic**

2 green onions, white and tender green parts, thinly sliced

¹/₂ **cup extra-virgin olive oil**

¹/₄ **cup soy sauce**

2 tablespoons seasoned rice vinegar

Salt and freshly ground black pepper

4 to 6 fresh chives, finely snipped

1 Slice the tenderloin ¹/₂ inch thick and lightly pound each slice with a rolling pin or the flat side of a meat pounder between 2 sheets of wax paper until about ¹/₄ inch thick. Each piece should be rectangular, about 1¹/₂ by 2¹/₂ inches. In a bowl, combine the sliced ginger, sliced garlic, green onions, and olive oil, stirring well. Add the beef and toss to coat. Cover and let marinate in the refrigerator for at least 8 hours.

2 Just before you prepare the grill, in a small bowl, combine the soy sauce, vinegar, grated ginger, and grated garlic, stirring with a whisk. Set aside. Soak 18 to 20 wooden skewers in water to cover for 30 minutes.

3 Prepare a grill for cooking over high heat. First, oil the grill rack. If using a charcoal grill, prepare a solid bed of hot coals. If using a gas grill, preheat to high.

4 Remove the beef from the marinade and discard the marinade. Thread the beef slices onto the soaked skewers and season to taste with salt and pepper. Lay the skewers on the grill rack. Close the lid if using a gas grill. Grill the beef just until seared, turning once, about 1 minute on each side. Serve the skewers drizzled with the ginger sauce and garnished with the chives.

Makes 18 to 20 mini skewers

CHEESY PIGS-in-a-BLANKET

Serve with an American-Style Premium Lager, such as Budweiser

All-purpose flour

1 package (1 pound) frozen pizza dough, thawed

4 regular-size hot dogs, each cut crosswise into thirds, or 12 cocktail-size hot dogs

3 teaspoons brown or coarse-grained mustard

³/₄ **cup shredded Monterey jack cheese**

1 large egg yolk

1 tablespoon water

1 Line a large baking sheet with parchment paper or aluminum foil.

2 Dust a large cutting board with flour and roll the pizza dough out into an 8-by-12-inch rectangle, making sure to patch any holes. Cut into 12 pieces, each 2 inches wide by 4 inches long, and arrange on the prepared baking sheet.

3 Place each hot dog piece crosswise on the short end of a dough rectangle. Brush each with ¹/₄ teaspoon of the mustard and sprinkle with 1 tablespoon of the cheese and roll the dough around it. Cover with a clean kitchen towel and let the dough rise until doubled in bulk, about 30 minutes.

4 Preheat the oven to 425°F. In a small bowl, mix together the egg yolk and water. Brush each roll with the egg mixture. Bake until the dough is golden brown, 13 to 15 minutes. Let rest for about 1 minute, then transfer with a spatula to a serving platter. Serve immediately.

Makes 4 servings

PORK POT STICKERS

Serve with a European-Style Pilsner, such as Harbin

$^1/_2$ **pound ground pork**

2 green onions, white and tender green parts, chopped, plus julienned green onion for garnish

1 tablespoon soy sauce

1 teaspoon sesame oil

Pinch of salt

1$^1/_2$ cups packaged shredded cabbage and carrot mix

$^1/_2$ teaspoon cornstarch

30 *gyoza* skins

4 tablespoons peanut oil

Plum sauce

1 Heat a large skillet over medium-high heat. Add the pork and cook, stirring to crumble, until no longer pink, about 6 minutes. Add the chopped green onions, soy sauce, sesame oil, and salt and cook for 30 seconds. Stir in the cabbage and carrot and cook, stirring often, until the cabbage wilts, about 30 seconds.

2 In a small bowl, combine 3 tablespoons water and the cornstarch, stirring with a whisk. Add the cornstarch mixture to the skillet and cook, stirring constantly, for 1 minute. Remove from the heat and let cool to room temperature.

3 Working with 1 *gyoza* skin at a time (cover the remaining skins to prevent drying), mound a scant 1 tablespoon of the pork mixture in the center of each skin. Moisten the edges of the skin with water. Fold in half, pinching the edges together to seal. Place on a baking sheet in a single layer (cover loosely with a towel to prevent drying). When all the skins are filled, remove the towel and cover with plastic wrap.

4 In a large skillet, heat 2 tablespoons of the peanut oil over medium heat. Arrange 15 pot stickers in the pan in a single layer and cook until browned on the bottoms, about 2 minutes. Add 1 cup water to the pan, cover, and cook for 5 minutes. Uncover and cook until the liquid evaporates, about 2 minutes longer. Transfer to a platter and keep warm. Repeat with the remaining pot stickers, using the remaining 2 tablespoons peanut oil and an additional 1 cup water. Serve immediately, garnished with the green onion strips. Put the plum sauce in small serving bowls and pass at the table.

Cook's Tip: Look for round *gyoza* skins or wonton wrappers in most supermarkets or in Asian groceries, where you can also find bottled plum sauce.

Makes 10 servings

Keeping Cool—Even though Anheuser-Busch was the first U.S. brewer to adopt pasteurization in the early 1870s, draught beer remained unpasteurized and required special attention when being transported throughout the nation. To that end, in the decade between 1876 (the year Budweiser was introduced) and 1886, the company developed a network of ice houses and refrigerated railcars. In the process, it established Budweiser as the country's first truly national beer.

ROASTED RED PEPPERS with GARLIC

Serve with an American-Style Light Lager, such as Busch Light

8 red bell peppers

2 garlic cloves, minced

1 teaspoon kosher or sea salt

¼ cup extra-virgin olive oil

½ teaspoon freshly ground black pepper

Fresh flat-leaf parsley

1 Preheat the broiler. Place the bell peppers on a baking sheet and broil 4 to 5 inches from the heat source until the skins are blackened and blistered all over, turning as needed, about 8 minutes. Transfer to a paper or plastic bag and close tightly. Let stand for 10 minutes (the steam will loosen the skins).

2 Meanwhile, on a cutting board, using the flat side of a chef's knife, mash the garlic with the salt, then transfer to a small bowl. Add the olive oil and pepper, stirring well to blend.

3 Peel, stem, and seed the roasted peppers and cut lengthwise into strips ³/₄ inch wide. Arrange the pepper strips on a platter and drizzle with the garlic oil, scraping it out of the bowl to get all the garlic. Garnish with the parsley and serve warm or at room temperature.

Cook's Tip: Roasting intensifies the flavors of vegetables, and red peppers are no exception. You can roast the peppers in the oven or on the grill. You can prepare these peppers up to a day ahead, then cover and refrigerate. Let them come to room temperature and drain off any excess liquid before serving. Be sure to use very fresh garlic, as old garlic will taste bitter and strong.

Makes 6 to 8 servings

GARLIC-STUFFED MUSHROOMS

Serve with an American-Style Light Lager, such as Bud Light

2 heads garlic, cloves separated and peeled

1 cup heavy cream

1 cup *panko* (Japanese bread crumbs; see Cook's Tip) or plain dried bread crumbs

1 teaspoon salt

24 large button or cremini mushrooms, stemmed

2 teaspoons olive oil

¼ teaspoon freshly ground black pepper

1 In a small saucepan, combine the garlic and cream over low heat. Slowly cook until the garlic is soft enough to mash with a spoon, about 45 minutes. (The cream will be reduced and thick.) Remove from the heat and mash the garlic into the cream with a fork, making a rough purée. Stir in the *panko* and salt, mixing thoroughly.

2 Preheat the oven to 450°F. Lay the mushroom caps, top side down, on a lightly oiled baking sheet. Brush the edges with the olive oil and fill the centers with the garlic mixture.

3 Bake until starting to brown, about 15 minutes. Remove from the oven and let stand for 5 to 10 minutes. Transfer the mushrooms to plates or a platter, discarding any released liquid. Sprinkle with the pepper and serve.

Cook's Tip: The vast amount of garlic here is tempered by being slowly cooked in cream, resulting in a rich, mild garlic stuffing. *Panko*, or Japanese bread crumbs, is very light and crunchy. You'll find it at Asian markets.

Makes 4 to 6 servings

GARLIC-POBLANO GUACAMOLE

Serve with an American-Style Light Lager, such as Michelob Ultra

6 garlic cloves, unpeeled

1 red bell pepper

1 poblano chile

1 ripe avocado, pitted, peeled, and coarsely mashed

$\frac{1}{4}$ cup finely chopped green onions, white and tender green parts

2 tablespoons chopped fresh cilantro

2 teaspoons fresh lime juice

$\frac{1}{4}$ teaspoon kosher salt

Tortilla chips

1 Preheat the oven to 450°F. Wrap the garlic cloves in aluminum foil. Bake until soft, about 15 minutes. Let cool slightly, then remove the skins. Place the roasted garlic in a serving bowl and mash with a fork.

2 Preheat the broiler. Place the bell pepper and chile on a baking sheet and broil 4 to 5 inches from the heat source until the skins are blackened and blistered all over, about 8 minutes. Remove from the broiler. Lower the oven temperature to 425°F.

3 Transfer the roasted pepper and chile to a paper or plastic bag and close tightly. Let stand for 10 minutes (the steam will loosen the skins), then peel, stem, and seed the pepper and the chile, and chop finely. Add the pepper, chile, avocado, green onions, cilantro, lime juice, and salt to the mashed garlic, stirring well. Serve the guacamole with the tortilla chips.

Cook's Tip: When storing this guacamole, press plastic wrap against its surface to help keep it from oxidizing and turning brown.

Makes 8 servings

WARM ARTICHOKE and AMBER BOCK DIP

Serve with an American-Style Amber Lager, such as Michelob Amber Bock

28 ounces (1$\frac{3}{4}$ pounds) drained canned artichoke hearts (water packed) or thawed frozen artichoke hearts

1 cup freshly grated Parmesan cheese

1 tablespoon grated lemon zest

1 tablespoon freshly ground black pepper

A few drops of hot-pepper sauce

1 package (8 ounces) light cream cheese

Egg white from 1 large egg

$\frac{1}{2}$ cup plain fresh or dried bread crumbs

1 cup Michelob Amber Bock

1 Preheat the oven 350°F. Combine all the ingredients in a food processor and process to a coarse purée. Scrape the mixture into a baking dish and bake until lightly browned and bubbling at the edges, about 30 minutes. Serve warm.

Cook's Tip: Beer can be used as a replacement for fat in certain dishes, and this version of a popular baked dip is a great example. Here artichoke hearts and Parmesan cheese are bound not by mayonnaise but by beer, bread crumbs, and egg white for a much less caloric rendition, one of Chef Sam Niemann's favorites.

Makes 12 servings

MUSHROOM-POTATO SOUP with PAPRIKA

 Serve with a Porter, such as Michelob Porter

$^{1}/_{2}$ ounce dried porcini mushrooms

$1^{1}/_{2}$ pounds fresh mushrooms such as shiitake, oyster, and *mitake*, or a combination

3 tablespoons olive oil

1 onion, halved and thinly sliced

$1^{1}/_{2}$ teaspoons salt

3 ounces pancetta, chopped

1 tablespoon smoked paprika *(pimentón)*

$2^{1}/_{2}$ cups chicken stock

3 russet or Yukon gold potatoes (about $1^{1}/_{2}$ pounds total), peeled and chopped

Salt and freshly ground black pepper

6 to 8 tablespoons crème fraîche or sour cream

1 In a small heatproof bowl, pour 1 cup boiling water over the dried porcini. Set aside.

2 Cut off the stems of the fresh mushrooms. Finely chop the stems and set aside. Slice the caps and set aside with the stems.

3 Using a slotted spoon, lift the porcini out of the bowl, pressing the excess liquid back into the bowl, and transfer to a cutting board. Finely chop the porcini and add to the stems and caps. Reserve the soaking liquid.

4 In a soup pot, heat the olive oil over medium-high heat. Add the onion and salt and cook, stirring, until the onion is soft, about 3 minutes. Add the pancetta and cook until the onion looks a bit creamy, about 2 minutes. Add the paprika and cook until very fragrant, about 2 minutes. Raise the heat to high and add all the mushrooms. Cook, stirring constantly, until the mushrooms start to give off their liquid, 3 to 5 minutes.

5 Add the reserved porcini soaking liquid (pour carefully to leave behind the sandy dregs), the chicken stock, 2 cups water, and the potatoes. Bring to a boil, then lower the heat to low and simmer, uncovered, until the potatoes are tender, 10 to 15 minutes. Season to taste with salt and pepper.

6 Ladle the soup into bowls and serve hot, with a dollop of crème fraîche.

Cook's Tip: Try using shiitake, oyster, and *mitake* (also called *maitake,* or "hen of the woods") for the fresh mushrooms here. The familiar button or cremini mushrooms work well, too.

Makes 6 to 8 servings

Liquid Bread—Near the turn of the twentieth century, Anheuser-Busch produced a number of beverages, including Liquid Bread, a common nickname for beer. This pure malt extract was brewed for an enterprising St. Louis physician named David Nicholson, who promoted the tonic's salutary health benefits to a willingly impressionable public.

ESCAROLE and WHITE BEAN SOUP

Serve with an English-Style Pale Ale, such as Michelob Pale Ale

¹/₂ pound escarole

1 tablespoon olive oil

1 large onion, chopped

2 garlic cloves, minced

2 ounces prosciutto or Westphalian ham, chopped (about ²/₃ cup)

5 cups chicken stock

1 can (15 ounces) cannellini (white kidney) beans, rinsed and drained

Salt and freshly ground black pepper

Freshly grated Parmesan cheese

1 Cut the base off the escarole, then rinse and drain the leaves. Cut the leaves crosswise into strips ¹/₄ inch wide. Set aside.

2 In a large saucepan, heat the olive oil over medium-high heat. Add the onion, garlic, and prosciutto. Cook, stirring often, until the onion is limp, 3 to 5 minutes. Add the stock and beans, raise the heat to high, cover, and bring to a boil. Stir in the escarole and cook just until wilted, about 1 minute. Season to taste with salt and pepper.

3 Ladle the soup into bowls and serve hot. Pass the Parmesan at the table to sprinkle on top of the soup.

Makes 4 servings

 CREAMY LAGER and JALAPEÑO SOUP

Serve with an American-Style Premium Lager, such as Budweiser

2 tablespoons butter

3 jalapeño chiles, seeded and finely chopped

¹/₂ onion, chopped

1 carrot, peeled and grated

2 tablespoons all-purpose flour

4 cups Budweiser

2 cups chicken stock

6 ounces half-and-half

2 tablespoons chopped fresh cilantro

1 teaspoon salt

1¹/₂ cups shredded Monterey jack cheese

1 In a large, heavy-bottomed saucepan, melt the butter over medium-high heat. When the foam subsides, stir in the jalapeños, onion, and carrot. Cook, stirring often, until the vegetables are softened, about 5 minutes.

2 Sprinkle in the flour and cook, stirring constantly, for 2 minutes. Pour the beer and stock into the pan in a slow, steady stream, whisking constantly. Bring to a boil. Reduce the heat to medium-low and simmer for 30 minutes. Strain through a fine-mesh sieve placed over a bowl. Reserve the solids and the saucepan.

3 Transfer the solids to a blender or food processor and process to a smooth purée. Return the purée to the saucepan along with the strained liquid and heat over medium-low heat. Pour in the half-and-half, stirring until well mixed and heated through. Remove from the heat and stir in the cilantro and salt.

4 Ladle the soup into bowls and serve hot, garnished with the cheese.

Cook's Tip: Chef Sam Niemann suggests leaving in the jalapeño seeds for a spicier soup.

Makes 6 servings

SAUSAGE and CABBAGE SOUP

 Serve with a Wheat Beer, such as Michelob Bavarian Style Wheat

12 ounces Portuguese linguiça or Polish sausage, sliced ¼ inch thick

1 onion, chopped

1 large garlic clove, minced

5 cups chicken stock

1 bottle (12 ounces) Michelob Bavarian Style Wheat

1 pound small thin-skinned potatoes, scrubbed and quartered

6 cups finely shredded cabbage

1 large carrot, peeled and sliced ¼ inch thick

1 teaspoon coriander seeds

½ teaspoon whole allspice

½ teaspoon black peppercorns

2 tablespoons chopped fresh flat-leaf parsley

Whole-grain mustard

1 In a large saucepan over medium-high heat, cook the sausage, stirring often, until lightly browned, 6 to 8 minutes. Spoon or pour off and discard all but 1 tablespoon fat in the pan. Add the onion and garlic and cook, stirring often, until limp, about 3 minutes. Raise the heat to high. Add the stock, beer, potatoes, cabbage, carrot, coriander seeds, allspice, and peppercorns (wrap and tie the spices in cheesecloth if desired). Cover and bring to a boil, then lower the heat to low and simmer until the potatoes are tender, 10 to 15 minutes. (Discard the spices if wrapped.) Stir in the parsley.

2 Ladle the soup into bowls and serve hot. Pass the mustard alongside for diners to add to their liking.

Makes 6 servings

ROASTED RED PEPPER and TOMATO SOUP

 Serve with an American-Style Light Amber Lager, such as Michelob Ultra Amber

3 red bell peppers (about 1½ pounds total)

3 tablespoons olive oil

1 large onion, chopped

2 garlic cloves, minced

1 can (28 ounces) whole San Marzano or other plum tomatoes

1 tablespoon smoked paprika (*pimentón*)

3 cups vegetable or chicken stock

2 teaspoons fresh lemon juice

Salt and freshly ground black pepper

Crème fraîche or plain yogurt

Chopped fresh flat-leaf parsley

1 Preheat the broiler. Place the bell peppers on a baking sheet and broil 4 to 5 inches from the heat source until the skins are blackened and blistered all over, turning as needed, about 8 minutes. Transfer to a paper or plastic bag and close tightly. Let stand for 10 minutes (the steam will loosen the skins). Peel, stem, and seed the peppers, reserving any juices.

2 In a soup pot, heat the olive oil over medium heat. Add the onion and cook, stirring often, until soft, about 5 minutes. Add the garlic and cook, stirring, until translucent, 1 to 2 minutes. Add the roasted peppers and any juices, the tomatoes along with their juices, and the paprika. Bring to a low simmer and cook, stirring occasionally, for about 3 minutes.

3 In a blender or food processor, purée the soup in batches until smooth. Return the purée to the pot over medium heat. Add the stock and lemon juice, stirring until hot. Season to taste with salt and pepper.

4 Ladle the soup into cups or bowls, top each with a dollop of crème fraîche, and garnish with the parsley. Serve hot.

Makes 10 to 12 servings

CORN and TOMATO SALAD

Serve with an American-Style Premium Lager, such as Budweiser

3 ears sweet corn

1 pound tomatoes, cored and diced

$\frac{1}{4}$ cup diced torpedo onion or red onion, rinsed in cold water and patted dry

1 tablespoon rice wine vinegar

$\frac{1}{4}$ cup chopped fresh basil

Salt and freshly ground black pepper

1 Over a large bowl, cut the kernels from the ears of corn. Scrape the remaining pulp from the cobs using the dull side of a knife, then discard the cobs.

2 Stir in the tomatoes and onion. Sprinkle with the vinegar and basil and toss to mix well. Season to taste with salt and pepper and serve.

Cook's Tip: Fresh corn is often so sweet and tender that there is no need to cook it. Be sure to use ripe tomatoes for the best flavor. Make this dish an hour or so in advance of serving so the flavor improves.

Makes 4 to 6 servings

MARINATED CUCUMBER SALAD

Serve with an American-Style Light Lager, such as Bud Light

1 cucumber, seeded and finely chopped

$\frac{1}{2}$ cup plain yogurt

2 tablespoons rice vinegar

2 tablespoons honey

2 teaspoons minced fresh mint, plus sprigs for garnish

$\frac{1}{8}$ teaspoon cayenne pepper

Salt and freshly ground black pepper

1 In a bowl, combine the cucumber, yogurt, vinegar, honey, minced mint, and cayenne. Season to taste with salt and black pepper. Toss gently. Garnish with the mint sprigs and serve.

Cook's Tip: You can serve this salad on its own or with grilled chicken or fish.

Makes 4 servings

Bud vs. Bud Light—The Bud Bowl was an ad disguised as a football game between computer-generated bottles of Budweiser and Bud Light, which squared off during the real Super Bowl (a can of beer scored a touchdown in 1994, but was tossed from the game for its excessive end-zone celebration). Here are the historic Bud Bowl stats:

1989—Budweiser 27, Bud Light 24

1990—Budweiser 36, Bud Light 34

1991—Bud Light 23, Budweiser 21

1992—Budweiser 27, Bud Light 24

1993—Budweiser 35, Bud Light 31

1994—Bud Light 20, Budweiser 14

1995—Budweiser 26, Bud Light 24

1997—Budweiser 27, Bud Light 24

CARROT, FETA, and BLACK OLIVE SALAD

Serve with an American-Style Premium Lager, such as Busch

5 large carrots, peeled and coarsely grated

1/2 cup fresh cilantro leaves, chopped

1 cup crumbled feta cheese

3/4 cup pitted black olives such as Kalamata

1/4 cup fresh lemon juice

1/3 cup extra-virgin olive oil

2 teaspoons toasted cumin seeds

1 In a serving bowl, combine the carrots, cilantro, feta, and olives and toss to mix well.

2 Pour the lemon juice into a small bowl, then slowly drizzle in the olive oil, whisking to blend. Pour the dressing over the carrot mixture and toss to combine. Sprinkle with the cumin seeds and serve.

Cook's Tip: You can serve this salad as a first course or side dish; it's excellent alongside grilled lamb chops.

Makes 4 to 6 servings

WARM SPINACH SALAD with APPLES and BACON

Serve with a Honey-Flavored Specialty Beer, such as Michelob Honey Lager

1 small Granny Smith apple, cored and thinly sliced

1 small red onion, thinly sliced

1/2 cup dried cranberries, chopped

1 package (10 ounces) baby spinach

1/3 cup balsamic vinegar

1 tablespoon sugar

2 tablespoons cranberry juice

1 teaspoon Dijon mustard

1/4 teaspoon salt

1/4 teaspoon freshly ground black pepper

2 tablespoons sour cream

2 bacon slices, cooked, drained, and crumbled

1 In a large bowl, combine the apple, onion, cranberries, and spinach and toss to mix well.

2 In a small saucepan, combine the vinegar, sugar, cranberry juice, mustard, salt, and pepper over medium heat. Bring to a boil and cook for 1 minute. Remove from the heat and stir in the sour cream. Drizzle the warm dressing over the salad and toss well. Sprinkle with the bacon. Serve immediately.

Cook's Tip: Toss the salad while the dressing is still hot to wilt the spinach leaves.

Makes 6 servings

MELON, SERRANO, and ARUGULA SALAD

Serve with a European-Style Pilsner, such as Kirin Ichiban

3 tablespoons sherry vinegar

1 tablespoon olive oil

1 teaspoon molasses

1 garlic clove, minced

1/4 teaspoon ground cumin

1/4 teaspoon salt

1/4 teaspoon freshly ground black pepper

8 cups loosely packed trimmed arugula

1 ripe cantaloupe, peeled and cut into thin slices

3 ounces serrano ham, thinly sliced

1/4 cup (1 ounce) shaved Manchego cheese

1 In a large bowl, combine the vinegar, oil, molasses, garlic, cumin, salt, and pepper, stirring well with a whisk.

2 Arrange the arugula in an even layer on a serving platter. Top with the cantaloupe slices and ham, and sprinkle evenly with the cheese. Pour over some of the dressing and serve immediately.

Cook's Tip: Serrano ham is an air-cured ham from Spain. You can find it in the deli section of many supermarkets, or you can substitute prosciutto.

Makes 6 servings

NORTHWEST WALDORF SALAD

Serve with an English-Style Pale Ale, such as Michelob Pale Ale

3/4 cup finely chopped celery

1/2 cup chopped dried cherries

1/4 cup chopped hazelnuts, toasted

1/3 cup plain yogurt

3 tablespoons sour cream

1 tablespoon fresh lemon juice

1/4 teaspoon salt

2 Bartlett pears (about 1 pound total)

1 In a large bowl, combine the celery, cherries, and hazelnuts.

2 In a small bowl, combine the yogurt, sour cream, lemon juice, and salt, stirring well with a whisk. Drizzle the yogurt mixture over the celery mixture and toss gently.

3 Peel, core, and chop the pears. Add the pears to the salad and toss gently. Cover and refrigerate for 1 hour. Serve chilled.

Makes 4 to 6 servings

GREEN BEAN and HAZELNUT SALAD

Serve with an American-Style Amber Lager, such as Michelob Amber Bock

³/₄ cup hazelnuts

8 cups packed green beans (about 1¹/₂ pounds total), stems trimmed

2 tablespoons chopped fresh mint

1 tablespoon grated lemon zest

2 teaspoons fresh lemon juice

¹/₂ teaspoon salt

¹/₄ cup hazelnut oil or extra-virgin olive oil

1 Preheat the oven to 375°F. Spread the nuts on a baking sheet and bake until golden under the skins (break one to test), 10 to 15 minutes. When the nuts are cool enough to handle, rub in a kitchen towel to remove as many skins as possible. Chop coarsely and set aside.

2 In a large pot over high heat, bring 3 quarts salted water to a boil. Add the green beans and cook just until crisp-tender, 4 to 7 minutes. Drain in a colander, then plunge the beans into a bowl of ice water to cool. Drain again and set aside.

3 In a small bowl, stir together the mint, lemon zest, lemon juice, and salt to make the dressing. Drizzle in the hazelnut oil, whisking constantly.

4 In a large bowl, gently toss the beans with the dressing and hazelnuts. Serve at room temperature.

Makes 6 servings

ROASTED BEET and CITRUS SALAD

Serve with a Wheat Beer, such as Michelob Bavarian Style Wheat

1 tablespoon olive oil, plus 1 tablespoon for the dressing

1¹/₂ pounds small golden beets, roots and 1 inch of stem intact

¹/₄ cup fresh orange juice

1 tablespoon cider vinegar

1 teaspoon honey

1 garlic clove, minced

¹/₄ teaspoon salt

¹/₄ teaspoon freshly ground black pepper

4 cups mixed salad greens

3 cups chopped beet greens

1¹/₂ cups tangerine or orange sections, halved crosswise (about 8 tangerines total)

2 tablespoons freshly shaved Parmesan cheese

1 tablespoon coarsely chopped walnuts, toasted

1 Preheat the oven to 400°F. Scrub the beets with a brush. Place the beets on the baking sheet and toss gently to coat with 1 tablespoon of the olive oil. Bake until tender, about 45 minutes. Let cool slightly. Trim off the roots and stems and rub off the skins. Cut the beets in half.

2 In a large bowl, combine the orange juice, vinegar, the remaining 1 tablespoon olive oil, honey, garlic, salt, and pepper, stirring with a whisk. Add the beets and toss gently to coat. Using a slotted spoon, transfer the beets to another bowl and set aside, reserving the orange juice mixture in the large bowl. Add the salad greens and beet greens to the large bowl and toss well.

3 Arrange about 1 cup of the greens mixture on individual salad plates. Top each salad with the beets, tangerine sections, cheese, and walnuts, dividing evenly. Serve immediately.

Makes 6 servings

FISH & SHELLFISH

🦅 **Chef's Specialty**

GRILLED TUNA NIÇOISE

Serve with an American-Style Amber Lager, such as Michelob Amber Bock

DRESSING

2 tablespoons red wine vinegar

1 tablespoon extra-virgin olive oil

¹/₂ teaspoon Dijon mustard

¹/₂ teaspoon chopped fresh tarragon

¹/₄ teaspoon salt

¹/₄ teaspoon freshly ground black pepper

¹/₂ pound green beans, stems trimmed

¹/₂ pound Yukon gold potatoes, quartered

6 yellowfin tuna steaks (about 6 ounces each)

¹/₄ teaspoon salt

¹/₄ teaspoon freshly ground black pepper

4 cups mixed salad greens

¹/₄ cup Niçoise olives

3 hard-boiled large eggs, quartered

1 To prepare the dressing, in a small bowl, combine the vinegar, olive oil, mustard, tarragon, salt, and pepper, stirring well with a whisk. Set aside.

2 In a large saucepan over high heat, bring 2 quarts salted water to a boil. Add the green beans and cook just until crisp-tender, 4 to 7 minutes. Remove with a slotted spoon and plunge into a bowl of ice water to cool. Drain the beans and set aside. Add the potatoes to the pan of boiling water and cook until tender when pierced with a knife, about 10 minutes. Drain the potatoes and set aside.

3 Prepare a grill for cooking over high heat. First, oil the grill rack. If using a charcoal grill, prepare a solid bed of hot coals. If using a gas grill, preheat to high (you can hold your hand 1 to 2 inches above grill level only 2 to 3 seconds).

4 Sprinkle the fish with the salt and pepper. Lay the fish on the grill rack. Close the lid if using a gas grill. Cook for about 3 minutes on each side for medium-rare, or until the desired degree of doneness.

5 In a large bowl, combine the beans, potatoes, salad greens, and olives. Drizzle with the dressing and toss well. Arrange the salad mixture on a large platter with the tuna steaks and egg halves. Serve immediately.

Cook's Tip: This version of the classic dish is a great outdoor meal. You can also cook the tuna in a grill pan.

Makes 6 servings

GRILLED TROUT with BACON and SPINACH

Serve with an American-Style Premium Lager, such as Michelob

4 bacon slices, cut into $1/2$-inch dice

4 trout fillets (about 6 ounces each), skin intact

$3/4$ teaspoon salt

$3/4$ teaspoon freshly ground black pepper

4 cups baby spinach

1 shallot, finely chopped

$1^1/2$ tablespoons sherry vinegar

San Francisco, 1906—One of the lesser-known facts about Adolphus Busch is that he was in San Francisco during the 1906 earthquake. "Fires started in all parts of the city, the main water pipes burst and flooded the streets," he wrote in a dispatch that was published in the St. Louis *Globe-Democrat.* "Then the worst happened. The fire spread over three-fourths of the city, and could not be controlled, no water to fight it, no light, and the earth still trembling. We were fortunate to secure two conveyances and fled to Nob Hill, from which we witnessed the indescribable drama. Block after block was devastated. The fires blazed like volcanoes, and all business houses, hotels, theatres, in fact, the entire business portion, lay in ruins, and two-thirds of the residences; but I trust 'Frisco will rise a phoenix from its ashes, that a new and more beautiful San Francisco will be born . . . We are now en route home with nothing saved but what is on our backs . . ."

1 Prepare a grill for cooking over high heat. First, oil the grill rack. If using a charcoal grill, prepare a solid bed of hot coals. If using a gas grill, preheat to high (you can hold your hand 1 to 2 inches above grill level only 2 to 3 seconds).

2 Meanwhile, in a skillet, cook the bacon over medium-high heat until crisp, about 6 minutes. Using a slotted spoon, transfer to paper towels to drain. Reserve the bacon fat in the skillet.

3 Brush the fillets on both sides with the reserved bacon fat and sprinkle the flesh side with $1/2$ teaspoon of the salt and $1/2$ teaspoon of the pepper. Lay the trout on the grill rack, flesh side down, and cook until beginning to brown, about 2 minutes. Using a large spatula (or two large spatulas), turn the fish and cook until opaque throughout, about 2 minutes longer. Transfer to a platter and cover to keep warm.

4 Put the spinach in a large bowl. Sprinkle with the remaining $1/4$ teaspoon each salt and pepper. Pour or spoon off and discard all but 2 tablespoons fat in the pan and heat the skillet over high heat. Add the shallot and cook until softened, about 3 minutes. Stir in the vinegar. Pour the warm vinaigrette over the spinach and toss to coat. Taste and adjust the seasoning. Divide the spinach between 4 serving plates, top each with a fillet, and sprinkle with the bacon bits. Serve immediately.

Cook's Tip: If you can find golden trout, use them in this recipe. They have gorgeous salmon-colored flesh and a wonderful flavor, perfect with the bacon and spinach in this recipe.

Makes 4 servings

BAJA-STYLE FRIED FISH TACOS

Serve with a European-Style Pilsner, such as Grolsch

CABBAGE AND CILANTRO SLAW

6 cups finely shredded cabbage (about 10 ounces)

1/3 cup chopped fresh cilantro

3 tablespoons fresh lime juice

2 tablespoons vegetable oil

1/4 teaspoon red pepper flakes

Salt

CHIPOTLE TARTAR SAUCE

2 tablespoons canned chipotle chiles in adobo, rinsed, stemmed, and seeded

1 cup mayonnaise

1/4 cup sweet pickle relish

1/4 cup chopped onion

Salt

1 cup Grolsch

1 cup all-purpose flour

1 teaspoon salt

1 1/2 pounds boneless and skinless firm, white-fleshed fish such as cod or tilapia

Vegetable oil

6 to 8 corn tortillas (8 inches in diameter), warmed

Lime wedges

1 To prepare the slaw, in a large bowl, mix together the cabbage, cilantro, lime juice, oil, red pepper flakes, and salt to taste. Set aside.

2 To prepare the tartar sauce, in a blender, purée the chiles with the mayonnaise, relish, and onion until smooth. Season to taste with salt and set aside.

3 Preheat the oven to 200°F. In a bowl, combine the beer, flour, and salt, whisking until well blended.

4 Rinse the fish and pat dry. Cut the fish crosswise into strips 1 inch wide.

5 In a large skillet with sides at least 2 inches high, pour in oil to a depth of about 1 inch. Bring the oil to 360°F on a deep-frying thermometer over medium-high heat. Using a fork, dip each piece of fish into the beer batter, lift out, and let drain briefly. Slip the fish into the oil, a few pieces at a time, and fry until golden (adjust the heat to maintain 360°F), turning to brown on all sides, 2 to 4 minutes for each batch. Using a slotted spoon, transfer to a baking sheet lined with paper towels. Keep warm in the oven while you fry the remaining fish.

6 To assemble the tacos, top each tortilla with a few pieces of fish, then a spoonful of cabbage and cilantro slaw. Serve with the chipotle tartar sauce and the lime wedges.

Makes 6 to 8 tacos

SALMON with CREAM and FRESH CHIVES

1 pound skinless salmon fillet, cut in half

1 cup chicken stock

1/2 cup Budweiser

1 bay leaf

1 sprig fresh thyme

1/4 cup heavy cream

1/4 cup minced fresh chives

1 Preheat the oven to 375°F. Place the salmon pieces in a single layer in a glass baking dish. Pour the stock and beer over the salmon and bake until opaque but still moist-looking in the center of the thickest part (cut to test), about 20 minutes. Transfer to a platter. Set aside and cover to keep warm.

2 Pour the liquid from the baking dish into a saucepan over medium-high heat. Add the bay leaf and thyme and bring to a simmer. Cook until reduced by one-fourth, about 2 minutes. Discard the bay leaf and thyme and stir in the cream and chives. Lower the heat to medium-low and simmer until the sauce thickens, about 2 minutes longer. Pour the sauce over the salmon and serve immediately.

Cook's Tip: Chef Sam Niemann likes to serve this dish at dinner parties. It makes an elegant presentation and is very easy to prepare. Keep a close eye on the salmon, as it can easily overcook.

Makes 4 servings

SEARED SALMON with ALMONDS and ORANGE

1/4 cup sliced almonds

4 salmon fillets (about 6 ounces each), skin intact

Salt

1 tablespoon olive oil

1/2 teaspoon grated orange zest

3/4 cup fresh orange juice

1/2 cup Michelob Bavarian Style Wheat

2 teaspoons chopped fresh thyme

1 In a large, dry skillet, stir the almonds over medium heat until lightly browned, 1 to 2 minutes. Transfer to a plate and set aside. Reserve the pan.

2 Rinse the salmon fillets and pat dry. Season them with 1/4 teaspoon salt. Place the skillet over medium-high heat and add the olive oil. When the oil is hot, add the salmon, skin side up, and cook until well browned on the bottoms, 3 to 5 minutes. Turn and cook until opaque but still slightly pink and moist-looking in the center of the thickest part (cut to test), 1 to 3 minutes longer, depending on the thickness of the fish. Transfer the salmon, skin side down, to individual plates or a serving platter and cover to keep warm.

3 Add the orange zest and juice and the beer to the pan. Boil, stirring and scraping to loosen any browned bits on the bottom of the pan, until reduced to 1/2 cup, about 6 minutes. Stir in the thyme. Season to taste with salt. Spoon the orange sauce over the salmon and sprinkle with the toasted almonds. Serve immediately.

Makes 4 servings

SALMON with PICHOLINE OLIVES

Serve with an American-Style Light Lager, such as Bud Light

1 cup dry vermouth

2 garlic cloves, chopped

1 large shallot, chopped

1 cup chicken or fish stock

1 cup heavy cream

$1/3$ cup chopped pitted picholine or other mild green olives (see Cook's Tip)

2 teaspoons chopped fresh thyme, plus sprigs for garnish

Salt and freshly ground black pepper

1 whole boneless and skinless salmon fillet (about 3 pounds)

1 tablespoon butter, cut into small pieces

1 tablespoon chopped fresh tarragon

1 Preheat the oven to 400°F. Lightly butter a 17-by-12-inch baking pan.

2 Pour the vermouth into a skillet and add the garlic and shallot. Bring to a boil over high heat and boil until reduced by about half, 5 to 8 minutes. Add $1/2$ cup of the stock and return to a boil.

3 Add the cream, olives, and chopped thyme. Boil, stirring occasionally, until the sauce is thick enough to coat the back of a spoon and is reduced to about $1^1/4$ cups, about 5 minutes. Season to taste with salt and pepper. Remove from the heat, cover, and set aside.

4 Rinse the salmon and pat dry. Using tweezers or needlenose pliers, pull out the pin bones. Lay the salmon in the prepared baking pan. Dot the salmon with the butter, drizzle with the remaining stock, and sprinkle with the tarragon. Sprinkle lightly with salt and pepper.

5 Bake until the salmon is opaque but still slightly pink and moist-looking in the center of the thickest part (cut to test), 13 to 18 minutes. Transfer the salmon to a serving platter.

6 If needed, reheat the sauce over medium-high heat, stirring until hot. Drizzle the salmon with some of the sauce and garnish with the thyme sprigs. Serve immediately, passing the remaining sauce at the table.

Cook's Tip: To pit the olives, crush them slightly with the flat side of a chef's knife, then remove the pits.

Makes 6 servings

Secretary of Beer—Napoleon said that an army marches on its stomach, but it was beer that helped fuel the rebels who fought the British in the Revolutionary War (the Continental Congress had mandated a ration of a quart a day for its soldiers). By the time that founding father James Madison became the young nation's fourth president, beer was an important enough part of American life that Madison proposed a national brewery and a Secretary of Beer, both of which were rejected by Congress.

GRILLED SALMON with CHERMOULA SAUCE

Serve with a Doppelbock, such as Brewmaster's Private Reserve

CHERMOULA SAUCE

$1/2$ **cup fresh lemon juice**

$1/4$ **cup olive oil**

$1/3$ **cup chopped fresh cilantro**

2 tablespoons paprika

1 tablespoon ground cumin

2 teaspoons ground coriander

$1/4$ **teaspoon cayenne pepper**

3 garlic cloves, minced

$1/2$ **teaspoon salt**

$1/2$ **teaspoon freshly ground black pepper**

2 pounds green or yellow zucchini, trimmed and cut crosswise into pieces 1 inch thick

2 red bell peppers (about 1 pound total), stemmed, seeded, and cut into 1-inch squares

1 whole boneless salmon fillet (about 3 pounds), skin intact

Lemon wedges

1 Soak 8 to 10 wooden skewers in water to cover for 30 minutes (see Cook's Tip page 161). Prepare a grill for cooking over indirect heat. First oil the grill rack. If using a charcoal grill, light 50 to 60 briquettes and let burn until covered with ash, 20 to 30 minutes, then mound them to one side. Place a drip pan on the side cleared of coals—this is the indirect heat area. Set the oiled grill rack in place. If using a gas grill, turn all the burners to high and close the lid. When the temperature inside the grill reaches 350° to 400°F, lift the lid, turn off one of the burners, and lower the other burner(s) to medium. Place a drip pan under the turned-off burner—this is the indirect heat area. Set the oiled grill rack in place.

2 To prepare the *chermoula* sauce, in a bowl, combine the lemon juice, olive oil, cilantro, paprika, cumin, coriander, cayenne, garlic, salt, and black pepper, stirring with a whisk.

3 In another bowl, combine the zucchini and bell peppers and drizzle with $2/3$ cup of the *chermoula* sauce, tossing to coat. Thread onto the soaked wooden skewers, alternating zucchini and peppers.

4 Rinse the salmon and pat dry. Using tweezers or needlenose pliers, pull out the pin bones. Lay a doubled sheet of heavy-duty aluminum foil slightly larger than the salmon on a 15-by-12-inch baking sheet. Lay the salmon, skin side down, on the foil. Trim the foil to within about an inch around the salmon, then fold the edges over and up to form a slight rim. Spread the remaining *chermoula* sauce evenly over the salmon.

5 Slide the salmon and foil off the baking sheet onto the grill rack over the indirect heat area. Lay the vegetable skewers directly over the heat. Close the lid. Cook the vegetables, turning once, until browned and tender when pierced with a knife, 10 to 15 minutes. Remove the skewers from the grill, close the lid again, and continue to cook the salmon until opaque but still slightly pink and moist-looking in the center of the thickest part (cut to test), 10 to 15 minutes longer.

6 Using a large, rimless baking sheet or several wide spatulas, transfer the foil and fish to a serving platter or board. Tuck the edges of the foil under the fish. Set the vegetable skewers alongside, garnish with the lemon wedges, and serve.

Cook's Tip: You can prepare the salmon and vegetables in advance (steps 2 through 4), then cover and refrigerate for up to 2 hours before grilling. If available, use Hungarian or Spanish paprika for the *chermoula* sauce.

Makes 8 to 10 servings

LEMON SOLE with LEMON-CAPER SAUCE

Serve with an English-Style Pale Ale, such as Michelob Pale Ale

1 tablespoon extra-virgin olive oil

4 skinless lemon sole fillets (about 6 ounces each)

$^1/_2$ teaspoon salt

$^1/_4$ teaspoon freshly ground black pepper

1 teaspoon butter

1 garlic clove, minced

$^3/_4$ cup chicken stock

2 tablespoons capers, rinsed, drained, and minced

1 tablespoon fresh lemon juice

1 tablespoon minced fresh flat-leaf parsley

1 In a large skillet, heat the olive oil over medium heat. Sprinkle the sole fillets with the salt and pepper. Lay the fillets in the pan and cook, turning once, until the fish flakes easily when tested with a fork, about 3 minutes on each side. Transfer the fillets to individual plates or a serving platter, cover, and keep warm.

2 In the same pan, melt the butter over medium heat. Add the garlic and cook until lightly browned, about 1 minute. Add the stock, scraping to loosen any browned bits on the bottom of the pan. Bring to a boil and cook until reduced to $^1/_4$ cup, about 6 minutes. Stir in the capers and lemon juice. Cook until the sauce is slightly thickened, about 3 minutes. Remove from the heat and stir in the parsley. Pour over the sole and serve immediately.

Cook's Tip: Lemon sole is an American variety of flatfish, which includes flounder. Most flatfish will work well here.

Makes 4 servings

STRIPED BASS with LEMONGRASS

Serve with a European-Style Pilsner, such as Kirin Ichiban

4 skinless striped bass fillets (about 8 ounces each)

$^1/_2$ teaspoon salt

$^1/_2$ teaspoon freshly ground black pepper

$^1/_2$ cup Kirin Ichiban

1 garlic clove, thinly sliced

2 stalks lemongrass, outer leaves and upper stalk discarded, cut into very thin julienne

1 shallot, thinly sliced

2 tablespoons chopped fresh cilantro

1 Preheat the oven to 350°F. In a large ovenproof skillet, arrange the fillets in a single layer and sprinkle with the salt and pepper. Pour in the beer and sprinkle with the garlic, lemongrass, and shallot. Place the pan over high heat and bring to a simmer. Cover with aluminum foil and transfer to the oven. Cook until the fillets are opaque throughout. Using a slotted spatula, transfer to individual plates. Sprinkle with the cilantro and serve.

Cook's Tip: You can substitute halibut, lingcod, Pacific cod, or black sea bass for the striped bass in this recipe.

Makes 4 servings

GRILLED SNAPPER PACKETS

Serve with an American-Style Premium Lager, such as Budweiser

1 large Yukon gold potato, peeled and cut into 8 slices

1 Vidalia or other sweet onion, thinly sliced

4 skinless red snapper fillets (about 6 ounces each)

8 tablespoons (1 stick) unsalted butter

1 shallot, minced

2 large garlic cloves, minced

4 small sprigs fresh tarragon

Salt and freshly ground black pepper

1 cup Budweiser

1 Prepare a grill for cooking over indirect heat. If using a charcoal grill, light 50 to 60 briquettes and let burn until covered with ash, then mound them to one side. If using a gas grill, turn all the burners to high and close the lid. When the temperature inside the grill reaches 350° to 400°F, lift the lid, turn off one of the burners, and lower the other burner(s) to medium.

2 Cut out four 12-by-18-inch pieces of aluminum foil and place on a work surface. Stack 2 potato slices in the middle of each piece of foil. Arrange one-fourth of the sliced onion on top of each and place a fillet on top. Place a 2-tablespoon chunk of butter on top of each fillet and sprinkle with the shallot and garlic. Top each with a tarragon sprig and season to taste with salt and pepper. Fold up the sides of the foil around the contents. Carefully pour 1/4 cup of the beer into each packet, then fold the opposite sides together to seal the packets tightly.

3 Lay the packets on the grill rack directly over the fire. If using a gas grill, close the lid. Cook until you hear the beer boiling, then move to the indirect heat area and cook until the fish is opaque throughout, about 20 minutes. Empty packets onto individual plates, and serve.

Cook's Tip: A variation on the French classic, here Chef Brent Wertz wraps snapper in foil to cook on the grill.

Makes 4 servings

SEARED SNAPPER PROVENÇALE

Serve with an English-Style Pale Ale, such as Michelob Pale Ale

2 cups grape tomatoes, halved

1/2 cup chopped roasted red bell pepper (see Cook's Tip page 150)

1/4 cup chopped pitted Niçoise or Kalamata olives

3 tablespoons chopped fresh basil

2 tablespoons chopped shallots

1 tablespoon balsamic vinegar

2 teaspoons extra-virgin olive oil

1/4 teaspoon salt

1 tablespoon olive oil

4 skinless red snapper fillets (about 6 ounces each)

1/4 teaspoon freshly ground black pepper

1 In a bowl, combine the tomatoes, roasted pepper, olives, basil, shallots, vinegar, and extra-virgin olive oil. Sprinkle with 1/8 teaspoon of the salt and toss well. Set aside.

2 In a large skillet, heat the olive oil over medium-high heat. Sprinkle the snapper fillets with the remaining 1/8 teaspoon salt and the pepper. Add the fish to the pan and cook, turning once, until the fish flakes easily when tested with a fork, about 4 minutes on each side. Serve with the tomato mixture.

Makes 4 servings

CORNMEAL-CRUSTED CATFISH

Serve with an American-Style Premium Lager, such as Busch

4 bacon slices

$1/3$ cup medium-ground yellow cornmeal

2 teaspoons Cajun seasoning

$1/2$ teaspoon salt

4 skinless catfish fillets (about 6 ounces each)

1 In a large skillet, cook the bacon over medium heat until crisp, about 6 minutes. Transfer the bacon to paper towels to drain. Spoon or pour off and discard all but 2 tablespoons of fat in the pan. (Crumble the bacon and reserve for another use.)

2 In a shallow dish, combine the cornmeal, Cajun seasoning, and salt, stirring with a whisk. Dredge the catfish fillets in the cornmeal mixture, shaking off any excess.

3 Heat the reserved bacon fat over medium-high heat. Add the catfish fillets and cook, turning once, until the fish flakes easily when tested with a fork, about 5 minutes on each side.

Cook's Tip: The bacon drippings used to cook the catfish lend this Southern family favorite authentic flavor. Use the crumbled bacon in a potato or spinach salad.

Makes 4 servings

SWORDFISH with SICILIAN FLAVORS

Serve with a Wheat Beer, such as Michelob Bavarian Style Wheat

2 tablespoons olive oil

4 swordfish steaks (about 6 ounces each)

$1/2$ teaspoon salt

$1/2$ teaspoon freshly ground black pepper

1 tablespoon sliced almonds

2 large garlic cloves, minced

2 tablespoons raisins

2 tablespoons fresh orange juice

$1^1/2$ tablespoons chopped pitted Kalamata olives

$1^1/2$ tablespoons chopped roasted red bell pepper (see Cook's Tip page 150)

1 In a large skillet, heat 1 tablespoon of the olive oil over medium-high heat. Sprinkle the swordfish steaks evenly with the salt and pepper. Lay the fish in the pan and cook, turning once, until the fish flakes easily when tested with a fork, about 5 minutes on each side. Transfer the fish to individual plates or a serving platter, cover, and keep warm.

2 In the same pan, heat the remaining 1 tablespoon olive oil over medium-high heat. Add the almonds and garlic and sauté for 30 seconds. Add the raisins, orange juice, olives, and roasted pepper. Cook until the liquid evaporates, about 1 minute. Spoon over the fish and serve.

Cook's Tip: You can substitute tuna steaks for the swordfish, if you like.

Makes 4 servings

LEMON-GARLIC SHRIMP SKEWERS

Serve with an American-Style Premium Lager, such as Michelob Golden Draft

2 tablespoons kosher salt

2 tablespoons sugar

2 to 2¹/₂ pounds jumbo shrimp, peeled and deveined

¹/₄ cup olive oil

¹/₄ cup chopped fresh flat-leaf parsley

1 tablespoon grated lemon zest

2 or 3 garlic cloves, minced

¹/₂ teaspoon freshly ground black pepper

Lemon wedges

Kraeusening—Kraeusening is a secondary fermentation process designed to create carbonation naturally. In Budweiser, which is the only major beer to go through a second ferment, kraeusening is achieved by letting beechwood chips from Anheuser-Busch tree farms in Kentucky and Tennessee soak in the cooling brew for about three weeks. More than imparting a distinct flavor to the beer, the chips create countless nooks and crannies to which the yeast clings and completely consumes the remaining sugars in the beer.

1 In a large bowl, stir together the salt and sugar. Add the shrimp and stir gently to coat. Cover and refrigerate for 45 minutes to 1 hour.

2 Meanwhile, prepare a grill for cooking over high heat. First, oil the grill rack. If using a charcoal grill, prepare a solid bed of hot coals. If using a gas grill, preheat to high (you can hold your hand 1 to 2 inches above grill level only 2 to 3 seconds). Soak 12 wooden skewers in water to cover for 30 minutes (see Cook's Tip page 161).

3 Rinse the shrimp well and drain. Rinse and dry the bowl, then return the shrimp to the bowl. Add the olive oil, parsley, lemon zest, garlic, and pepper. Stir gently to coat. Thread the shrimp onto the soaked skewers, running a skewer through the body once near the tail and once near the head end of each shrimp so it looks like the letter C.

4 Lay the skewers on the grill rack. Close the lid if using a gas grill. Cook, turning once, until the shrimp are bright pink and opaque but still moist-looking in the center of the thickest part (cut to test), about 3 minutes on each side. Serve with lemon wedges.

Cook's Tip: A brief cure in salt and sugar not only adds flavor to the shrimp and makes them more tender but also acts as a mild preservative. You can assemble the skewers up to a day ahead, then cover and refrigerate until ready to grill.

Makes 6 to 8 servings

MUSSELS and CLAMS with GREEN CURRY

Serve with an American-Style Light Lager, such as Michelob Ultra

1 package (7 ounces) rice noodles

1 tablespoon olive oil

1 large garlic clove, minced

1 serrano chile, seeded and thinly sliced

1 can (14 ounces) coconut milk

1 cup chicken stock

1 tablespoon green curry paste

1 teaspoon peeled and finely grated fresh ginger

1½ pounds mussels, scrubbed and debearded

1½ pounds littleneck clams, scrubbed

2 cups grape or cherry tomatoes

1 cup chopped fresh cilantro

¼ cup fresh lime juice

Lime wedges

1 In a bowl, soak the noodles in warm water to cover for 15 minutes.

2 Meanwhile, in a large Dutch oven, heat the olive oil over medium heat. Add the garlic and chile and sauté for 1 minute. Stir in the coconut milk, stock, curry paste, and ginger. Bring to a boil and add the mussels and clams, discarding any that do not close to the touch. Cover, lower the heat to medium-low, and simmer until the shells open, about 5 minutes. Remove from the heat, discarding any shellfish that failed to open. Stir in the tomatoes, ½ cup of the cilantro, and the lime juice, tossing well.

3 Drain the noodles and divide among 4 individual shallow bowls. Top each with the mussels and clams. Drizzle the sauce evenly over shellfish and sprinkle each bowl with 2 tablespoons of the remaining cilantro. Serve with lime wedges.

Cook's Tip: If you don't have a serrano chile, substitute ¼ teaspoon red pepper flakes.

Makes 4 servings

SHRIMP GARAM MASALA

Serve with an English-Style Pale Ale, such as Michelob Pale Ale

1½ pounds large shrimp, peeled and deveined

1½ teaspoons garam masala

1½ tablespoons canola oil

1 green bell pepper, stemmed, seeded, and chopped

1 onion, chopped

⅓ cup Michelob Pale Ale

4 tablespoons chopped fresh cilantro

¼ teaspoon salt

¼ teaspoon freshly ground black pepper

Lime wedges

1 Sprinkle the shrimp evenly with the garam masala and let stand for 5 minutes.

2 In a large skillet, heat the oil over medium-high heat. Add the bell pepper and onion and sauté until crisp-tender, about 5 minutes. Add the shrimp and sauté until bright pink, about 3 minutes. Stir in the beer, 3 tablespoons of the cilantro, and the salt and pepper. Cook for 30 seconds longer, then remove from the heat. Sprinkle with the remaining 1 tablespoon cilantro. Serve with the lime wedges.

Cook's Tip: Find the peppery Indian spice blend garam masala in the spice aisle of large grocery stores. If you can't find garam masala, substitute equal parts ground cumin, black pepper, cloves, and nutmeg. Ladle these shrimp over basmati rice.

Makes 4 servings

PASTA with SCALLOPS, TOMATOES, and CAPERS

Serve with an American-Style Premium Lager, such as Rolling Rock

$^1/_3$ **cup extra-virgin olive oil**

6 large garlic cloves, thinly sliced

1$^1/_4$ pounds sea scallops, quartered and patted dry

$^1/_2$ **teaspoon salt**

$^1/_4$ **teaspoon freshly ground black pepper**

3 plum tomatoes, seeded and diced

3 tablespoons capers, rinsed and drained

Pinch of red pepper flakes

1 pound dried *trottole, rotelle,* or fusilli

$^1/_4$ **cup chopped fresh flat-leaf parsley**

1 In a large, heavy skillet, heat the olive oil over high heat. Add the garlic and cook until golden and crisp, 2 to 3 minutes. Set aside.

2 Using a slotted spoon, transfer to paper towels to drain. Add the scallops to the hot pan. Sprinkle with the salt and pepper and cook until lightly browned on the bottoms, 1 to 2 minutes. Turn the scallops and add the tomatoes, capers, and red pepper flakes. Cook until the scallops are just opaque throughout, about 1 minute longer.

3 Meanwhile, in a large pot over high heat, bring about 4 quarts water to a boil. Add the pasta and cook until al dente, 7 to 9 minutes. Drain well. Pour the drained pasta into a large bowl. Add the scallop mixture, the reserved garlic chips, and the parsley and toss gently to mix. Serve immediately.

Cook's Tip: You can use frozen scallops if fresh aren't available. Just defrost the scallops, wrapped tightly, in a bowl of cold water or overnight in the fridge. *Trottole* are large, plump twists, like fusilli that have been inflated with a bicycle pump. If you can't find them, use regular fusilli or *rotelle.*

Makes 4 servings

SCALLOPS with BLACK BEAN SAUCE

Serve with a Porter, such as Michelob Porter

$^1/_2$ **cup Michelob Porter**

2 tablespoons soy sauce

1 tablespoon black bean sauce (see Cook's Tip)

1 teaspoon cornstarch

$^1/_2$ **teaspoon brown sugar**

2 tablespoons vegetable oil

$^3/_4$ **pound sea scallops, quartered if large**

1 tablespoon peeled and minced fresh ginger

1 bunch broccolini, cut into 2-inch pieces

4 green onions, white and tender green parts, thinly sliced

Steamed rice

1 In a small bowl, whisk together the beer, soy sauce, black bean sauce, cornstarch, and brown sugar. Set aside.

2 In a large skillet or wok, heat 1 tablespoon of the oil over high heat until almost smoking. Add the scallops and cook, turning once, until almost opaque throughout, about 30 seconds on each side. Transfer to a plate.

3 Add the remaining 1 tablespoon oil, the ginger, and the broccolini and stir-fry until the vegetables are crisp and tender, 2 to 3 minutes. Return the scallops to the pan and add the beer mixture and green onions. Stir-fry until the sauce thickens slightly, about 30 seconds longer. Serve with the rice.

Cook's Tip: You can find several varieties of jarred black bean sauce in the supermarket, and they make wonderful stir-fries. Here the sauce is spruced up with fresh ginger and cooked with green onions and broccolini, a tender, sweet vegetable resembling broccoli but actually a hybrid of broccoli and cabbage. The sauce is also terrific with shrimp or a combination of shrimp and scallops.

Makes 4 servings

GRILLED LOBSTER with BEER BUTTER

Serve with an American-Style Premium Lager, such as Budweiser

4 lobster tails, thawed if frozen, or 4 live
   Maine lobsters (1¼ to 1½ pounds each)

1 cup Budweiser

1 tablespoon finely chopped shallot

½ teaspoon fresh thyme leaves

Pinch of kosher salt

Pinch of white pepper

½ teaspoon vanilla extract

½ cup unsalted butter, at room temperature

1. Prepare a grill for cooking over high heat. First, oil the grill rack. If using a charcoal grill, prepare a solid bed of hot coals. If using a gas grill, preheat to high (you can hold your hand 1 to 2 inches above grill level only 2 to 3 seconds).

2. If using lobster tails, cut them in half lengthwise. If using live lobsters, cook them in boiling salted water for 2 minutes and drain. Cut the lobsters in half lengthwise and crack the claws with a nutcracker or hammer.

3. In a saucepan, combine the beer, shallot, thyme, salt, and white pepper over medium-high heat and bring to a boil. Lower the heat to medium-low and simmer gently until the liquid is reduced by half. Still at a low simmer, add the vanilla and whisk in the butter in small amounts until all the butter is added and the sauce is smooth.

4. Brush the cut sides of the lobsters with the butter sauce and arrange, cut sides down, on the grill rack. If using a gas grill, close the lid. Cook for about 6 minutes. Turn and cook, brushing the cut sides with the butter, until the flesh is opaque throughout, 3 to 5 minutes longer. Serve hot with the remaining butter sauce.

Cook's Tip: Chef Sam Niemann's butter sauce is great on grilled or boiled lobster alike.

Makes 4 servings

CLASSIC CIOPPINO

Serve with a European-Style Pilsner, such as Grolsch

1 large fennel bulb

3 tablespoons olive oil

1 large onion, chopped

2 garlic cloves, minced

4 tablespoons chopped fresh flat-leaf parsley

3 cans (15 ounces each) diced tomatoes

1 bottle (12 ounces) Grolsch

3 tablespoons tomato paste

1 tablespoon dried basil

½ teaspoon dried oregano

½ teaspoon red pepper flakes

12 clams, scrubbed

2 cooked Dungeness crabs (about 2 pounds each),
   cleaned and cracked

1 pound medium shrimp, peeled and deveined

Salt and freshly ground black pepper

1. Trim off and discard the tough stems and base of the fennel bulb. Rinse the fennel, core, and chop.

2. In a large saucepan, heat the olive oil over medium-high heat. Add the fennel, onion, garlic, and 2 tablespoons of the parsley. Cook until the onion is softened, 8 to 10 minutes. Add the tomatoes along with their juices, the beer, tomato paste, basil, oregano, and red pepper flakes. Raise the heat to high and bring to a boil. Cover, lower the heat to low, and simmer until the flavors are well blended, about 15 minutes.

3. Add the clams, crab, and shrimp, discarding any clams that do not close to the touch. Cover and bring to a boil over high heat, then lower the heat to medium-low and simmer until the clams open, the shrimp turn pink, and the crab is hot, about 5 minutes. Discard any clams that failed to open. Season to taste with salt and pepper. Ladle into wide bowls. Sprinkle with the remaining 2 tablespoons parsley and serve hot.

Makes 4 to 6 servings

ÉTOUFÉE with SAUSAGE and SHRIMP

Serve with a Dry Stout, such as Bare Knuckle Stout

7 tablespoons butter, plus 1 cup (2 sticks)

³/₄ cup all-purpose flour

1 pound andouille sausage, cut into ¹/₂-inch dice

1 pound smoked sausage, cut into ¹/₂-inch dice

¹/₂ onion, diced

1 celery rib, diced

¹/₂ green bell pepper, seeded and diced

3 cups dry stout

2 cups chicken stock

¹/₂ cup Creole seasoning

2 pounds jumbo shrimp, peeled and deveined

1 pound bay scallops

1. In a skillet, melt the 7 tablespoons butter over medium-high heat; be careful not to let it burn. Add the flour gradually, whisking until smooth. Lower the heat to low and continue to cook, whisking constantly, until the mixture is dark brown, about 8 minutes. Set the roux aside.

2. In a large saucepan, melt the 1 cup butter over medium-high heat. Add the andouille sausage, smoked sausage, onion, celery, and bell pepper. Cook, stirring often, until the vegetables are softened, about 10 minutes. Add the beer, stock, and Creole seasoning and bring to a boil. Add the roux and whisk until smooth. Lower the heat to medium-low and simmer gently, still stirring often, for 15 minutes. Add the shrimp and scallops and cook until the flavors have blended and the shrimp and scallops are opaque throughout, about 15 minutes longer. Taste and adjust the seasoning. Ladle the étoufée into bowls and serve hot.

Cook's Tip: The cooked butter-and-flour mixture Chef Sam Niemann uses here is called a *roux*, a classic, flavorful base for thickening sauces and stews. He uses smoked bratwurst for extra-rich flavor.

Makes 4 to 6 servings

Repeal—Immediately after the repeal of Prohibition on April 7, 1933, the first air shipment of Budweiser was loaded onto a waiting TWA Tri-Motor aircraft at St. Louis's Lambert Field. The event was covered by a local radio station because the recipient of this special delivery would be President Roosevelt and other government officials, including former New York Governor Al Smith. August Busch, Sr., believed Smith deserved a special thank you for his longtime, and vocal, opposition to Prohibition.

POULTRY

🦅 Chef's Specialty

THAI SATAY with PINEAPPLE RELISH

Serve with a European-Style Pilsner, such as Tiger

2 tablespoons soy sauce

1 tablespoon *each* light brown sugar, fresh lime juice, and vegetable oil

1 garlic clove, minced

1/2 teaspoon salt

1 pound boneless, skinless chicken thighs, cut into strips about 2 inches long and 1 inch wide

PINEAPPLE RELISH

3 cups fresh pineapple chunks

3/4 cup diced red bell pepper

1 shallot, thinly sliced

2 tablespoons rice wine vinegar

1 tablespoon light brown sugar

1/2 teaspoon salt

Pinch of red pepper flakes

2 tablespoons chopped fresh mint or cilantro

Chopped peanuts (optional)

1 In a shallow dish or glass pie plate, combine the soy sauce, brown sugar, lime juice, oil, garlic, and salt, stirring well. Add the chicken and toss to coat. Cover and let stand at room temperature for 15 minutes or marinate in the refrigerator for up to 4 hours. Meanwhile, prepare the pineapple relish: In a bowl, combine the pineapple, bell pepper, shallot, vinegar, brown sugar, salt, red pepper flakes, and mint and toss to mix well.

2 Soak 8 to 10 wooden skewers in water to cover for 30 minutes. If using a charcoal grill, prepare a solid bed of hot coals. If using a gas grill, preheat to high. Thread the chicken pieces lengthwise onto the soaked skewers, leaving a small space between each piece. Lay the skewers on the grill rack. If using a gas grill, close the lid. Cook, turning as needed, until opaque throughout (cut to test), 10 to 12 minutes total. Serve with the pineapple relish. Sprinkle with the peanuts, if you like.

Makes 4 servings

CHICKEN SKEWERS with ONION and BAY

Serve with an American-Style Light Lager, such as Bud Light

1 1/4 pounds boneless, skinless chicken thighs, cut into 1-inch pieces

2 very large red onions, each cut into 8 wedges

12 fresh or dried imported bay leaves

1 pound large white mushrooms, halved

1/4 cup extra-virgin olive oil

1/2 teaspoon salt

1/2 teaspoon freshly ground black pepper

1 In a large nonreactive bowl or zip-top plastic bag, combine the chicken, onion wedges, bay leaves, mushrooms, olive oil, salt, and pepper, stirring or turning in the bag to coat completely. Marinate in the refrigerator for at least 2 hours or up to overnight.

2 Soak 10 to 14 wooden skewers in water to cover for 30 minutes. Prepare a grill for cooking over high heat. First, oil the grill rack. If using a charcoal grill, prepare a solid bed of hot coals. If using a gas grill, preheat to high (you can hold your hand 1 to 2 inches above grill level only 2 to 3 seconds).

3 Thread the chicken pieces onto the soaked skewers, alternating with the pieces of onion, the bay leaves, and the mushroom halves and leaving a small space between each piece.

4 Lay the skewers on the grill rack. If using a gas grill, close the lid. Cook, turning as needed, until the onions and mushrooms are nicely browned and the chicken is opaque throughout (cut to test), 10 to 12 minutes total. Serve immediately.

Cook's Tip: The more assertive flavor of dark-meat chicken is complemented by the classic earthy combination of onions and mushrooms. Basmati rice is a great accompaniment.

Makes 4 servings

SPICED CHICKEN KEBABS

Serve with a Doppelbock, such as Brewmaster's Private Reserve

KEBABS

¾ cup plain yogurt

1 tablespoon peeled and grated fresh ginger

2 teaspoons ground coriander

2 teaspoons paprika

1 teaspoon ground cumin

¼ teaspoon ground cardamom

¼ teaspoon ground turmeric

¼ teaspoon saffron threads, crushed

⅛ teaspoon ground cinnamon

⅛ teaspoon ground cloves

3 garlic cloves, minced

2 pounds boneless, skinless chicken thighs, cut into 1-inch pieces

1 large red onion, cut into 1-inch pieces

1 large red bell pepper, stemmed, seeded, and cut into 1-inch pieces

1 large zucchini, cut into 1-inch pieces

2 tablespoons olive oil

½ teaspoon salt

½ teaspoon freshly ground black pepper

RAITA

½ cup plain yogurt

⅓ cup diced seeded tomato

¼ cup cucumber, peeled, seeded, grated, and squeezed dry

¼ cup sour cream

1 tablespoon minced seeded jalapeño chile

1½ teaspoons chopped fresh cilantro

¼ teaspoon ground cumin

¼ teaspoon salt

1 To prepare the kebabs, in a large zip-top plastic bag, combine the yogurt, ginger, coriander, paprika, cumin, cardamom, turmeric, saffron, cinnamon, cloves, and garlic. Add the chicken, seal the bag, and turn to coat. Marinate in the refrigerator overnight, turning the bag occasionally.

2 Soak 8 wooden skewers in water to cover for 30 minutes (see Cook's Tip page 161). Prepare a grill for cooking over medium-high heat. First, oil the grill rack. If using a charcoal grill, prepare a solid bed of medium-hot coals. If using a gas grill, preheat to high and close the lid, then open the lid and lower the heat to medium-high (you can hold your hand 1 to 2 inches above grill level only 3 to 4 seconds).

3 Remove the chicken from the bag and discard the marinade. Thread the chunks of chicken, onion, bell pepper, and zucchini alternately onto the soaked skewers. Brush the kebabs with the olive oil and sprinkle with the salt and pepper.

4 Lay the kebabs on the grill rack. If using a gas grill, close the lid. Cook, turning as needed, until the vegetables are nicely browned and the chicken is opaque throughout (cut to test), 10 to 12 minutes total. Transfer the kebabs to a serving platter and keep warm.

5 To prepare the *raita,* in a small bowl, combine the yogurt, tomato, cucumber, sour cream, chile, cilantro, cumin, and salt, stirring well. Serve with the kebabs.

Makes 8 servings

ORANGE-OLIVE CHICKEN SCALOPPINE

Serve with a Wheat Beer, such as Michelob Bavarian Style Wheat

4 boneless, skinless chicken breast halves (about 6 ounces each)

Salt and freshly ground black pepper

1 cup buttermilk

$1/2$ cup all-purpose flour

5 teaspoons olive oil

$1/3$ cup slivered almonds or pine nuts

$1/4$ cup chopped shallots

$1/2$ cup chicken stock

1 teaspoon grated orange zest

$1/2$ cup fresh orange juice

$1/4$ cup pitted Kalamata olives

1 tablespoon chopped fresh flat-leaf parsley

Orange wedges

1 Rinse the chicken breasts and pat dry with paper towels. Place each piece between 2 sheets of wax paper. Using a rolling pin or the flat side of a meat mallet, lightly pound each breast until about $1/4$ inch thick. Sprinkle both sides of the chicken with salt and pepper. Place the chicken in a large zip-top plastic bag, pour in the buttermilk, and seal the bag. Marinate in the refrigerator for 2 hours, turning the bag occasionally.

2 Remove the chicken from the bag and discard the marinade. Pat the chicken dry with paper towels. Spread the flour in a shallow bowl and dredge the chicken in the flour, shaking off any excess.

3 In a large skillet, heat 3 teaspoons of the olive oil over medium-high heat. Add the chicken and cook, turning once, until opaque throughout (cut to test), about 3 minutes on each side. Transfer the chicken to a serving platter and keep warm.

4 In the same pan, heat another 1 teaspoon of the olive oil over medium heat. Add the nuts, stirring until golden, 30 seconds to 1 minute. Using a slotted spoon, transfer the nuts to a plate and set aside.

5 In the same pan, heat the remaining 1 teaspoon olive oil over medium-high heat. Add the shallots, stirring until softened, about 2 minutes. Add the stock, orange zest, orange juice, and olives, stirring until the mixture is boiling. Continue to boil, stirring occasionally, until the liquid is slightly reduced, 1 to $1^{1}/_{2}$ minutes.

6 Spoon the sauce over the chicken. Sprinkle with the nuts and parsley. Season to taste with salt and pepper. Garnish with the orange wedges and serve.

Makes 4 servings

A tavern sign from the 1940s, depicting a wreath of barley and hops.

SPICY CHICKEN with SWEET PEPPERS

 Serve with a Porter, such as Michelob Porter

CHICKEN

6 boneless, skinless chicken breast halves (about 6 ounces each)

2 teaspoons chopped fresh thyme

2 teaspoons chopped fresh rosemary

2 teaspoons chopped fresh sage

1 teaspoon fennel seeds, coarsely crushed

½ teaspoon red pepper flakes

1 teaspoon extra-virgin olive oil

4 garlic cloves, minced

3 tablespoons fresh lemon juice

1 teaspoon salt

½ teaspoon freshly ground black pepper

PEPPERS

2 red bell peppers, halved, stemmed, and seeded

2 yellow bell peppers, halved, stemmed, and seeded

2 orange bell peppers, halved, stemmed, and seeded

1 tablespoon chopped fresh basil

3 tablespoons fresh lemon juice

1 tablespoon extra-virgin olive oil

1 tablespoon balsamic vinegar

1 garlic clove, thinly sliced

½ teaspoon salt

¼ teaspoon freshly ground black pepper

1 To prepare the chicken, rinse the chicken breasts and pat dry with paper towels. In a large zip-top plastic bag, combine the thyme, rosemary, sage, fennel seeds, red pepper flakes, olive oil, and garlic. Add the chicken, seal the bag, and turn to coat. Marinate in the refrigerator for at least 8 hours or up to overnight, turning the bag occasionally. Add the lemon juice to the bag and shake well. Marinate in the refrigerator for 20 minutes longer.

2 Prepare a grill for cooking over medium-high heat. First, oil the grill rack. If using a charcoal grill, prepare a solid bed of medium-hot coals. If using a gas grill, preheat to high and close the lid, then open the lid and lower the heat to medium-high (you can hold your hand 1 to 2 inches above grill level only 3 to 4 seconds).

3 Remove the chicken from the bag and discard the marinade. Sprinkle the chicken evenly with the salt and pepper. Lay the chicken on the grill rack. If using a gas grill, close the lid. Cook, turning once, until opaque throughout (cut to test), about 6 minutes on each side. Transfer to a cutting board and let cool slightly. Cut the chicken crosswise into thin slices.

4 To prepare the peppers, place the pepper halves, skin side up, on a work surface and flatten with your hand. Lay the peppers, skin side down, on the grill rack. Cook until the skins are blackened and blistered all over, about 15 minutes. Transfer the peppers to a paper or plastic bag, close the bag tightly, and let stand for 10 minutes (the steam will loosen the skins). Peel the peppers and cut into strips.

5 In a bowl, combine the pepper strips, basil, lemon juice, olive oil, vinegar, garlic, salt, and pepper. Arrange the pepper mixture on a serving platter, top with the chicken, and serve.

Cook's Tip: You can prepare the peppers, omitting the basil so it doesn't darken and wilt, up to 2 days in advance. Add the basil right before serving.

Makes 8 servings

GRILLED CHICKEN with CHIPOTLE-LIME BUTTER

Serve with an American-Style Premium Lager, such as Michelob

4 bone-in chicken breast halves, skin intact

1 teaspoon salt

¼ cup butter, at room temperature

½ minced chipotle chile

1 teaspoon fresh lime juice

1 Rinse the chicken breasts and pat dry with paper towels. Sprinkle all over with ½ teaspoon of the salt, including some under the skin. Cover and refrigerate for at least 2 hours or up to overnight.

2 In a small bowl, combine the butter, chile, lime juice, and the remaining ½ teaspoon salt, mixing well. Rub the butter mixture over the chicken breasts, including some under the skin. Let the chicken come to room temperature for 30 minutes before grilling.

3 Prepare a grill for cooking over indirect heat. First, oil the grill rack. If using a charcoal grill, light 50 to 60 briquettes and let burn until covered with ash, about 20 to 30 minutes, then mound them to one side. Place a drip pan on the side cleared of coals—this is the indirect heat area. Set the oiled grill rack in place. If using a gas grill, turn all the burners to high and close the lid. When the temperature inside the grill reaches 350° to 400°F, lift the lid, turn off one of the burners, and lower the other burner(s) to medium. Place a drip pan under the turned-off burner—this is the indirect heat area. Set the oiled grill rack in place.

4 Lay the chicken skin side down on the indirect heat area. If using a gas grill, close the lid. Cook for 15 minutes, then turn the chicken over, re-covering the gas grill, and cook for 10 minutes longer. Move chicken over the direct heat area and cook, turning once, until the skin is nicely browned and crisp and the meat is opaque throughout (cut to test), 3 to 5 minutes longer. Serve immediately.

Makes 4 servings

Michelob was introduced in 1896 as a premium draught beer that was sold only in taverns and restaurants. According to records in the Anheuser-Busch archives, in 1908 a Chicago branch office manager was allowed to bottle two barrels of Michelob. This diamond sunburst label was produced for this special bottling. It wasn't until 1961 that a pasteurized, bottled version of this popular brew was produced.

SEARED CHICKEN with TOMATILLO SALSA

Serve with an American-Style Light Lager, such as Michelob Golden Draft Light

3 tomatillos (about 4 ounces total)

1 cup peeled and chopped avocado

1/2 cup sliced radish

1/4 cup chopped fresh cilantro

2 tablespoons fresh lime juice

1/2 teaspoon salt

1/4 teaspoon red pepper flakes

4 boneless, skinless chicken breast halves (about 6 ounces each)

1 1/2 teaspoons poultry seasoning

2 tablespoons olive oil

Sour cream

1 Remove and discard the husks and stems from the tomatillos and finely chop. In a bowl, combine the tomatillos, avocado, radish, cilantro, lime juice, salt, and red pepper flakes, mixing gently.

2 Rinse the chicken breasts and pat dry with paper towels. Sprinkle the chicken evenly with the poultry seasoning.

3 In a large skillet, heat the olive oil over medium-high heat. Add the chicken and cook for 5 minutes. Turn the chicken over, lower the heat to medium, and cook until the meat is opaque throughout (cut to test), 5 to 10 minutes longer. Serve the chicken with the tomatillo salsa and pass the sour cream.

Cook's Tip: It's important to prepare the salsa before the chicken so that its flavor has time to develop.

Makes 4 servings

DEVILED CHICKEN WINGS

Serve with an American-Style Premium Lager, such as Budweiser Select

3 tablespoons extra-virgin olive oil

3 tablespoons fresh lemon juice

2 teaspoons grated lemon zest

1 teaspoon freshly ground black pepper

1 teaspoon red pepper flakes

3 garlic cloves, smashed

1 1/4 teaspoons kosher salt

4 pounds chicken wings, tips cut off and discarded, wings split into 2 pieces through the joint

1 In a large bowl, combine the olive oil, 2 tablespoons of the lemon juice, the zest, black pepper, red pepper flakes, garlic, and 1 teaspoon of the salt, stirring well. Add the chicken and toss to coat. Cover and marinate in the refrigerator for at least 4 hours or up to overnight.

2 Prepare a grill. First, oil the grill rack. If using a charcoal grill, prepare a solid bed of medium-hot coals. If using a gas grill, preheat to high and close the lid, then open the lid and lower the heat to medium (you can hold your hand 1 to 2 inches above grill level only 4 to 5 seconds).

3 Lay the chicken wings on the grill rack. If using a charcoal grill, place them on a cooler area of the grill; if using a gas grill, close the lid. Cook, turning once, for about 8 minutes on each side. If using a charcoal grill, move the chicken to the hotter area of the grill. If using a gas grill, raise the heat to medium-high. Grill until the skin is nicely browned and crisp and the meat is opaque throughout (cut to test), 2 to 3 minutes longer on each side.

4 Drizzle with the remaining 1 tablespoon lemon juice, sprinkle with the remaining 1/4 teaspoon salt, and serve.

Makes 4 to 6 servings

LEMONGRASS ROASTED CHICKEN

Serve with a European-Style Pilsner, such as Harbin

1 stalk lemongrass, outer leaves and upper stalk discarded

1 garlic clove, chopped

1 shallot, chopped

4 tablespoons unsalted butter

1 teaspoon salt

1/2 teaspoon freshly ground black pepper

4 chicken drumsticks

4 bone-in chicken thighs

1 Thinly slice the lemongrass and chop as finely as possible. In a food processor or blender, process the lemongrass, garlic, and shallot until finely chopped. Add the butter, 1/2 teaspoon of the salt, and 1/4 teaspoon of the pepper and pulse until well combined.

2 Preheat the oven to 500°F. Line a large, shallow baking pan with aluminum foil.

3 Gently loosen the skin of the chicken pieces and stuff the butter mixture underneath the skin of each. Sprinkle with the remaining 1/2 teaspoon salt and 1/4 teaspoon pepper. Roast until the skin is golden, an instant-read thermometer inserted into the thickest part of a thigh away from the bone registers 160°F, and the juices run clear when a thigh is pierced with a fork, 30 to 35 minutes. Serve immediately.

Cook's Tip: The outer stalk and upper part of lemongrass are extremely tough and fibrous. Just discard them and chop the tender part of the stalk.

Makes 4 servings

OVEN-FRIED CHICKEN

Serve with an American-Style Light Lager, such as Michelob Light

1 cup buttermilk

2 large eggs, lightly beaten

1 cup all-purpose flour

1/3 cup medium-ground yellow cornmeal

1 teaspoon salt

3/4 teaspoon freshly ground black pepper

1/4 teaspoon cayenne pepper

2 bone-in chicken breast halves (about 1 pound total)

2 bone-in chicken thighs (about 1/2 pound total)

2 chicken drumsticks (about 1/2 pound total)

1/4 cup canola oil

1 Preheat the oven to 425°F. Line a large baking sheet with parchment paper.

2 In a shallow dish, combine the buttermilk and eggs, stirring well with a whisk. In a separate shallow dish, combine the flour, cornmeal, 1/2 teaspoon of the salt, the black pepper, and the cayenne, stirring well.

3 Rinse the chicken pieces and pat dry with paper towels. Sprinkle the chicken evenly with remaining 1/2 teaspoon salt. Dip the chicken pieces first in the buttermilk mixture, then dredge in the flour mixture.

4 In a large skillet, heat the oil over medium-high heat. Add the chicken and cook, turning once, until lightly browned, about 4 minutes on each side. Arrange the chicken on the prepared baking sheet.

5 Bake until the skin is golden, an instant-read thermometer inserted into the thickest part of a thigh away from the bone registers 160°F, and the juices run clear when a thigh is pierced with a fork, 30 to 35 minutes.

Makes 4 servings

CHICKEN with AMBER LAGER and HONEY

Serve with an American-Style Amber Lager, such as Michelob Amber Bock

1 onion, finely chopped

5 tablespoons Michelob Amber Bock

3 tablespoons fresh lemon juice

2 tablespoons vegetable oil

2 tablespoons honey

1 tablespoon soy sauce

4 boneless, skinless chicken breast halves
   (about 6 ounces each)

1 In a small bowl, combine the onion, beer, lemon juice, oil, honey, and soy sauce, stirring well.

2 Place the chicken in a shallow dish. Pour about 1/2 cup of the beer mixture over the chicken and turn to coat. Cover and marinate in the refrigerator for 4 hours. Cover the remaining beer mixture and set aside.

3 Prepare a grill for cooking over medium-high heat. First, oil the grill rack. If using a charcoal grill, prepare a solid bed of medium-hot coals. If using a gas grill, preheat to high and close the lid, then open the lid and lower the heat to medium-high (you can hold your hand 1 to 2 inches above grill level only 3 to 4 seconds).

4 Meanwhile, in a saucepan over medium-high heat, bring the remaining beer mixture to a simmer and cook, stirring occasionally, until reduced and thickened to a glaze, 5 to 6 minutes. Set aside.

5 Remove the chicken from the marinade and gently pat dry with paper towels. Discard the marinade. Lay the chicken on the grill rack. Cover and cook for 3 or 4 minutes, then brush with the glaze, re-cover, and cook for 4 minutes longer. Turn the chicken and repeat the same steps, cooking until the chicken is cooked through (cut to test) and the juices run clear. Transfer to a platter, pour the remaining glaze over the chicken, and serve.

Makes 4 servings

MESQUITE-GRILLED CHICKEN

Serve with an American-Style Premium Lager, such as Budweiser

1 cup mesquite chips

2 bottles (12 ounces each) Budweiser, plus
   more for soaking the wood chips

4 garlic cloves, smashed

1 bay leaf

2 tablespoons teriyaki sauce

2 teaspoons kosher salt

2 teaspoons freshly ground black pepper

6 boneless, skinless chicken breast halves
   (about 6 ounces each)

1 Place the wood chips in a small, shallow dish and add lager to cover. Soak for at least 1 hour.

2 In a large bowl, combine the 2 bottles lager, the garlic, bay leaf, teriyaki sauce, salt, and pepper. Add the chicken and turn to coat. Cover and marinate in the refrigerator for at least 2 hours or up to overnight.

3 Prepare a grill for cooking over medium-high heat. First, oil the grill rack. If using a charcoal grill, prepare a solid bed of medium-hot coals. If using a gas grill, preheat to high and close the lid, then open the lid and lower the heat to medium-high (you can hold your hand 1 to 2 inches above grill level only 3 to 4 seconds). Drain the wood chips and place in a foil pan directly on the heat in the corner for a gas grill, or scatter them over the coals if using a charcoal grill.

4 Remove the chicken from the marinade and pat dry gently with paper towels. Discard the marinade. Lay the chicken on the grill rack. Cover and cook for 6 minutes. Uncover, turn the chicken, and cook until cooked through (cut to test) and the juices run clear, 6 to 8 minutes longer. Serve immediately.

Cook's Tip: Chef Sam Niemann uses mesquite chips, which soak up the beer quickly. Larger chunks of mesquite need several hours to soak.

Makes 6 servings

SMOKE-ROASTED CHICKEN

Serve with an American-Style Premium Lager, such as Budweiser

1 cup hickory, mesquite, applewood, or beechwood chips

12 garlic cloves

1 tablespoon chili powder

$1/3$ cup chopped fresh thyme

$1/3$ cup chopped fresh rosemary

$1/4$ cup olive oil

1 tablespoon salt

1 tablespoon freshly ground black pepper

1 whole chicken ($3^1/2$ to 4 pounds)

By the 1950s, Anheuser-Busch marketers had set their sights on the newly prosperous inhabitants of post-war suburbia. In this charming magazine ad from 1951, enterprising hubby has devised a foot pedal so he can have his rotisserie chicken and enjoy his Bud, too.

1 Place the chips in a bowl and add water to cover. Let soak for at least 30 minutes, then drain just before using.

2 In a food processor, combine the garlic, chili powder, thyme, rosemary, olive oil, salt, and pepper. Process until the mixture forms a paste.

3 Rinse chicken inside and out, then pat dry with paper towels. Press down on the breastbone of the chicken to flatten the bird slightly. Rub the spice paste evenly over all the skin.

4 Prepare a grill for cooking over indirect heat. First, oil the grill rack. If using a charcoal grill, light 50 to 60 briquettes and let burn until covered with ash, about 20 to 30 minutes, then mound them to one side. Place a drip pan on the side cleared of coals—this is the indirect heat area. Set the oiled grill rack in place. If using a gas grill, turn all the burners to high and close the lid. When the temperature inside the grill reaches 350° to 400°F, lift the lid, turn off one of the burners, and lower the other burner(s) to medium. Place a drip pan under the turned-off burner—this is the indirect heat area. Set the oiled grill rack in place. If using wood chips, place all the chips in the metal smoking box or in a foil pan directly on the heat in a corner. If using a charcoal grill, scatter half of the chips over the coals.

5 Lay the chicken on the grill rack over the drip pan, breast side down. Close the lid on the grill. If using a charcoal grill, adjust the vents to halfway open. Cook for 40 minutes, then turn the chicken over (if using charcoal, scatter another 20 briquettes over the coals, along with the remaining wood chips). Cover the lid again. Continue to cook until an instant-read thermometer inserted in the thickest part of a thigh away from the bone registers 160°F and the juices run clear, about 40 minutes longer. Transfer to a carving board, loosely tent with aluminum foil, and let rest for 10 minutes. Carve the chicken and serve.

Cook's Tip: This dish is delicious served with Grilled Spicy Sweet-Potato Packets, page 258.

Makes 4 servings

ROAST CHICKEN with WILD RICE STUFFING

Serve with a Wheat Beer, such as Michelob Bavarian Style Wheat

2 tablespoons olive oil

1/2 onion, chopped

3/4 cup long-grain and wild rice blend

1 garlic clove, minced

1/3 cup chopped dried figs

1 1/2 tablespoons pine nuts, toasted

3/4 teaspoon salt

1 whole chicken (3 1/2 to 4 pounds)

2 tablespoons butter, at room temperature

3/4 teaspoon ground cumin

1/2 teaspoon ground coriander

1/2 teaspoon red pepper flakes

1/4 teaspoon ground cinnamon

1 Preheat the oven to 375°F. Lightly oil a roasting rack and set it in a roasting pan.

2 In a saucepan, heat the olive oil over medium-high heat. Add the onion and sauté for 4 minutes. Add the rice and garlic and sauté for 1 minute. Add 1 1/2 cups water to pan and bring to a boil. Cover, lower the heat to low, and simmer until the rice is almost tender, about 20 minutes. Stir in the figs, pine nuts, and 1/4 teaspoon of the salt.

3 Remove and discard the giblets and neck from the chicken and trim any excess fat. Rinse the chicken inside and out, then pat dry with paper towels. Starting at the neck cavity, loosen the skin from the breasts and drumsticks by inserting your fingers, gently pushing between the skin and meat.

4 In a small bowl, combine the butter, cumin, coriander, red pepper flakes, cinnamon, and the remaining 1/2 teaspoon salt. Rub the seasoning mixture under the loosened skin and over the breasts and drumsticks. Stuff the rice mixture in the chicken cavity. Tie the ends of the legs together with kitchen string. Lift the wing tips up and over the back and tuck them under the chicken. Place the chicken, breast side up, on the rack in the roasting pan.

5 Roast for 40 minutes. Raise the oven temperature to 450°F and continue to roast until an instant-read thermometer inserted in the thickest part of a thigh away from the bone registers 160°F and the juices run clear, about 20 minutes longer. Transfer to a carving board, tent loosely with aluminum foil, and let rest for 10 minutes. Carve the chicken and serve with the stuffing.

Cook's Tip: Pack the stuffing loosely in the cavity so that air circulates and the stuffing cooks properly.

Makes 4 servings

ROAST CHICKEN with BALSAMIC GLAZE

Serve with an English-Style Pale Ale, such as Michelob Pale Ale

1 whole chicken (3 1/2 to 4 pounds), cut into 8 serving pieces

1 1/2 tablespoons olive oil

1 teaspoon kosher salt

1/2 teaspoon freshly ground black pepper

3/4 cup balsamic vinegar

1/4 cup soy sauce

1 1/2 teaspoons sugar

5 thin slices (1/8 inch thick) peeled fresh ginger

Early Innovation—Think of the word "pasteurization" and a tall glass of fresh, wholesome milk probably comes to mind. In fact, Louis Pasteur's Études sur la Bière was published in 1876 to explain how harmful microorganisms in beer could be killed by flash-heating after fermentation. Significantly, Anheuser-Busch was the first brewer to pasteurize its beer, doing so even before the legendary scientist took the time to publish the text whose contents would forever be associated with his name.

1 Preheat the oven to 500°F. Line a large, shallow baking pan with aluminum foil.

2 Pat the chicken pieces dry with paper towels, then put in a large bowl and toss with the olive oil, salt, and pepper. Transfer to the prepared pan, skin side up. Roast until the skin is golden, an instant-read thermometer inserted into the thickest part of a thigh away from the bone registers 160°F, and the juices run clear, about 35 minutes.

3 While the chicken is roasting, in a saucepan, combine the vinegar, soy sauce, sugar, and ginger over medium-high heat. Bring to a simmer and cook, stirring occasionally, until reduced to about 1/3 cup, about 10 minutes.

4 When the chicken is done, transfer to a clean large bowl. Add the glaze and toss to coat. Let stand for 5 minutes, then toss again and serve.

Cook's Tip: You can make this salty-sweet and gingery chicken with any chicken parts as long as they are bone-in.

Makes 4 servings

CHICKEN DIVAN

Serve with a European-Style Pilsner, such as Grolsch

1¹/₂ pounds boneless, skinless chicken breasts

2¹/₂ cups chicken stock, plus more if needed (optional)

1 large bunch (about 1¹/₂ pounds) broccoli, trimmed and cut into florets with 4-inch-long stems

4 tablespoons unsalted butter

¹/₃ cup all-purpose flour

¹/₄ cup heavy cream

¹/₄ cup Grolsch

2 teaspoons fresh lemon juice

³/₄ teaspoon salt

¹/₄ teaspoon freshly ground black pepper

Pinch of cayenne pepper

1¹/₂ cups (6 ounces) shredded Gruyère or Swiss cheese

1 In a large saucepan, combine the chicken and stock and bring to a simmer over medium-high heat. Cook until opaque throughout (cut to test), 8 to 12 minutes. Using a slotted spoon, transfer the chicken to a cutting board. Pour the cooking liquid into a large glass measuring pitcher and reserve the pan. You should have about 2 cups stock. If there is less than 2 cups, add enough additional stock or water to make up the difference.

2 Meanwhile, put the broccoli in a steamer basket fitted into a saucepan over (but not touching) boiling water or in a large skillet with ¹/₂ inch boiling water and steam just until just tender, 6 to 8 minutes. (Alternatively, arrange the broccoli in a single layer on a microwave-safe plate, sprinkle with 3 tablespoons water, and microwave on high, covered with a paper towel, until just tender, about 3 minutes.)

3 Preheat the oven to 375°F. In a saucepan over low heat, melt the butter. Whisk in the flour and cook, whisking constantly, for 2 to 3 minutes. Raise the heat to medium-high and add the reserved stock in a slow, steady stream, again whisking constantly. Bring to a boil, then lower the heat and simmer, whisking occasionally, until slightly thickened, about 10 minutes. Whisk in the cream, ale, lemon juice, salt, black pepper, cayenne, and 1 cup of the Gruyère, stirring until the cheese is melted and the sauce is smooth.

4 Arrange the broccoli in the bottom of a 2-quart gratin dish or other shallow baking dish. Pour 1 cup of the sauce over. Cut the chicken breasts crosswise into thin slices and layer over the sauce. Pour the remainder of the sauce over and sprinkle with the remaining ¹/₂ cup Gruyère. Bake until heated through, about 15 minutes. Turn the oven to broil or preheat the broiler and broil about 5 inches from the heat source until lightly browned and bubbling, about 4 minutes. Serve hot.

Cook's Tip: This 1930s casserole is a wonderful combination of chicken, broccoli, and cheese sauce. Traditionally the sauce was flavored with sherry and Parmesan, but here it's updated with shredded Gruyère cheese and beer.

Makes 6 servings

CHICKEN with SESAME NOODLES

Serve with a European-Style Pilsner, such as Tiger

2 boneless, skinless chicken breast halves (5 to 6 ounces each)

8 ounces dried Asian wheat noodles

1 teaspoon vegetable oil

3 tablespoons sesame seeds

1 tablespoon minced garlic

½ cup rice vinegar

⅓ cup soy sauce

2 tablespoons sugar

¼ teaspoon cayenne pepper

2 carrots, peeled and cut into 2-inch-long matchsticks

2 stalks celery, rinsed and thinly sliced diagonally

4 cups bean sprouts, rinsed and drained

⅓ cup chopped fresh cilantro

1 In a large saucepan, bring $2\frac{1}{2}$ to 3 quarts water to a boil over high heat. Add the chicken and return to a boil, then cover and remove from the heat. Let stand until the chicken is opaque throughout (cut to test), about 18 minutes. If still pink, return the water to a simmer, cover, remove from the heat, and let stand for a few minutes longer. Using tongs, lift the chicken from the water, set aside, and let cool. Tear the chicken into shreds ½ inch thick.

2 Return the water to a boil over high heat. Add the noodles and cook, stirring occasionally, until barely tender to the bite, 3 to 4 minutes. Drain, rinse with cold water until cool, and drain again thoroughly. Rinse and dry the pan.

3 In the same pan, heat the oil over medium heat. Add the sesame seeds and stir until golden, 2 to 4 minutes. Stir in the garlic and remove from heat. Stir in the vinegar, soy sauce, sugar, and cayenne. Spoon 3 tablespoons of the sesame vinaigrette into a small bowl and reserve. Add the noodles and half of the carrots, celery, bean sprouts, and cilantro to the pan, mixing well.

4 Divide the noodle mixture among 4 plates. Pour any dressing left in the pan into the bowl of reserved dressing. Top the noodle mixture with the remaining carrots, celery, and bean sprouts, then top with all the chicken. Sprinkle with the remaining cilantro. Serve with the reserved dressing to drizzle over the chicken.

Cook's Tip: This tasty dish comes together quickly if you rinse and cut the carrots, celery, and bean sprouts while cooking the chicken and noodles.

Makes 4 servings

PASTA with SAUSAGE and BROCCOLI RABE

Serve with an American-Style Amber Lager, such as Michelob Amber Bock

2 tablespoons pine nuts

1/4 cup extra-virgin olive oil

1/2 pound smoked chicken or turkey sausage

4 garlic cloves, lightly crushed with a chef's knife and peeled but left whole

1 head broccoli rabe, tough stems trimmed, cut into 2-inch lengths

1/4 cup pitted Kalamata olives, chopped

1/2 teaspoon salt, plus 2 tablespoons

Pinch of red pepper flakes

12 ounces dried bow-tie pasta

Freshly grated Pecorino Romano cheese

1 In a large skillet over medium heat, toast the pine nuts, stirring often, until lightly browned, about 6 minutes. Transfer to a plate.

2 In the same skillet, heat the olive oil over medium-high heat. Add the sausage and cook, turning often, until browned on all sides, about 5 minutes. Transfer to a plate. Add the garlic and cook until light golden brown, about 2 minutes. Add the broccoli rabe, olives, the 1/2 teaspoon salt, and the red pepper flakes and stir to mix. Cook until the broccoli rabe is crisp-tender, 6 to 8 minutes. Thinly slice the sausage and add to the pan along with the pine nuts. Cook, stirring, until the broccoli rabe is tender and the sausage is warmed through, about 5 minutes longer.

3 Meanwhile, in a large pot over high heat, bring about 3 quarts water to a boil and add the 2 tablespoons salt. Add the pasta and cook until al dente, 6 to 8 minutes. Drain, reserving 1/4 cup of the pasta water, and add both the pasta and reserved cooking water to the skillet. Lower the heat to medium and toss the pasta with the sauce until well mixed. Divide between 4 bowls. Serve with the Pecorino Romano.

Cook's Tip: Broccoli rabe is known by several names, such as bitter broccoli, broccoletti, and rapini. It's much stronger than regular Italian broccoli and is a great match for other bold flavors such as the smoked sausage and olives in this pasta.

Makes 4 servings

George Washington's Beer—From Colonial times into the early part of the nineteenth century, many American households made batches of their own "small beer," which was a common low-alcohol variation on the drink we enjoy today. Among the fans of this people's brew was George Washington, whose handwritten 1757 recipe calls for thirty gallons of water that have been boiled with bran hops "to your Taste," three gallons of molasses, and a quart of yeast. One contemporary brewer who tried to re-create Washington's brew pronounced it undrinkable by modern standards.

SPICY RICE NOODLES with CHICKEN

Serve with a European-Style Pilsner, such as Harbin

4 cups chicken stock

6 to 7 ounces Chinese rice noodles, rinsed

1/4 cup plus 1 teaspoon vegetable oil

1 large egg, well beaten

1 boneless, skinless chicken breast half (about 4 ounces), cut into very thin matchsticks (2 inches long)

2 tablespoons Japanese noodle soup base (see Cook's Tip)

1 tablespoon Harbin

1 teaspoon light brown sugar

2 cups carrot matchsticks (2 inches long)

2 cups thinly sliced fresh shiitake mushroom caps

5 cups finely shredded green cabbage

Salt

1 In a saucepan, bring the stock to a boil over high heat. Add the rice noodles, stir to submerge, and remove from the heat. Let soak until tender to the bite, about 15 minutes. Pour the noodles into a colander set over a bowl to drain and reserve the stock.

2 Meanwhile, in a large skillet, heat 1 teaspoon of the oil over medium-high heat. Pour in the egg and swirl to make a paper-thin pancake. Cook until set, about 1 minute. Slide onto a cutting board and let cool, then cut into thin strips.

3 In a small bowl, combine the chicken, noodle soup base, beer, and sugar. In a large wok or a frying pan with sides at least 2 1/2 inches high, heat 2 tablespoons of the oil over high heat. Add the chicken mixture and cook, stirring, until the chicken is opaque throughout, about 1 minute. Add the carrots and cook until crisp-tender, 1 to 2 minutes. Add the mushrooms and cook until beginning to brown but still firm to the bite, about 1 minute. Add the cabbage and cook until barely wilted, about 30 seconds. Transfer the chicken and vegetables to a bowl.

4 Lower the heat to medium-high, add the remaining 2 tablespoons oil to the pan, and pour in the softened noodles. Stir vigorously to separate, then cook until heated through, 2 to 3 minutes. Add the chicken-vegetable mixture and stir until heated through and mixed well, adding a little of the reserved chicken stock if the mixture seems too dry (reserve the remaining stock for another use). Season to taste with salt. Transfer the noodle mixture to a serving dish and top with strips of egg. Serve immediately.

Cook's Tip: Chinese black vinegar *(Chinkiang)* and Sriracha hot sauce may be used to season each bowl to taste. If you can't find the Japanese noodle soup base, substitute a mixture of 2 tablespoons soy sauce, 2 teaspoons Chinese black vinegar *(Chinkiang)* or rice vinegar, 1 teaspoon sugar, and 1/2 teaspoon Asian fish sauce.

Makes 4 to 6 servings

CHICKEN and POTATO SOUP with DUMPLINGS

Serve with an American-Style Light Amber Lager, such as Michelob Ultra Amber

4 skinless bone-in chicken thighs (about 1½ pounds total)

8 cups chicken stock

5 fresh sage leaves, plus 2 teaspoons finely chopped fresh sage

2 leeks (about 1 pound total)

5 russet potatoes (about 2½ pounds total), peeled and diced

2 stalks celery, trimmed and diced

2 carrots, peeled and diced

1 cup all-purpose flour

½ cup cornmeal

1½ teaspoons baking powder

1 teaspoon salt

⅓ cup milk

1 large egg plus 1 large egg white, lightly beaten together

2 tablespoons melted butter

1 Rinse the chicken thighs and pat dry with paper towels. In a large pot, combine the chicken, stock, and whole sage leaves over high heat. Bring to a boil, then lower the heat to low, cover, and simmer, skimming off and discarding any foam that rises to the surface, until the chicken is opaque throughout (cut to test), about 30 minutes.

2 Meanwhile, cut off and discard the root ends and dark green tops from the leeks. Cut the white and pale green parts in half lengthwise and rinse well under running water. Thinly slice crosswise.

3 Using tongs, lift the chicken from the stock, set aside, and let cool, reserving the stock in the pot. Tear the chicken into shreds and discard the bones.

4 Add the leeks, potatoes, celery, carrots, and 2 cups water to the pot. Bring to a boil over high heat, then lower heat to medium, cover, and simmer until the vegetables are tender when pierced with a knife, 20 to 30 minutes. Stir in the shredded chicken.

5 Meanwhile, in a large bowl, combine the flour, cornmeal, baking powder, salt, and chopped sage, stirring with a whisk. Stir in the milk, beaten egg and egg white, and melted butter just until combined.

6 Drop 12 to 14 heaping tablespoon portions of the dumpling batter on the surface of the simmering soup. Cover the pot, reduce the heat to medium-low, and simmer (do not let boil) until a knife inserted in the center of a dumpling comes out clean, about 10 minutes. Ladle into bowls and serve hot.

Cook's Tip: Use a wide pot in order to have adequate surface area to make the dumplings. You can make the soup through step 4 up to a day ahead, then let cool, cover airtight, and refrigerate. Before serving, bring the soup to a simmer over medium heat, stirring occasionally, then proceed with making the dumplings.

Makes 6 to 8 servings

CAJUN JAMBALAYA with WILD RICE

Serve with an American-Style Premium Lager, such as Budweiser

4 tablespoons olive oil

1 pound smoked ham, cut into ½-inch dice

1 pound andouille sausage, cut into slices about ¼ inch thick

2 green bell peppers, stemmed, seeded, and diced

1 large onion, diced

5 stalks celery, diced

5 garlic cloves, minced

3 pounds boneless, skinless chicken thighs, cut into ½-inch dice

2 pounds jumbo shrimp, peeled and deveined

6 cups Budweiser

3 cups chicken stock

4 cans (28 ounces each) diced tomatoes

3 tablespoons Cajun seasoning, or to taste

1 bay leaf

2 cans (6 ounces each) tomato paste

6 cups cooked wild rice

Salt

1 In a soup pot, heat the olive oil over medium-high heat. Add the ham, sausage, bell peppers, onion, celery, and garlic and cook, stirring often, until the vegetables are softened, about 10 minutes. Add the chicken and shrimp and cook, stirring, until the shrimp are opaque throughout, about 10 minutes longer.

2 Add the beer, stock, diced tomatoes, Cajun seasoning, and bay leaf to the pot and bring to a boil. Lower the heat to medium-low and simmer, stirring often, 15 to 20 minutes. Add the tomato paste and wild rice. Simmer, still stirring often, until the flavors have blended and the rice is heated through, 15 to 20 minutes longer.

3 Taste and adjust the seasoning with Cajun seasoning or salt, if you like. Discard the bay leaf. Ladle the jambalaya into bowls and serve hot.

Cook's Tip: Chef Sam Niemann uses boneless chicken thighs, instead of breasts, for richer flavor.

Makes 8 to 10 servings

Clydesdales—Originally a gift from the Busch sons to their father, August Busch, Sr., the Clydesdales made their first public appearance in 1933 when they delivered a post-Prohibition case of beer to President Franklin D. Roosevelt. Marching down Pennsylvania Avenue, the horses were an immediate hit. Today, as many as fifteen Clydesdale foals are born per year at Grant's Farm, the St. Louis stable where several hundred of the prize horses are stabled and cared for. But not every Clydesdale born at Grant's Farm grows up to be a Budweiser Clydesdale. To make the grade, a horse must:

- Stand eighteen hands tall (about six feet) at the shoulders
- Weigh between 2,000 and 2,500 pounds
- Have a bay body, black mane, and black tail
- Sport a blaze of white on its face
- And have white feathering on its legs and feet

GREEN CHILE CHICKEN STEW

Serve with a Wheat Beer, such as Michelob Bavarian Style Wheat

1 chicken (3 to 4 pounds), cut into 8 pieces

2 bay leaves

1 tablespoon whole black peppercorns

5 teaspoons salt

1 package (16 ounces) frozen corn, thawed and drained

2 green bell peppers, stemmed, seeded, and halved

4 Anaheim or New Mexico green chiles, stemmed, seeded, and halved

4 serrano chiles, stemmed, seeded, and halved

3 tablespoons canola oil

2 large yellow onions, chopped

2 tablespoons minced garlic

1 tablespoon ground cumin

1 tablespoon ground coriander

2 cans (12 to 15 ounces each) posole or hominy, rinsed and drained

2 cans (15 ounces each) white beans, rinsed and drained

1 can (28 ounces) whole tomatillos, drained and coarsely chopped

Chopped fresh cilantro

Lime wedges

Tortilla chips

1 Rinse the chicken pieces and pat dry with paper towels. In a large pot, combine the chicken, bay leaves, peppercorns, and 2 teaspoons of the salt. Add water to cover the chicken by 2 inches. Bring to a boil over high heat, then lower the heat to low and simmer, adding water as needed to keep the chicken covered, until the chicken is opaque throughout (cut to test), 35 to 45 minutes. Transfer the chicken to a platter and let cool. Pour the cooking liquid through a fine-mesh sieve and reserve, discarding the spices. Set the stock aside to cool, then skim off as much fat as you can.

2 Meanwhile, preheat the oven to 400°F. Spread the corn in a baking pan and roast until it begins to turn golden, 15 to 20 minutes. Remove from the oven and let cool. Preheat the broiler.

3 Arrange the bell peppers and chiles cut side down on a large baking sheet. Broil 4 to 5 inches from the heat source until the skins are blackened and blistered all over, turning as needed, about 8 minutes. Transfer to a paper or plastic bag and close tightly. Let stand for 10 minutes (the steam will loosen the skins), then peel and coarsely chop.

4 In a large pot, heat the oil over medium-high heat. Add the onions, garlic, cumin, coriander, and the remaining 3 teaspoons salt. Cook, stirring, until the onions are translucent, about 4 minutes. Add the bell peppers, chiles, and corn and cook for 3 minutes. Add the posole, beans, tomatillos, and 7 cups of the reserved cooking liquid (freeze the remainder for another use). Bring the stew to a boil, then lower the heat to low and simmer for 10 minutes.

5 When the chicken is cool enough to handle, remove and discard the skin. Using 2 forks, shred the meat off the bone. Add the meat to the pot and simmer until the chicken is warmed through, about 10 minutes. Serve topped with cilantro and accompanied with lime wedges and tortilla chips.

Cook's Tip: Although loaded with chiles and peppers, this stew has a gentle heat. For a stronger punch, double the number of chiles. This stew is best made up to 2 days in advance. Reheat in a cast-iron or other heavy-bottomed pot over low heat.

Makes 10 servings

CHICKEN STEW
with SAFFRON

Serve with an American-Style Light Amber Lager, such as Michelob Ultra Amber

2 tablespoons extra-virgin olive oil, or as needed

4 chicken legs

4 chicken thighs

$^1/_2$ teaspoon salt

$^1/_2$ teaspoon freshly ground black pepper

1 extra-large yellow onion, chopped

2 bulbs fennel, trimmed and coarsely chopped, fronds reserved

1 teaspoon anise seeds, lightly crushed

$^1/_2$ teaspoon dried thyme

1 can (15 ounces) diced tomatoes

Pinch of saffron

2 fresh or dried bay leaves

2 cups chicken stock

$^3/_4$ pound Yukon gold or Yellow Finn potatoes, peeled and cut into $1^1/_2$-inch chunks

1 In a large Dutch oven or heavy casserole with a lid, heat the olive oil over medium-high heat. Sprinkle the chicken with the salt and pepper. Working in batches, add the chicken to the hot oil and cook until browned, about 5 minutes on each side. Transfer the chicken pieces to a plate as they are finished. Repeat with the remaining chicken, adding more oil to the pan if needed.

2 Add the onion and fennel to the same pot and cook, stirring occasionally until the vegetables are golden, about 6 minutes. Stir in the anise, thyme, tomatoes, saffron, bay leaves, and stock. Return the chicken and any accumulated juices on the plate to the pot. Cover, bring to a simmer, and cook for 30 minutes. Add the potatoes and simmer, uncovered, until the potatoes are tender when pierced with a knife, 20 to 25 minutes. Chop 2 tablespoons of the reserved fennel fronds and stir in. Discard the bay leaves. Taste and adjust the seasoning with salt. Serve immediately.

Makes 4 to 6 servings

CHICKEN STEW with
MUSHROOMS and ALE

Serve with an English-Style Pale Ale, such as Michelob Pale Ale

6 strips (about 6 ounces) thick-sliced bacon, cut into $^1/_2$-inch pieces

1 whole chicken (3 to 4 pounds), cut into 8 serving pieces

$^1/_2$ teaspoon salt

$^1/_4$ teaspoon freshly ground black pepper

2 leeks, white and tender green parts, thinly sliced

12 ounces cremini mushrooms, quartered

$^1/_2$ teaspoon dried savory or thyme

1 bottle (12 ounces) Michelob Pale Ale

2 tablespoons brown sugar

1 In a large, deep skillet, cook the bacon over medium-high heat until crisp, about 6 minutes. Using a slotted spoon, transfer to paper towels to drain. Pour or spoon off all but 2 tablespoons fat in the pan and return to medium-high heat. Sprinkle the chicken with the salt and pepper. Working in batches, add the chicken pieces to the hot fat and cook until browned on both sides, about 5 minutes on each side. Transfer the chicken pieces to a plate as they are finished.

2 Add the leeks and mushrooms to the same pan and cook, scraping to loosen any browned bits on the bottom of the pan, until the mushrooms are softened, about 6 minutes. Stir in the savory, beer, and brown sugar. Return the chicken and any accumulated juices on the plate to the pan. Simmer, covered, until the chicken is opaque throughout (cut to test), about 20 minutes. Transfer the chicken to a serving platter and tent with aluminum foil to keep warm.

3 Raise the heat to high and boil the pan juices until slightly thickened, about 8 minutes. Pour over the chicken and sprinkle with the bacon. Taste and adjust the seasoning. Serve immediately.

Makes 6 servings

CHICKEN STEW with OLIVES and LEMON

Serve with a Wheat Beer, such as Michelob Bavarian Style Wheat

1 pound boneless, skinless chicken thighs

2 tablespoons all-purpose flour

Salt and freshly ground black pepper

2 tablespoons olive oil

2 large garlic cloves, minced

1 tablespoon capers, rinsed, drained, and minced

Grated zest and juice of 1 lemon

1/2 cup Michelob Bavarian Style Wheat

1 3/4 cups chicken stock

1 pound Yukon gold potatoes, cut into 3/4-inch cubes

1 package (8 ounces) frozen artichoke hearts, thawed, quartered if large

1 cup finely chopped fresh flat-leaf parsley

1 cup pitted green olives

Lemon wedges

1 Rinse the chicken thighs and pat dry with paper towels. Cut each thigh into 2 or 3 chunks. In a large zip-top plastic bag, combine the flour with salt and pepper to taste. Add the chicken, seal the bag, and shake to coat. Remove the chicken, shaking off any excess flour.

2 In a large pot, heat the olive oil over medium-high heat. Add the chicken in a single layer and cook, turning once, until browned, 4 to 5 minutes. Transfer to a plate and set aside.

3 Lower the heat to medium. Add the garlic, capers, and lemon zest to the pot, stirring just until fragrant, about 30 seconds. Add the beer and simmer, scraping up any browned bits from the bottom, until reduced by half, about 2 minutes. Add the stock, potatoes, and chicken and return to a simmer. Lower the heat slightly to maintain a simmer, cover, and cook for 10 minutes. Add the artichokes and stir. Cover and cook until the potatoes are tender when pierced with a knife, 8 to 10 minutes. Stir in the parsley, lemon juice to taste, and olives. Season to taste with salt and pepper. Serve hot, with lemon wedges on the side.

Cook's Tip: Boned and skinned chicken thighs are an excellent choice for braising and a tasty alternative to chicken breasts.

Makes 4 servings

LIGHT SWEDISH MEATBALLS

Serve with an American-Style Light Lager, such as Michelob Ultra

2 slices rye bread

1 pound boneless, skinless chicken breast halves, cut into chunks

$3/4$ teaspoon salt

$1/4$ teaspoon freshly grated nutmeg

$1/4$ teaspoon freshly ground black pepper

1 large egg white

1 tablespoon canola oil

1 cup chicken stock

1 tablespoon all-purpose flour

1 cup sour cream

2 tablespoons chopped fresh flat-leaf parsley

1 In a food processor, pulse the bread until coarse crumbs measure 1 cup. Place in a bowl and set aside.

2 In the food processor, pulse the chicken until ground. Add the chicken to the bowl of bread crumbs, then stir in $1/2$ teaspoon of the salt, the nutmeg, pepper, and egg white until combined. Shape the mixture into 16 meatballs $1/2$ inches in diameter.

3 In a large skillet, heat the oil over medium-high heat. Add the meatballs and cook, browning on all sides, about 6 minutes. Transfer the meatballs to a plate and keep warm.

4 Add the remaining $1/4$ teaspoon salt, the stock, and the flour to the pan, stirring with a whisk until combined. Bring to a boil and cook, stirring constantly, until slightly thickened, about 1 minute. Stir in the sour cream and return the meatballs to the pan. Lower the heat to medium-low and cook until the meatballs are cooked through (cut to test) and the sauce is thick, about 10 minutes. Sprinkle with the parsley and serve.

Cook's Tip: You can substitute white or whole-wheat bread for the rye to bind the meatballs, if you like.

Makes 4 servings

SLOW-COOKER CHICKEN PAPRIKASH

Serve with an English-Style Pale Ale, such as Michelob Pale Ale

3 tablespoons all-purpose flour

2 pounds boneless, skinless chicken breasts, rinsed and patted dry, then cut into $1/2$-inch strips

$1/4$ cups chicken stock

8 ounces mushrooms, sliced

1 large onion, chopped

1 cup chopped red bell pepper

$1/2$ cup shredded carrot

2 large garlic cloves, minced

2 tablespoons Hungarian sweet paprika

1 teaspoon salt

1 teaspoon freshly ground black pepper

$1/4$ cups sour cream

1 In a bowl, combine the flour and chicken, tossing well to coat.

2 In an electric slow-cooker, combine the chicken mixture, stock, mushrooms, onion, bell pepper, carrot, garlic, paprika, salt, and pepper. Cover and cook on low heat for 8 hours. Just before serving, stir in the sour cream.

Cook's Tip: Serve this traditional dish with egg noodles, mashed potatoes, or orzo.

Makes 6 servings

PULLED CHICKEN SANDWICHES

Serve with an American-Style Light Amber Lager, such as Michelob Ultra Amber

2 tablespoons dark brown sugar

1 teaspoon paprika

1 teaspoon chili powder

³/₄ teaspoon ground cumin

¹/₂ teaspoon ground chipotle chile

¹/₂ teaspoon salt

¹/₄ teaspoon ground ginger

2 pounds boneless, skinless chicken thighs

8 sandwich rolls, halved and lightly toasted

16 hamburger dill chips

SAUCE

2 teaspoons canola oil

¹/₂ onion, finely chopped

2 tablespoons dark brown sugar

1 teaspoon chili powder

¹/₂ teaspoon garlic powder

¹/₂ teaspoon dry mustard

¹/₄ teaspoon ground allspice

¹/₈ teaspoon cayenne pepper

1 cup ketchup

2 tablespoons cider vinegar

1 tablespoon molasses

1 Prepare a grill for cooking over medium-high heat. First, oil the grill rack. If using a charcoal grill, prepare a solid bed of medium-hot coals. If using a gas grill, preheat to high and close the lid, then open the lid and lower the heat to medium-high (you can hold your hand 1 to 2 inches above grill level only 3 to 4 seconds).

2 In a small bowl, combine the brown sugar, paprika, chili powder, cumin, ground chipotle chile, salt, and ginger. Rub the spice mixture evenly over the chicken.

3 Lay the chicken on the grill rack. Close the lid if using a gas grill. Cook, turning occasionally, until an instant-read thermometer inserted in the thickest part of a thigh away from the bone registers 160°F and the juices run clear, about 20 minutes. Transfer the chicken to a cutting board and let stand for 5 minutes, then shred with 2 forks.

4 To prepare the sauce, in a saucepan, heat the oil over medium heat. Add the onion and cook, stirring occasionally, until tender, about 5 minutes. Stir in the brown sugar, chili powder, garlic powder, dry mustard, allspice, and cayenne and cook for 30 seconds. Stir in the ketchup, vinegar, and molasses. Bring to a boil, then lower the heat to low and simmer, stirring occasionally, until slightly thickened, about 10 minutes. Stir in the chicken and cook until thoroughly heated, about 2 minutes.

5 Place about ¹/₃ cup chicken mixture on the bottom half of each sandwich roll, then top with 2 pickle chips and the top roll half. Serve immediately.

Cook's Tip: These sandwiches make an easy main course for a casual get-together. The chicken and sauce can be made up to 2 days in advance and stored in the refrigerator. Reheat the mixture in a saucepan before serving.

Makes 8 sandwiches

GAME HENS with TAPENADE

Serve with a European-Style Pilsner, such as Kirin Ichiban

5 tablespoons unsalted butter, at room temperature

2 tablespoons store-bought tapenade

3 tablespoons chopped fresh flat-leaf parsley

2 Cornish game hens (about 2 pounds each), thawed if frozen, halved lengthwise

1 teaspoon salt

1/2 teaspoon freshly ground black pepper

3/4 cup chicken stock

1 Preheat the oven to 500°F. In a bowl, combine 4 tablespoons of the butter with the tapenade and parsley and mix well. Working with 1 hen half at a time, slide your fingers under the skin on each breast and around the leg, including the drumstick, being careful not to tear the skin. Place a scant 2 tablespoons of the tapenade butter under the skin of each hen half, then massage to spread the butter over the thigh, drumstick, and breast.

2 Place the hen halves, skin side up, in a baking pan. Sprinkle with the salt and pepper and roast until an instant-read thermometer inserted into the thickest part of a thigh away from the bone registers 160°F, the juices run clear when a thigh or breast is pierced with a fork, and the hens are nicely browned, about 35 minutes.

3 Transfer the hens to a platter and cover to keep warm. Place the roasting pan over medium-high heat on 2 burners. Add the stock and stir, scraping to loosen any browned bits on the bottom of the pan. Swirl in the remaining 1 tablespoon butter. Taste and adjust the seasoning. Serve the birds with the sauce.

Cook's Tip: Most game hens found in the supermarket are frozen solid, so you'll have to plan ahead to make this dish.

Makes 4 servings

GRILLED GAME HENS with HERBS

Serve with an English-Style Pale Ale, such as Michelob Pale Ale

3 large garlic cloves

1 teaspoon kosher salt

2 tablespoons fresh lemon juice

Grated zest of 1 lemon

2 tablespoons extra-virgin olive oil

4 teaspoons chopped fresh rosemary

Pinch of cayenne pepper

2 Cornish game hens (about 2 pounds each), backbone removed and birds flattened

1 On a cutting board, using the flat side of a chef's knife, mash the garlic with the salt, then transfer to a shallow baking dish. Add the lemon juice and zest, olive oil, rosemary, and cayenne. Add the hens and turn to coat. Cover and marinate in the refrigerator for at least 2 hours or up to overnight.

2 Prepare a grill for cooking over medium-low heat. First, oil the grill rack. If using a charcoal grill, prepare a solid bed of medium-low coals. If using a gas grill, preheat to high and close the lid, then open the lid and lower the heat to medium-low (you can hold your hand 1 to 2 inches above grill level only 5 to 6 seconds).

3 Lay the hens on the grill rack, skin side up. If using a gas grill, close the lid. Grill for 20 minutes, then turn skin side down and cook until an instant-read thermometer inserted into the thickest part of a thigh away from the bone registers 160°F, the juices run clear when a thigh or breast is pierced with a fork, and the hens are nicely browned, 8 to 10 minutes longer. Serve immediately.

Cook's Tip: The best way to grill these hens is slowly, skin side up for most of the cooking time. This way the fat doesn't cause flare-ups and the birds don't burn over the fire. After they're almost cooked, you simply turn them and brown the skin side so it's golden and crispy.

Makes 4 servings

CRISP ROAST DUCK

Serve with an American-Style Amber Lager, such as Michelob Amber Bock

1 whole Long Island Duck (5 to 6 pounds)

$1^{1}/_{2}$ teaspoons salt

$^{3}/_{4}$ teaspoon freshly ground black pepper

$^{1}/_{2}$ cup dried cherries

$^{1}/_{2}$ cup Michelob Amber Bock

1 cup thinly sliced shallots

1 pound Savoy cabbage, cored and shredded

1 Preheat the oven to 425°F. Remove and reserve any excess fat from the duck body cavity and neck. Prick the skin all over with a fork. Folding the neck skin under the body, put the duck, breast side up, on a rack set in a roasting pan. Rub all over with 1 teaspoon of the salt and $^{1}/_{2}$ teaspoon of the pepper.

2 Roast for 20 minutes and remove from the oven. Protecting your hands with kitchen towels or washable oven mitts, turn the duck breast side down. Roast for 20 minutes longer. Turn the duck breast side up again and roast until an instant-read thermometer inserted into the thickest part of a thigh away from the bone registers 160°F, the juices run clear when a thigh or breast is pierced with a fork, and the duck is nicely browned, about 20 minutes longer (the total roasting time will be about 1 hour). Transfer the duck to a cutting board, tent loosely with aluminum foil, and let rest for 15 minutes before carving.

3 Meanwhile, in a microwave-safe dish, combine the cherries and beer and microwave on high until almost boiling, about 30 seconds. Cover and set aside. After the duck has cooked for 2 hours, spoon off $^{1}/_{4}$ cup fat from the roasting pan and transfer to a large skillet over medium-high heat. Add the shallots and cook, stirring often, for 3 minutes. Stir in the cherries and beer and the cabbage. Cook, stirring often, until the cabbage is tender, about 15 minutes. Season with the remaining $^{1}/_{2}$ teaspoon salt and $^{1}/_{4}$ teaspoon pepper and serve with the duck.

Makes 4 to 6 servings

GRILLED AMBER DUCK

Serve with an American-Style Amber Lager, such as Michelob Amber Bock

2 bottles (12 ounces each) Michelob Amber Bock

Juice of 1 lemon

1 tablespoon pure maple syrup

1 teaspoon soy sauce

$^{1}/_{4}$ cup chopped fresh thyme

2 shallots, minced

2 garlic cloves, minced

1 teaspoon freshly ground black pepper

4 boneless duck breast halves (6 ounces each), skin on

2 cups (about 8 ounces) beechwood chips

Salt to taste

1 In a bowl, combine $^{3}/_{4}$ cup of the beer, the lemon juice, maple syrup, soy sauce, thyme, shallots, garlic, and pepper. Add the duck breasts and turn to coat. Cover and marinate in the refrigerator for 1 hour.

2 Place the wood chips in a small bowl and add $1^{3}/_{4}$ cups of the beer. Soak for at least $^{1}/_{2}$ hour. If using a charcoal grill, prepare a solid bed of medium coals. If using a gas grill, preheat to high and close the lid, then open the lid and lower the heat to medium. Drain the wood chips and place in a foil pan directly on the heat in the corner for a gas grill, or scatter them over the coals if using charcoal.

3 Remove the duck from the marinade and pat dry with paper towels. Season with salt and pepper. Discard the marinade. Lay the duck breasts on the grill rack, skin side down. If using a gas grill, close the lid. Cook, basting occasionally with the remaining $^{1}/_{2}$ cup beer, until the skin is crisp and nicely browned, 7 to 10 minutes. Turn and cook, again basting with beer, until reddish pink for medium-rare, about 5 minutes longer. Transfer to a cutting board, tent loosely with foil, and let rest for about 5 minutes. Slice very thinly across the grain. Serve immediately.

Cook's Tip: Chef Brent Wertz suggests using applewood chips if beechwood chips are not available.

Makes 4 servings

QUESADILLA with CRANBERRY CHUTNEY

Serve with an English-Style Pale Ale, such as Michelob Pale Ale

CRANBERRY CHUTNEY

2 tablespoons butter

¹/₃ cup minced red onion

3 cups fresh cranberries

3 tablespoons honey

1 small bunch fresh tarragon, finely chopped

¹/₂ cup Michelob Pale Ale

4 flour tortillas (12 inches in diameter)

4 ounces diced cooked pheasant or chicken

1 cup (4 ounces) shredded white Cheddar cheese

1 tablespoon diced canned green chiles, drained

¹/₄ cup fresh corn kernels

1 tablespoon butter

1 To prepare the chutney, in a saucepan over medium heat, melt the butter. Add the onion and cook until lightly golden. Add the remaining ingredients and bring to a simmer. Cook until the cranberries are soft, about 10 minutes. Remove from the heat and let cool.

2 Place 2 of the tortillas on a work surface. Arrange half of the pheasant on each tortilla, leaving about a 1-inch border. Sprinkle each with the cheese, chiles, and corn kernels. Top each with 2 tablespoons of the cranberry chutney. Place the remaining 2 tortillas on top and press to pack gently. In a large frying pan over medium-high heat, melt the 1 tablespoon butter. Place a quesadilla in the hot butter and cook until browned and crispy on the bottom, about 4 minutes. Turn and cook until browned on the second side, about 4 minutes longer. Repeat to cook the second quesadilla. Cut each in half and serve immediately, passing some of the remaining chutney at the table.

Cook's Tip: Chef Brent Wertz uses leftover chutney with other light meats, such as grilled chicken or pork.

Makes 2 servings

UPLAND GAME CHILI

Serve with an American-Style Premium Lager, such as Budweiser

1 pound dried navy beans, soaked overnight and drained

4 cups chicken stock

3 bottles (12 ounces each) Budweiser

1 onion, chopped

1 garlic clove, minced

¹/₂ teaspoon salt

¹/₂ teaspoon freshly ground black pepper

¹/₂ teaspoon ground cumin

1 teaspoon chili powder

1 pound cooked pheasant, cut into ¹/₂-inch dice

1 pound cooked quail, cut into ¹/₂-inch dice

1 In a soup pot, combine the beans, stock, beer, onion, garlic, salt, and pepper and bring to a boil over high heat. Lower the heat to low, cover, and simmer, stirring often to avoid scorching, until the beans are almost tender, 1 to 1¹/₂ hours.

2 Add the cumin, chili powder, and pheasant and quail meat. Return to a simmer and cook until the beans are tender and the flavors have blended, about 30 minutes longer. Taste and adjust the seasoning. Ladle the chili into bowls and serve hot.

Cook's Tip: Upland game are nonmigratory grassland birds such as pheasant, quail, partridge, woodcock, wild turkey, and grouse. Chef Sam Niemann advises adding more stock or beer, or both, to this warm and rustic dish if it seems dry.

Makes 8 servings

PARMESAN-BREADED TURKEY CUTLETS

Serve with a European-Style Pilsner, such as Tiger

2 boneless, skinless turkey tenders (about 10 ounces each)

1/2 teaspoon salt

1/4 teaspoon freshly ground pepper

3 slices whole-wheat or white bread, torn into small pieces

1 tablespoon coarsely chopped fresh rosemary

3 tablespoons freshly grated Parmesan cheese

2 large eggs

1/4 cup all-purpose flour

3 tablespoons extra-virgin olive oil, or as needed

Lemon wedges

1 Cut each turkey piece in half crosswise. Butterfly each piece by cutting horizontally into the turkey and opening it like a book. Using a rolling pin or the flat side of a meat pounder, lightly pound each piece between 2 sheets of wax paper until about 1/4 inch thick. Sprinkle on both sides with the salt and pepper and set aside.

2 In a food processor, combine the bread, rosemary, and Parmesan and process until finely chopped. Transfer the bread-crumb mixture to a pie plate. In a bowl, beat the eggs until well blended. Put the flour on a piece of wax paper.

3 In a large, heavy skillet, heat the olive oil over medium-high heat. Dredge a turkey cutlet in the flour and shake off the excess. Dip it in the egg, then in the bread-crumb mixture. Repeat with the remaining cutlets. When the oil is hot, add 2 cutlets and cook until nicely browned on the first side, about 2 minutes. Turn and cook until browned on the second side, 2 to 3 minutes longer. Transfer to a platter and cover to keep warm. Repeat to cook the remaining 2 cutlets, adding more oil to the pan if needed. Serve with the lemon wedges.

Cook's Tip: These crispy cutlets are made from turkey tenderloins. If tenders are not available, you can cut slices from a breast of turkey. First remove the skin, then carve the turkey off the bone. Cut 1/2-inch slices and pound them to make cutlets of about 1/4-inch thickness.

Makes 4 servings

Budweiser coaster, circa 1940.

TURKEY SAUSAGE with WHITE BEANS

Serve with an English-Style Pale Ale, such as Michelob Pale Ale

1/2 pound dried cannellini or Great Northern beans, soaked overnight and drained

6 large garlic cloves

1 bay leaf

1 teaspoon salt

1/4 teaspoon freshly ground black pepper

1/2 cup chopped fresh flat-leaf parsley

3 tablespoons extra-virgin olive oil

1 pound mild Italian turkey sausage

1 Preheat the oven to 375°F. In a Dutch oven or large, heavy ovenproof saucepan, combine the beans, garlic, bay leaf, and cold water to cover by 3 inches. Bring to a boil over high heat. Cover and place in the oven. Bake for 30 minutes, then add the salt. Cover and bake until the beans are tender, 20 to 30 minutes longer. Drain the beans, discarding the bay leaf, and return the beans to the pot. Add the pepper, parsley, and olive oil. Set aside.

2 Prepare a grill for cooking over medium-high heat. First, oil the grill rack. If using a charcoal grill, prepare a solid bed of medium-hot coals. If using a gas grill, preheat to high and close the lid, then open the lid and lower the heat to medium-high (you can hold your hand 1 to 2 inches above grill level only 3 to 4 seconds).

3 Prick the sausage several times with a fork and lay it on the grill rack. If using a gas grill, close the lid. Grill the sausage, turning as needed, until lightly browned on all sides and no longer pink inside (cut to test), about 10 minutes. Serve with the beans.

Cook's Tip: You can quickly presoak the beans for this dish by bringing them to a boil and letting them sit, covered, for 1 hour. But if you're really stuck for time, substitute 3 cups of drained canned cooked beans and just warm them in a saucepan with the olive oil, parsley, 1 minced clove of garlic, and salt and pepper.

Makes 4 servings

TURKEY MEATBALL SUBS

Serve with an American-Style Premium Lager, such as Michelob Golden Draft

1 pound ground turkey, preferably dark meat

1/4 cup plain fresh bread crumbs

1/4 cup chopped fresh flat-leaf parsley

1/4 cup (1 ounce) freshly grated Parmesan cheese

2 garlic cloves, minced

1 large egg

1/2 teaspoon salt

1/4 teaspoon freshly ground black pepper

2 tablespoons extra-virgin olive oil

1 cup tomato sauce

1 baguette, cut crosswise into 4 pieces (each 5 to 6 inches long), split horizontally

1 cup (4 ounces) shredded provolone cheese

1 In a large bowl, combine the turkey, bread crumbs, parsley, Parmesan, garlic, egg, salt, and pepper. Using your hands, mix well. Shape the turkey mixture into meatballs 1 1/2 inches in diameter.

2 Preheat the broiler. In a large, heavy skillet (preferably 12-inch), heat the olive oil over medium heat. Add the meatballs and cook, turning gently as needed to brown on all sides, until opaque throughout (cut to test), 5 to 8 minutes. Add the tomato sauce. Bring to a simmer and cook until heated through, about 5 minutes longer.

3 Pile the meatballs onto the bottoms of the baguette pieces, dividing evenly, and sprinkle with the provolone. Broil until the cheese melts. Serve hot.

Cook's Tip: Ground dark-meat turkey makes very tender, flavorful meatballs. As you brown them, turn the meatballs gently or they'll break apart.

Makes 4 sandwiches

PORK, BEEF & LAMB

Chef's Specialty

CHILE VERDE

Serve with an English-Style Pale Ale, such as Michelob Pale Ale

4 pounds boned pork shoulder (butt), trimmed of excess fat and cut into 2-inch cubes

2 tablespoons vegetable oil, if needed

3 onions (about 2 pounds total), cut into wedges 1/4 inch thick

5 large garlic cloves, minced

3 tablespoons ground cumin

1 can (28 ounces) whole tomatoes

1 3/4 cups chicken stock

10 Anaheim or poblano chiles (about 1 1/2 pounds total), stemmed, roasted, peeled, and chopped (see Cook's Tip), or 4 cans (7 ounces each) whole green chiles, drained and chopped

2 tablespoons chopped fresh oregano

Salt and freshly ground black pepper

Chopped fresh cilantro

Lime wedges

1 Rinse the pork cubes, place in a large saucepan, and add 1/3 cup water. Cover and cook over medium-high heat, stirring occasionally, until the pork is very juicy, 15 to 20 minutes. Uncover, raise the heat to high, and cook, stirring often, until the liquid is evaporated and the pork is browned, 20 to 30 minutes. Transfer the pork to a bowl and set aside.

2 Lower the heat to medium. If there is leftover pork fat in the pan, spoon or pour off and discard all but 3 tablespoons (if not, add the oil). Add the onions, garlic, and cumin. Stir, then cover and cook, stirring occasionally, until the onions are softened, about 8 minutes.

3 Return the pork and any accumulated juices to the pan. Add the tomatoes and stock, breaking up the tomatoes with a spoon. Bring to a simmer, then lower the heat to low, cover, and simmer for 1 hour.

4 Stir in the chiles and oregano. Cover and continue to simmer until the pork is very tender when pierced with a knife and the flavors are blended, about 15 minutes longer. Season to taste with salt and pepper. Serve topped with the cilantro and garnished with the lime wedges.

Cook's Tip: To roast and peel chiles or bell peppers, place them on a baking sheet and broil 4 to 5 inches from the heat source until the skins are blackened and blistered all over, turning as needed, 5 to 8 minutes. Transfer to a paper or plastic bag, close tightly, and let stand for 10 minutes (the steam will loosen the skins). Peel, stem, seed, and cut as needed.

Makes 6 to 8 servings

BRAISED PORK with LEMON and SAGE

Serve with a European-Style Pilsner, such as Harbin

3 pounds boned pork shoulder roast, trimmed of excess fat

2 tablespoons all-purpose flour

1½ tablespoons kosher salt

2 teaspoons freshly ground black pepper

2 tablespoons olive oil

4 garlic cloves, minced

5 fresh sage leaves

3½ cups whole milk

1 teaspoon grated lemon zest

1 Rinse the pork roast and pat dry with paper towels. In a small bowl, combine the flour, salt, and pepper. Sprinkle the flour mixture over the pork.

2 In a large skillet, heat the olive oil over medium-high heat. Add the pork and cook, turning until well browned on all sides, about 15 minutes. Transfer the pork and any juices to a large electric slow-cooker.

3 Let the pan cool slightly, then add the garlic and sage to the fat remaining in the pan. Stir over medium-low heat until the garlic turns golden, about 1 minute. Add the garlic mixture, milk, and lemon zest to the slow-cooker.

4 Cover the crock and cook on high heat for 4 to 5 hours, then uncover and continue to cook until the pork is tender when pierced with a knife and the sauce is golden brown and reduced by about half, about 3 hours longer.

5 Transfer the pork to a carving board and slice. Serve with the sauce on the side.

Cook's Tip: The traditional Italian method used for this dish makes a rather lumpy, toffee-colored sauce, but it is one of the most succulent ways to cook pork. You'll need to uncover the slow-cooker for the last 3 hours of cooking, so plan ahead. Serve with polenta and a green salad.

Makes 6 servings

A Michelob coaster widely used from the late 1950s through the 1960s.

PORK LOIN BRAISED with CABBAGE

Serve with an American-Style Amber Lager, such as Michelob Amber Bock

4 teaspoons Hungarian sweet paprika

2 teaspoons chopped fresh thyme

1^1/$_2$ teaspoons kosher salt

1^1/$_2$ teaspoons freshly ground black pepper

1 teaspoon chopped fresh sage

1 boneless pork loin (2 pounds), trimmed of excess fat

1 tablespoon olive oil

4 ounces Canadian bacon, diced

2 pounds red or green cabbage, thinly sliced

2 onions, thinly sliced

1 carrot, peeled and thinly sliced

1 tablespoon tomato paste

^{1}/$_2$ teaspoon caraway seeds

1 bottle (12 ounces) Michelob Amber Bock

1 Preheat the oven to 350°F. Combine 2 teaspoons of the paprika, 1 teaspoon of the thyme, 1 teaspoon each of the salt and pepper, and the sage. Rinse the pork loin and pat dry with paper towels. Rub the spice mixture over the pork. In a large ovenproof Dutch oven, heat the olive oil over medium-high heat. Add the pork and cook, turning until well browned on all sides, about 5 minutes. Transfer the pork to a platter and set aside.

2 Add the bacon to the pan and cook for 3 minutes. Add the cabbage, onions, and carrot. Cover, lower the heat to medium, and cook, stirring occasionally, until the cabbage begins to wilt, about 15 minutes. Stir in the tomato paste, the remaining 2 teaspoons of paprika, the remaining 1 teaspoon of thyme, the remaining ^{1}/$_2$ teaspoon of pepper, the caraway seeds, and beer. Return the pork to the pan and cover.

3 Bake the pork until tender, about 2 hours. Sprinkle with the remaining ^{1}/$_2$ teaspoon salt and serve.

Makes 8 servings

HOISIN PORK and SNOW PEA STIR-FRY

Serve with a European-Style Pilsner, such as Kirin Ichiban

4 ounces rice noodles

1 pork tenderloin (about 1 pound), trimmed of excess fat and thinly sliced

2 tablespoons soy sauce

^{3}/$_4$ cup chicken stock

^{1}/$_4$ cup hoisin sauce

1 tablespoon cornstarch

1 tablespoon honey

4 teaspoons dark sesame oil

8 ounces snow peas, trimmed

^{1}/$_2$ cup sliced red bell pepper

1 tablespoon peeled and minced fresh ginger

1 teaspoon minced garlic

^{1}/$_2$ cup chopped green onions, white and tender green parts

1 In a bowl, soak the noodles in warm water to cover for 15 minutes. Drain and keep warm. Meanwhile, rinse the pork slices and pat dry with paper towels. Place the pork in a bowl and drizzle with 1 tablespoon of the soy sauce, tossing to coat. Set aside.

2 In another bowl, combine the remaining 1 tablespoon soy sauce, the stock, hoisin sauce, cornstarch, and honey, stirring with a whisk until smooth.

3 In a large skillet, heat 1 tablespoon of the sesame oil over medium-high heat. Add the pork and sauté until browned, about 3 minutes. Transfer the pork to a plate. Add the remaining 1 teaspoon sesame oil to the pan. Stir in the snow peas, bell pepper, ginger, and garlic and sauté for 30 seconds. Return the pork to the pan. Stir in the stock mixture and simmer, stirring occasionally, until thick, about 2 minutes. Remove from the heat and stir in the green onions. Serve the pork over the noodles.

Makes 4 servings

PEAR and CRANBERRY STUFFED PORK ROAST

Serve with a Wheat Beer, such as Michelob Bavarian Style Wheat

2 teaspoons olive oil

¼ cup sliced onion

½ teaspoon dried thyme

½ teaspoon dried rubbed sage

2 garlic cloves, minced

½ cup chicken stock

2 pears, peeled, cored, and chopped

¼ cup dried cranberries

¼ cup apple juice

1 boneless pork loin roast (about 2 pounds), trimmed of excess fat and butterflied

1 teaspoon salt

1 teaspoon freshly ground black pepper

1 In a large skillet, heat the olive oil over medium-high heat. Add the onion, thyme, sage, and garlic. Sauté until the onion is tender, about 3 minutes. Stir in the stock, scraping to loosen any browned bits from the bottom of the pan. Cook until the liquid is almost evaporated, about 5 minutes. Add the pears and cook, stirring often, until lightly browned, about 5 minutes. Stir in the cranberries and apple juice. Cook until the liquid is absorbed, about 5 minutes. Remove from the heat and let cool to room temperature.

2 Preheat the oven to 400°F. Lightly oil a roasting rack set inside a roasting pan.

3 Unroll the pork roast, rinse, and pat dry with paper towels. Sprinkle both sides of the pork with the salt and pepper. Spread the pear mixture over the roast, stopping 2 inches from the outside edges. Roll up the roast, jelly-roll fashion, starting with the short side. Secure at 1-inch intervals with twine. Place the roast on the rack in the roasting pan.

4 Roast for 15 minutes. Lower the oven temperature to 325°F (do not remove the pork from the oven) and roast until an instant-read thermometer inserted in the thickest part registers 160°F and the meat is slightly pink in the center (cut to test), about 1 hour and 10 minutes longer. Let stand for 10 minutes. Slice the pork into 1-inch-thick slices and serve.

Cook's Tip: If your butcher can't butterfly the roast for you and time is short, buy a tied loin roast. Separate it into two pieces, spread the filling between the halves, and truss tightly.

Makes 8 servings

PORK MEDALLIONS with PORCINI SAUCE

Serve with a Porter, such as Michelob Porter

1¹/₂ cups dried porcini mushrooms (1¹/₂ ounces)

1 pork tenderloin (about 1 pound), trimmed of
    excess fat and cut crosswise into 8 pieces

1 teaspoon salt

1 teaspoon freshly ground black pepper

1 teaspoon minced fresh rosemary

1 garlic clove, crushed

2 teaspoons olive oil

1 teaspoon butter

³/₄ cup diced red onion

¹/₂ cup Michelob Porter

1 cup chicken stock

Fresh rosemary sprigs (optional)

1 Place the mushrooms in a bowl and pour in 1¹/₂ cups boiling water. Cover and let stand until tender, about 30 minutes. Drain in a colander set over a bowl, reserving 1 cup soaking liquid. Finely chop the mushrooms and set aside.

2 Rinse the pork pieces and pat dry with paper towels. Place each piece between 2 sheets of wax paper. Using a rolling pin or the flat side of a meat mallet, pound until ¹/₂ inch thick. Sprinkle both sides of the pork with ¹/₄ teaspoon of the salt and the 1 teaspoon of pepper.

3 In a small bowl, combine the minced rosemary, the remaining ³/₄ teaspoon of salt, and garlic, mashing with a fork into a paste.

4 In a large skillet, heat the olive oil and butter over medium-high heat. Add the garlic paste and sauté for 30 seconds. Add the pork and cook for 2 minutes on each side. Transfer the pork to a plate and set aside.

5 Add the onion to the pan and sauté until tender, about 5 minutes. Stir in the mushrooms and beer and cook for 1 minute. Add the reserved mushroom soaking liquid and stock. Bring to a boil and cook until reduced to 1¹/₂ cups, about 10 minutes. Lower the heat to medium-low. Return the pork to the pan and cook until thoroughly heated, about 3 minutes. Garnish with rosemary sprigs, if you like, and serve.

Cook's Tip: Dried porcini mushrooms keep up to 6 months in an airtight container. Water used to reconstitute the mushrooms becomes a flavorful stock. Serve the pork with steamed carrots, squash, and zucchini.

Makes 4 servings

Suds, it seems, were Eberhard Anheuser's destiny. Before he acquired the Bavarian Brewery—which he promptly renamed after himself—in 1860, the Prussia-born businessman ran St. Louis's biggest soap factory.

SPICE-RUBBED PORK with TOMATOES

Serve with a Wheat Beer, such as Michelob Bavarian Style Wheat

1 tablespoon brown sugar

1 teaspoon ground coriander

1/2 teaspoon garlic powder

1/2 teaspoon freshly ground black pepper

1/4 teaspoon salt

1/4 teaspoon ground cumin

1/8 teaspoon ground ginger

1 pork tenderloin (about 1 pound), trimmed of excess fat

1 teaspoon chile paste

16 cherry tomatoes

2 tablespoons soy sauce

1 teaspoon dark sesame oil

1. Soak 16 wooden skewers in water to cover for 30 minutes. Prepare a grill for cooking over medium-high heat. First, oil the grill rack. If using a charcoal grill, prepare a solid bed of medium-hot coals. If using a gas grill, preheat to high and close the lid, then open the lid and lower the heat to medium-high (you can hold your hand 1 to 2 inches above grill level only 3 to 4 seconds).

2. Meanwhile, in a small bowl, combine the brown sugar, coriander, garlic powder, pepper, salt, cumin, and ginger. Rinse the pork tenderloin and pat dry with paper towels. Cut the pork in half crosswise, then cut each half into 8 lengthwise strips. In a shallow dish, combine the pork strips and chile paste, tossing to coat. Sprinkle the brown sugar mixture evenly over the pork, tossing to coat. Let the pork stand for 10 minutes.

3. Thread 1 strip of pork and 1 tomato onto each soaked skewer. Lay the skewers on the grill rack. Cook, turning once, until browned and still slightly pink in the center (cut to test), about 3 minutes on each side. In a small bowl, stir together the soy sauce and sesame oil, then drizzle over the pork skewers and serve.

Makes 4 servings

PORK SKEWERS with MOROCCAN SPICES

Serve with an American-Style Light Lager, such as Bud Light

1 1/4 pounds ground pork

1 1/2 tablespoons minced garlic

2 teaspoons ground cumin

2 teaspoons ground paprika

1/3 cup finely chopped onion

1 1/2 teaspoons salt

1 teaspoon freshly ground black pepper

1. Soak 8 wooden skewers in water to cover for 30 minutes. Prepare a grill for cooking over medium heat. First, oil the grill rack. If using a charcoal grill, prepare a solid bed of medium coals. If using a gas grill, preheat to high and close the lid, then open the lid and lower the heat to medium (you can hold your hand 1 to 2 inches above grill level only 4 to 5 seconds).

2. Meanwhile, in a bowl, combine the pork, garlic, cumin, paprika, onion, salt, and pepper, mixing well. Form the mixture into small meatballs, each about the size of a golf ball, then thread the meatballs onto the soaked skewers, dividing them equally among the skewers.

3. Lay the skewers on the grill rack. If using a gas grill, close the lid. Cook, turning as needed, until browned on all sides and still slightly pink in the center (cut to test), about 8 minutes total. Serve warm.

Cook's Tip: Soaking the wooden skewers in water to cover while the grill heats helps prevent them from burning on the grill. Drain the skewers and pat them dry before threading with the meat (or other ingredients).

Makes 4 to 6 servings

CUBAN PORK with PINEAPPLE

Serve with a European-Style Pilsner, such as Tiger

¹/₃ cup pineapple juice

¹/₄ cup soy sauce

1 tablespoon brown sugar

1 tablespoon vegetable oil

1 teaspoon ground ginger

¹/₂ teaspoon ground allspice

¹/₂ teaspoon red pepper flakes

¹/₂ teaspoon dry mustard

4 pork loin rib chops (about ³/₄ inch thick and 6 ounces each)

12 ounces peeled and cored pineapple

1 large red onion

2 tablespoons chopped fresh mint

Lime wedges

1 In a bowl, combine the pineapple juice, soy sauce, brown sugar, oil, ginger, allspice, red pepper flakes, and dry mustard, stirring with a whisk to blend. Rinse the pork and pat dry with paper towels. Place the chops in a large zip-lock plastic bag and pour in all but ¹/₄ cup juice mixture. Seal the bag and turn to coat. Let stand, turning the bag occasionally, for at least 20 minutes, or refrigerate for up to 24 hours.

2 Prepare a grill for cooking over high heat. First, oil the grill rack. If using a charcoal grill, prepare a solid bed of hot coals. If using a gas grill, preheat to high (you can hold your hand 1 to 2 inches above grill level only 2 to 3 seconds).

3 Meanwhile, cut the pineapple into slices ¹/₂ inch thick. Peel the onion and cut crosswise into slices ¹/₂ inch thick, discarding the ends. Arrange the pineapple and onion slices in a single layer on a rimmed baking sheet and drizzle evenly with the reserved ¹/₄ cup juice mixture. Let stand for about 20 minutes, turning the slices once.

4 Remove the pork chops from the bag and discard the marinade. Lay the chops, pineapple, and onion on the grill rack. If using a gas grill, close the lid. Cook, turning once, until the pineapple and onion are browned and the pork is browned and still slightly pink in the center (cut to test), 2 to 4 minutes on each side.

5 Transfer the chops to plates. Garnish with the grilled pineapple and onion. Sprinkle with the mint and serve with lime wedges.

Cook's Tip: For more intense flavor, marinate the pork in the refrigerator overnight. Serve with black beans and a spicy vinegar-dressed coleslaw seasoned with cumin seeds, chopped fresh cilantro, and minced garlic.

Makes 4 servings

PORK CHOPS with CAROLINA RUB

Serve with an American-Style Premium Lager, such as Michelob

1 teaspoon garlic powder

1 teaspoon onion powder

1 teaspoon sugar

1 teaspoon paprika

1 teaspoon chili powder

1 teaspoon freshly ground black pepper

1/2 teaspoon salt

4 center-cut pork loin chops (6 ounces each)

1/4 cup barbecue sauce

1 Prepare a grill for cooking over medium-high heat. First, oil the grill rack. If using a charcoal grill, prepare a solid bed of medium-hot coals. If using a gas grill, preheat to high and close the lid, then open the lid and lower the heat to medium-high (you can hold your hand 1 to 2 inches above grill level only 3 to 4 seconds).

2 In a bowl, combine the garlic powder, onion powder, sugar, paprika, chili powder, pepper, and salt. Rinse the pork chops and pat dry with paper towels. Rub the pork with the spice mixture and let stand for 10 minutes.

3 Place the pork on the grill rack. If using a gas grill, close the lid. Cook the chops for 4 minutes on the first side, then turn and cook on the other side for 2 minutes. Brush each chop with 1 tablespoon barbecue sauce and cook until still slightly pink in the center (cut to test), about 2 minutes longer. Serve immediately.

Cook's Tip: Season the chops and let them stand for about 10 minutes before grilling. This allows the meat to absorb the flavorful spice rub.

Makes 4 servings

PORK CHOPS with COUNTRY GRAVY

Serve with an American-Style Amber Lager, such as Michelob Amber Bock

1/4 cup all-purpose flour

3/4 teaspoon salt

1/4 teaspoon dried marjoram or basil

1/4 teaspoon dried thyme

1/4 teaspoon dried rubbed sage

4 boneless center-cut pork loin chops (each about 3/4 inch thick and 4 ounces)

1 tablespoon butter

1 1/2 cups milk

1 In a shallow dish, combine the flour, salt, marjoram, thyme, and sage, stirring with a whisk. Rinse the pork chops and pat dry with paper towels. Dredge the pork in the flour mixture, turning to coat and shaking off any excess. Reserve the remaining flour mixture.

2 In a large skillet, melt the butter over medium-high heat. Add the pork chops and cook until browned, about 2 minutes on each side. Lower the heat to medium and cook, turning once, until still slightly pink in the center (cut to test), about 5 minutes on each side. Transfer the chops to a plate and keep warm.

3 In a small bowl, combine the reserved flour mixture and milk, stirring with a whisk until blended. Add the milk mixture to the pan and bring to a boil over medium-high heat, scraping to loosen any browned bits from the bottom of the pan. Lower the heat to low and simmer, stirring constantly, until slightly thickened, about 2 minutes. Serve the gravy with the chops.

Cook's Tip: This recipe makes enough gravy to smother the pork chops, or you can spoon half over the chops and half over mashed potatoes.

Makes 4 servings

SPICY PORK RIBS

Serve with an American-Style Premium Lager, such as Budweiser

³/₄ cup *harissa* paste

3 tablespoons fresh lemon juice

1 tablespoon minced garlic

2 slabs baby back ribs (about 1¹/₂ pounds each)

Kosher salt and freshly ground black pepper

2 bottles (12 ounces each) Budweiser

1 In a small bowl, stir together the *harissa* paste, lemon juice, and garlic. Set aside.

2 Rinse the ribs and pat dry with paper towels. Using a dull butter knife, loosen the thin papery membrane that runs along underside of the ribs, then pull it off with your fingers. Rub the ribs generously on both sides with salt and pepper, then slather all over with the *harissa* mixture. Wrap the ribs in plastic wrap and refrigerate for at least 8 hours and up to 24 hours.

3 Prepare a grill for cooking over indirect heat. First, oil the grill rack. If using a charcoal grill, light 50 to 60 briquettes and let burn until covered with ash, about 20 to 30 minutes, then mound them to one side. Place a drip pan on the side cleared of coals—this is the indirect heat area. Set the oiled grill rack in place. If using a gas grill, turn all the burners to high and close the lid. When the temperature inside the grill reaches 350° to 400°F, lift the lid, turn off one of the burners, and lower the other burner(s) to medium. Place a drip pan under the turned-off burner—this is the indirect heat area. Set the oiled grill rack in place.

4 Place the ribs, bone side down, over the indirect-heat area of the grill and close the lid. Cook, basting gently with the beer on both sides every 10 minutes (leave bone side down and try to keep the *harissa* mixture on the ribs while basting) until the ribs are tender and cooked through and the meat has shrunk back from the ends of the bones, 40 to 50 minutes. Serve the ribs hot.

Cook's Tip: *Harissa,* a Tunisian spice paste, is available at gourmet food stores and Middle Eastern markets. You can marinate the ribs for up to 2 days before cooking.

Makes 8 servings

What's in a Name?—The word "Budweiser" was coined in 1876 by Adolphus Busch, who wanted a moniker for his new national beer brand that would be easy to pronounce and suggest old-country roots (German immigrants were among Anheuser-Busch's biggest customers at the time).

BAKED POLENTA with SAUSAGE and TOMATO

Serve with a Porter, such as Michelob Porter

5¹/₂ tablespoons olive oil

1 can (28 ounces) crushed tomatoes

1 tablespoon chopped fresh oregano

1 yellow onion, cut lengthwise into thin wedges

1 yellow, red, or orange bell pepper, stemmed,
  seeded, and cut lengthwise into thin slices

2 garlic cloves, minced

¹/₂ teaspoon salt

¹/₂ teaspoon freshly ground black pepper

¹/₂ teaspoon red pepper flakes

1 pound bulk Italian sweet or spicy sausage or
  1 pound Italian sausage links, casings removed

2 packages (16 ounces each) prepared polenta,
  sliced into rounds ¹/₂ inch thick

8 ounces fresh mozzarella, drained and sliced
  into rounds ¹/₄ inch thick

1 Preheat the broiler. Coat the bottom of a 9-by-13-inch baking pan with 1¹/₂ tablespoons of the olive oil.

2 In a saucepan, heat 3 tablespoons of the olive oil over medium heat. Add the tomatoes and oregano and simmer for 15 minutes.

3 Meanwhile, in a skillet, heat the remaining 1 tablespoon olive oil over medium-high heat. Add the onion, bell pepper, garlic, salt, pepper, and red pepper flakes, stirring to combine. Cover, lower the heat to medium, and cook until the vegetables are softened, about 5 minutes. Add the sausage and cook, stirring and breaking it into small pieces with a wooden spoon, about 5 minutes. Cover and cook until the vegetables are tender and the sausage is cooked through, 5 to 8 minutes longer. Add the tomato mixture and simmer for 10 minutes.

4 Add the polenta slices to the prepared baking pan and turn to coat with the oil, then arrange the slices lengthwise in 3 slightly overlapping rows. Broil the polenta about 4 inches from the heat source until golden brown and crisp, 10 to 15 minutes.

5 Pour the sauce over the broiled polenta, then arrange the mozzarella slices over the top. Broil until the cheese is melted and beginning to brown, about 2 minutes. Let cool slightly before serving.

Cook's Tip: Using ready-made polenta saves you the step of making it from scratch, and the quick tomato sauce can be cooked in just 30 minutes. All you need is a fresh green salad and a loaf of crusty Italian bread to round out the meal.

Makes 6 servings

BRATWURST with CARAMELIZED ONIONS

Serve with an American-Style Premium Lager, such as Budweiser

3 tablespoons unsalted butter

2 extra-large yellow onions, thinly sliced (about 1½ pounds total)

Pinch of sugar

½ teaspoon salt

¼ teaspoon freshly ground black pepper

1 teaspoon caraway seeds

¼ cup Budweiser

3 tablespoons coarse-grained mustard

1 pound uncooked bratwurst

1 Prepare a grill for cooking over medium-high heat. First, oil the grill rack. If using a charcoal grill, prepare a solid bed of medium-hot coals. If using a gas grill, preheat to high and close the lid, then open the lid and lower the heat to medium-high (you can hold your hand 1 to 2 inches above grill level only 3 to 4 seconds).

2 In a large skillet, melt the butter over medium-high heat. Add the onions, sugar, salt, pepper, caraway, and 2 tablespoons of the beer. Stir to coat the onions and cover. Lower the heat to medium-low and cook, stirring occasionally, until the onions are very tender, about 35 minutes (remove the cover for a few minutes if any liquid remains).

3 In a bowl, stir together the remaining 2 tablespoons beer and the mustard and spread over the bratwurst. Let stand at room temperature for 15 minutes. Lay the bratwurst on the grill rack. If using a gas grill, close the lid. Grill until lightly browned on all sides and cooked through (cut to test), 8 to 10 minutes. Serve immediately with the onions.

Cook's Tip: This dish is great made with uncooked bratwurst, but it will work with fully cooked brats as well. Just cook the sausages until lightly browned and warmed through, about 5 minutes total grilling time.

Makes 4 servings

THE ULTIMATE BACON, LETTUCE, and TOMATO

Serve with an English-Style Pale Ale, such as Michelob Pale Ale

BASIL AIOLI

1 cup loosely packed basil leaves

½ cup extra-virgin olive oil

½ cup canola oil

2 egg yolks

2 cloves garlic, minced

½ teaspoon *each* dried mustard, lemon juice, salt, and pepper

8 slices artisan levain or sourdough bread, cut ¼ to ½ inch thick

12 applewood-smoked thick-cut bacon slices, cooked until crisp and drained

4 ripe tomatoes, sliced

1 cup loosely packed arugula leaves

8 ounces fresh mozzarella, drained and sliced

Salt and freshly ground black pepper

1 To make the basil aioli, bring a large pot of salted water to a boil. Plunge the basil leaves into the boiling water for 20 seconds. Drain and squeeze out as much excess water as possible. In a blender, purée the blanched basil leaves with olive and canola oils. Empty into a measuring cup or small pitcher and set aside. In a bowl, whisk together the egg yolks, garlic, mustard, lemon juice, salt, and pepper. Whisk in a drop of the basil oil. Continue adding drops of oil, whisking until the mixture thickens to a mayonnaise-like consistency. Continuing to whisk, pour in the remaining basil oil in a very thin stream. Season with salt and pepper to taste

2 Spread one side of each slice of bread with the aioli. On 1 slice of the bread, stack 3 slices of bacon and one-fourth of the tomato slices, arugula leaves, and fresh mozzarella slices. Sprinkle with salt and pepper. Top with another slice of bread. Repeat for the remaining ingredients and serve.

Makes 4 sandwiches

VIETNAMESE SKEWERS with DIPPING SAUCE

Serve with a European-Style Pilsner, such as Grolsch

1 stalk lemongrass, outer leaves and upper stalk
   discarded, thinly sliced

1 shallot, thinly sliced

1 garlic clove, coarsely chopped

1 tablespoon light brown sugar

2 tablespoons fish sauce

1 pound skirt steak (3/4 to 1 inch thick), trimmed
   of excess fat

DIPPING SAUCE

1 garlic clove

1/4 teaspoon red pepper flakes

1 tablespoon light brown sugar

2 tablespoons *each* fresh lime juice, rice vinegar,
   and fish sauce

1 tablespoon *each* shredded daikon and peeled
   and shredded carrot

1 In a food processor or blender, combine the lemongrass, shallot, garlic, brown sugar, and fish sauce and process until finely chopped. Spread the mixture over both sides of the steak and let stand at room temperature for 30 minutes.

2 Soak 8 wooden skewers in water to cover for 30 minutes. Prepare a grill for cooking over high heat. First, oil the grill rack. If using a charcoal grill, prepare a solid bed of hot coals. If using a gas grill, preheat to high.

3 Meanwhile, prepare the dipping sauce. On a cutting board, mince together the garlic, red pepper flakes, and brown sugar. Transfer to a bowl and stir in the remaining ingredients. Set aside.

4 Cut the steak into slices about 1/4 inch thick. Thread the beef slices onto the soaked skewers. Lay the skewers on the grill rack. Cook, turning once, just until seared and still pink in the center for medium-rare (cut to test), 1 to 2 minutes on each side. Serve with the sauce.

Makes 4 servings

MOROCCAN-STYLE BEEF KEBABS

Serve with an English-Style Pale Ale, such as Michelob Pale Ale

1 teaspoon ground cumin

1 teaspoon smoked paprika *(pimentón)*

Pinch of cayenne pepper

1 teaspoon salt

1 pound beef sirloin, trimmed of excess fat and
   cut into 1-inch cubes

1/2 red bell pepper, seeded and cut into 1-inch
   chunks

1/2 yellow bell pepper, seeded and cut into 1-inch
   chunks

Warm flat bread

Plain Greek yogurt (optional)

1 In a large bowl, combine the cumin, paprika, cayenne, and salt, stirring well. Add the beef and toss to coat. Let stand at room temperature for 30 minutes.

2 Soak 8 wooden skewers in water to cover for 30 minutes. Prepare a grill for cooking over high heat. First, oil the grill rack. If using a charcoal grill, prepare a solid bed of hot coals. If using a gas grill, preheat to high (you can hold your hand 1 to 2 inches above grill level only 2 to 3 seconds).

3 Thread the beef and pepper pieces onto the soaked skewers, alternating one by one. Lay the skewers on the grill rack. If using a gas grill, close the lid. Cook, turning once, until browned on the outside but still pink in the center for medium-rare (cut to test), 3 to 4 minutes on each side. Serve with the flat bread and the yogurt, if desired.

Cook's Tip: A fresh cucumber salad would make a great accompaniment to these kebabs. If you can't find smoked paprika, substitute regular paprika.

Makes 4 servings

HOT-and-SOUR ASIAN BEEF SALAD

Serve with a European-Style Pilsner, such as Harbin

1 beef flank steak (about 1 pound)

8 ounces dried thin rice noodles

1/2 cup fresh lime juice

1/4 cup Asian fish sauce or soy sauce

1/4 cup sugar (2 tablespoons if using soy sauce)

1 tablespoon minced garlic

3 to 4 teaspoons minced fresh serrano chiles

8 cups salad greens (about 5 ounces)

1 cup cherry tomatoes, stemmed and halved

1/2 red onion, thinly sliced

1/3 cup fresh mint leaves

1/3 cup fresh cilantro leaves

1 Prepare a grill for cooking over high heat. First, oil the grill rack. If using a charcoal grill, prepare a solid bed of hot coals. If using a gas grill, preheat to high (you can hold your hand 1 to 2 inches above grill level only 2 to 3 seconds).

2 Rinse the steak and pat dry with paper towels. Lay the steak on the grill rack. If using a gas grill, close the lid. Cook, turning once, until browned on the outside but still pink in the center for medium-rare (cut to test), about 4 minutes on each side. Transfer to a carving board, tent loosely with aluminum foil, and let rest for 5 minutes.

3 Meanwhile, in a large saucepan, bring 2 1/2 to 3 quarts water to a boil over high heat. Add the noodles and cook, stirring occasionally, until barely tender to the bite, 3 to 4 minutes. Drain, rinse with cold water until cool, and drain again thoroughly.

4 In a small bowl, combine 1/2 cup water (use 1/4 cup water if substituting soy sauce for fish sauce), the lime juice, fish sauce, sugar, and garlic, stirring with a whisk. Add the chiles to taste.

5 Thinly slice the beef across the grain at a 45 degree angle, then cut the slices into strips 3 to 4 inches long. On individual plates, layer equal portions of salad greens, noodles, tomatoes, onion, mint, and cilantro.

6 Top the salads with the strips of beef. Drizzle half the dressing over the salads and serve, passing the remaining dressing at the table.

Cook's Tip: You can prepare this salad through step 5 up to 4 hours in advance of serving. Cover and refrigerate the dressing, beef, and plated salads separately, then finish assembly just before serving.

Makes 4 servings

GORGONZOLA BURGERS

Serve with an American-Style Premium Lager, such as Rolling Rock

1½ pounds freshly ground chuck

1 teaspoon salt

12 tablespoons softened Gorgonzola dolce cheese

1 ripe tomato, sliced

1 small red onion, thinly sliced

4 hamburger rolls

1 In a large bowl, pull the meat apart into small chunks, add the salt, and toss gently with your fingers spread apart until loosely mixed. (Mix in the salt very, very gently. The more you handle the meat, the tougher your burgers will be.)

2 Using wet hands, divide the meat into 8 equal portions and form into patties ¼ to ½ inch thick, making them thinner in the center. Divide the cheese into 4 equal portions, then shape each into a disk and put on a patty. Top the cheese disks with the remaining 4 patties and seal the edges of the patties around the cheese. Gently shape the patties so that they are about ¼ inch thinner in the center than the edges. (They'll shrink and even out during cooking.) Refrigerate the patties.

3 Prepare a grill for cooking over high heat. First, oil the grill rack. If using a charcoal grill, prepare a solid bed of hot coals. If using a gas grill, preheat to high (you can hold your hand 1 to 2 inches above grill level only 2 to 3 seconds).

4 Lay the patties on the grill rack. If using a gas grill, close the lid. Cook the burgers, turning once without pressing, for 2 minutes on each side for rare, 3 minutes for medium-rare, 4 minutes for medium, and 5 minutes for well-done. (Pressing or constant turning will toughen and dry out the meat, and if you flip too soon, the burgers will stick.)

5 Remove the burgers from the heat and let them rest for a few minutes before serving. This allows them to finish cooking and allows their juices, which have collected on the surface during grilling, to redistribute throughout the meat.

6 Split the rolls with a knife and assemble the burgers. Top each burger with tomato and onion slices and serve immediately.

Cook's Tip: For juicy burgers, look for ground chuck with a fat content of at least 18 percent. Lean or extra-lean meat makes tough, dry burgers. Also, the more freshly ground the meat is, the more tender and flavorful the burger. If your store has butchers, ask them to grind the meat fresh for you.

Makes 4 burgers

Anheuser-Busch owned the St. Louis Cardinals from 1953 until 1995. During that time, future Hall of Famers such as Red Schoendienst, Bob Gibson, Lou Brock, and Ozzie Smith wore Cardinal red. But no Cardinal Hall of Famer was a steadier presence in the field and at the plate than Stan Musial, who played his entire career for the team from 1941 until 1963, and served as its general manager in 1967, when the Redbirds won the World Series.

SAUSAGE and POTATO SKILLET

Serve with a Maerzen Beer, such as
Michelob Marzen

½ cup olive oil

2 red bell peppers, stemmed, seeded, and cut into
    julienne

2 yellow bell peppers, stemmed, seeded, and cut
    into julienne

2 green bell peppers, stemmed, seeded, and cut
    into julienne

2 onions, cut into julienne

1 pound smoked elk sausage, cut into ½-inch slices

1 pound smoked bison sausage, cut into ½-inch
    slices

1 pound smoked pheasant sausage, cut into ½-inch
    slices

1 pound smoked venison sausage, cut into ½-inch
    slices

4 Yukon gold potatoes, peeled and diced

1 bottle (12 ounces) Michelob Marzen

Pinch of kosher salt

1 In a large cast-iron skillet, heat the olive oil over
medium heat. Add the bell peppers and onions and
cook, stirring often, until softened, about 10 minutes.

2 Add the sausages and cook, stirring often, until
brown, about 10 minutes. Add the potatoes and
cook, stirring often, 10 minutes longer. Stir in the beer
and salt, lower the heat to low, and simmer gently until
the potatoes are tender, about 15 minutes longer. Serve
hot directly from the skillet.

Cook's Tip: Chef Sam Niemann uses smoked sausages
for their flavor and to cut down on cooking time. You can
substitute smoked chicken, turkey, or pork sausages if
game sausages are not available, but make the effort to
find them for this hearty, earthy dish.

Makes 10 servings

SPICY SHREDDED BEEF SANDWICHES

Serve with an English-Style Pale Ale, such as
Michelob Pale Ale

2½ pounds boneless beef chuck

1 can (14½ ounces) chopped tomatoes

1 can (7 ounces) chipotle sauce
    or 7 ounces spicy salsa

1 can (4 ounces) diced jalapeño chiles, drained

1 onion, chopped

3 garlic cloves, minced

2 tablespoons ground dried New Mexico chile
    or regular chili powder

1 tablespoon honey

2½ teaspoons kosher salt

1 teaspoon ground cumin

2 cups beef stock

6 crusty French-bread rolls, split

1 Rinse the beef and pat dry with paper towels. Trim
off any excess fat. Place the beef in a large electric
slow-cooker. Stir in the tomatoes with juice, chipotle
sauce, jalapeño chiles, onion, garlic, ground chile, honey,
salt, and cumin. Pour the stock over the top.

2 Cover the crock and cook on low heat until the
beef is very tender when pierced with a knife, 8 to
10 hours. If desired, remove the lid for the last 30 minutes to let the sauce reduce and thicken.

3 Using a heavy fork, transfer the meat to a carving
board or plate. Shred with 2 forks. Ladle out half the
sauce and reserve for another use. Return the shredded
beef to the remaining sauce in the slow-cooker, cover,
and let warm. Pile onto rolls and serve.

Cook's Tip: These sandwiches are delicious topped with
shredded cabbage, red onion, sliced tomato, cilantro, and
sour cream.

Makes 6 sandwiches

STEAK TACOS with GREEN SALSA

Serve with an American-Style Light Lager, such as Busch Light

1 canned chipotle chile in adobo, minced

1 tablespoon red wine vinegar

3 garlic cloves, minced

1 teaspoon dried oregano

1 teaspoon salt

½ teaspoon ground coriander

1 pound skirt steak (¾ to 1 inch thick), trimmed of excess fat

SALSA

½ pound tomatillos, husked and rinsed

1 serrano chile, seeded and coarsely chopped

1 garlic clove, chopped

⅓ cup cilantro leaves

2 tablespoons fresh lime juice

1 avocado, pitted, peeled, and diced

1 teaspoon salt

Fresh corn tortillas

Crumbled *queso fresco*

1 In a small bowl, combine the chipotle chile, vinegar, garlic, oregano, salt, and coriander, stirring well. Spread the mixture over both sides of the steak and let stand at room temperature for 30 minutes.

2 Prepare a grill for cooking over high heat. First, oil the grill rack. If using a charcoal grill, prepare a solid bed of hot coals. If using a gas grill, preheat to high (you can hold your hand 1 to 2 inches above grill level only 2 to 3 seconds).

3 Meanwhile, preheat the oven to 250°F. To prepare the salsa, in a food processor, combine the tomatillos, serrano chile, garlic, and cilantro and pulse until coarsely chopped. Transfer to a bowl and stir in the lime juice, avocado, and salt. Let stand at room temperature. Wrap the tortillas in aluminum foil and place in the oven to warm, about 15 minutes.

4 Lay the steak on the grill rack. If using a gas grill, close the lid. Cook, turning once, until the meat is browned on the outside but still pink in the center for medium-rare (cut to test), 3 to 4 minutes on each side. Transfer the steak to a carving board or serving platter, tent loosely with aluminum foil, and let rest for 5 minutes. Slice the meat thinly across the grain. Serve with the salsa, warm tortillas, and *queso fresco*.

Cook's Tip: These classic tacos with fresh tomatillo salsa are delicious served with fresh corn tortillas. Chipotle chiles in adobo are smoked jalapeños in adobo sauce, classically a mixture of tomatoes, garlic, vinegar, salt, and spices; you'll find them in cans at Mexican groceries and well-stocked supermarkets.

Makes 4 servings

Spuds MacKenzie—Spuds made his debut as the mascot for Bud Light in 1986. Playing the role of a benignly macho, gal-happy party animal, Spuds, a bull terrier, was actually a gal himself, whose real name was Honey Tree Evil Eye.

BISTEC ARGENTINO al CHIMICHURRI

Serve with an American-Style Amber Lager, such as Michelob Amber Bock

CHIMICHURRI

¹/₂ cup packed chopped fresh cilantro

6 tablespoons balsamic vinegar

2 tablespoons olive oil

2 garlic cloves, minced

1 teaspoon adobo seasoning (see Cook's Tip)

¹/₂ teaspoon dried oregano

¹/₂ teaspoon freshly ground black pepper

¹/₄ teaspoon red pepper flakes

2 boneless beef rib-eye or top loin (New York strip) steaks (about 1¹/₂ to 2 pounds total), trimmed of excess fat

1 teaspoon salt

1 teaspoon freshly ground black pepper

2 tablespoons butter

1 To prepare the *chimichurri,* in a bowl, combine the cilantro, vinegar, olive oil, garlic, adobo seasoning, oregano, black pepper, and red pepper flakes, mixing well. Set the *chimichurri* sauce aside.

2 Rinse the steaks and pat dry with paper towels. In a small bowl, combine the salt and pepper. Rub the steaks all over with the salt and pepper.

3 In a large skillet, melt 1 teaspoon of the butter over medium-high heat. Lay the steaks in the pan and cook, turning as needed, until browned on all sides, including the edges, and still red in the center for rare (cut to test), about 10 minutes total. For medium-rare, cook for 2 or 3 minutes longer. To reduce spattering, wipe the fat from the pan as needed with paper towels.

4 Transfer the steaks to a platter and keep warm. If any dark charred bits remain in the pan, wipe out with a paper towel. Add the remaining 5 teaspoons butter to the pan and melt over medium-high heat. When the butter is melted, add the *chimichurri* sauce.

5 Cut the steaks into 4 portions and place on individual plates. Stir the meat juices from the platter into the pan, then ladle the sauce over the steaks. Serve immediately.

Cook's Tip: *Chimichurri,* a tangy herb paste used as both a marinade and a sauce, is the national condiment of Argentina. You can make the *chimichurri* sauce 1 day in advance of serving, then cover and refrigerate. If you can't find adobo seasoning, you can substitute ¹/₂ teaspoon garlic salt, ¹/₂ teaspoon onion powder, and ¹/₄ teaspoon red pepper flakes.

Makes 4 servings

FLANK STEAK with CHERMOULA

Serve with a Doppelbock, such as Brewmaster's Private Reserve

CHERMOULA

1 cup fresh flat-leaf parsley leaves

1 cup fresh cilantro leaves

3 tablespoons beef stock

2 tablespoons fresh lime juice

1 tablespoon extra-virgin olive oil

1 tablespoon paprika

1 teaspoon ground cumin

$1/2$ teaspoon ground coriander

$1/4$ teaspoon salt

$1/4$ teaspoon cayenne pepper

2 garlic cloves, peeled

1 flank steak ($1^1/2$ pounds), trimmed of excess fat

$1/4$ teaspoon salt

$1/4$ teaspoon freshly ground black pepper

Olive oil

1 To prepare the *chermoula*, in a food processor, combine the parsley, cilantro, stock, lime juice, extra-virgin olive oil, paprika, cumin, coriander, salt, cayenne, and garlic. Process until finely chopped, scraping the sides of the bowl occasionally. Set aside.

2 Sprinkle both sides of the steak with the salt and pepper. Heat a cast-iron grill pan over high heat and coat the pan with olive oil. Lay the steak in the pan and cook until browned on the outside but still pink in the center for medium-rare (cut to test), about 4 minutes on each side. Transfer to a serving platter or a carving board, tent with aluminum foil, and let rest for 5 minutes. Cut the steak diagonally across the grain into thin slices. Serve with the *chermoula* sauce.

Cook's Tip: *Chermoula* is a versatile North African herb-and-spice sauce. Use a cast-iron grill pan for this dish, as a nonstick grill pan can't handle high heat.

Makes 6 servings

Bock Beer—Bock beer derives its name from the German town of Einbeck, where the malty-sweet, bottom-fermented brew has been a springtime specialty since the fourteenth century. It is thought that the name Einbeck gave way to Ein Bock ("one goat" in German), which is probably why many Bock beer labels feature billy goats. This rare Budweiser Bock can from the early 1950s is highly prized among collectors because it was produced only between 1951 and 1954.

CHICKEN FRIED STEAK with CREAM GRAVY

Serve with an American-Style Premium Lager, such as Budweiser Select

1 pound beef bottom round roast, trimmed of excess fat and cut into 4 slices (each 1/2 inch thick)

1/2 cup plus 2 tablespoons all-purpose flour

1 teaspoon dried oregano

Salt and freshly ground black pepper

2 large eggs

5 tablespoons heavy cream

Vegetable oil for frying

1 tablespoon unsalted butter

1 serrano chile, seeded and chopped

1 cup chicken stock

1 plum tomato, seeded and chopped

1 Using a rolling pin or the flat side of a meat mallet, lightly pound each beef slice between 2 sheets of wax paper until about 1/4 inch thick. In a pie plate, whisk together the 1/2 cup flour, the oregano, 1 teaspoon salt, and 1/2 teaspoon pepper. In another pie plate, whisk together the eggs and 2 tablespoons of the heavy cream.

2 In a large, heavy skillet (preferably 12-inch), heat 1/4 inch of oil over medium-high heat. Dip the steaks into the egg mixture, then into the flour mixture, coating evenly. When the oil is hot, add 2 or 3 pieces of steak (do not crowd the pan) and fry until golden brown, about 2 minutes on each side. Repeat with the remaining steak(s). Cover and keep warm.

3 Pour or spoon off and discard all but 2 tablespoons fat in the pan and whisk in the 2 tablespoons flour and the butter. Cook for 2 minutes, whisking constantly. Whisk in the chile, stock, and remaining 3 tablespoons cream and bring to a simmer. Season with salt and pepper to taste and stir in the tomato. Serve the steaks with the hot gravy.

Makes 4 servings

ROADHOUSE STEAKS with ANCHO CHILE RUB

Serve with an English-Style Pale Ale, such as Michelob Pale Ale

1 tablespoon freshly ground black pepper

2 teaspoons ancho chile powder

4 teaspoons Worcestershire sauce

1 teaspoon Dijon mustard

1/2 teaspoon salt

1/2 teaspoon ground cumin

1/8 teaspoon cayenne pepper

2 garlic cloves, minced

4 beef tenderloin steaks (6 ounces each), trimmed of excess fat

1 Prepare a grill for cooking over medium-high heat. First, oil the grill rack. If using a charcoal grill, prepare a solid bed of medium-hot coals. If using a gas grill, preheat to high and close the lid, then open the lid and lower the heat to medium-high (you can hold your hand 1 to 2 inches above grill level only 3 to 4 seconds).

2 In a small bowl, combine the pepper, chile powder, Worcestershire sauce, mustard, salt, cumin, cayenne, and garlic, stirring with a whisk. Rinse the beef steaks and pat dry with paper towels. Rub the spice mixture evenly over the steaks and let stand for 10 minutes.

3 Lay the steaks on the grill rack. If using a gas grill, close the lid. Cook, turning once, until browned on the outside but still pink in the center for medium-rare (cut to test), about 5 minutes on each side. Transfer to a platter, tent loosely with aluminum foil, and let rest for 5 minutes before serving.

Cook's Tip: Ancho chile powder is made from ground, smoked, dried poblano chiles, and it gives this rub a subtle smoky heat. For a milder flavor, cut back on the ground black pepper or ancho chile powder and omit the cayenne.

Makes 4 servings

BEECHWOOD-SMOKED ST. LOUIS STRIP

Serve with an American-Style Premium Lager, such as Budweiser

BEER BUTTER

1 pound (4 sticks) unsalted butter, at room temperature

³/₄ cup Budweiser

Juice of 1 lemon

¹/₄ cup chopped fresh tarragon

¹/₄ cup chopped fresh thyme

¹/₄ cup chopped fresh marjoram

¹/₄ cup chopped fresh oregano

¹/₂ cup chopped fresh flat-leaf parsley

2 shallots, minced

3 cloves garlic, minced

1 tablespoon salt

1 teaspoon freshly ground black pepper

2 cups (about 8 ounces) beechwood or applewood chips

2 bottles (12 ounces each) Budweiser

1¹/₂ pounds sirloin steak (about 2 inches thick), trimmed of excess fat

2 teaspoons olive oil

Salt and freshly ground black pepper

1 To prepare the butter, in a bowl, using an electric mixer set on medium speed, beat the butter until softened. Add the ³/₄ cup of beer, lemon juice, herbs, shallots, garlic, salt, and pepper and beat until the mixture is smooth and well blended.

2 Place the wood chips in a small bowl and add 1 bottle of the beer. Soak for at least ¹/₂ hour. Meanwhile, prepare a grill for cooking over high heat. First, oil the grill rack. If using a charcoal grill, prepare a solid bed of hot coals. If using a gas grill, preheat to high (you can hold your hand 1 to 2 inches above grill level only 2 to 3 seconds). Drain the wood chips and place in the metal smoking box or in a foil pan directly on the heat in the corner for a gas grill, or scatter them over the coals if using a charcoal grill.

3 Brush the steak on all 4 sides with the olive oil and season generously with salt and pepper. Lay the steak on the grill rack. If using a gas grill, close the lid. Cook, turning once, until the meat is still slightly pink in the center for medium-rare (cut to test), about 5 minutes on each side. Turn the steak on its sides and grill just until the whole steak is marked. As the steak cooks, baste it occasionally with the remaining beer.

4 Transfer to a carving board or serving platter, tent loosely with aluminum foil, and let stand for about 10 minutes. Using a sharp knife, slice very thinly across the grain. Serve immediately with the beer butter.

Cook's Tip: Chef Brent Wertz suggests serving this flavorful butter at room temperature for best flavor. Let the butter firm up a bit in the fridge and then shape into a log before storing, if you like. Store, covered tightly, in the refrigerator for up to 7 days, or wrap tightly in plastic, place in a zip-top plastic freezer bag, and freeze for up to 1 month. When you are ready to use the butter, simply take it out of the freezer and cut off what you need. You can also serve this butter as a sauce on pasta, pieces of fish, beef, chicken, or whatever you like.

Makes 1 or 2 servings

MAERZEN-BRAISED SHORT RIBS

 Serve with a Maerzen Beer, such as Michelob Marzen

2 cups Budweiser Beechwood Barbecue Sauce or another store-bought barbecue sauce

2 cups beef stock

2 bottles (12 ounces each) Michelob Marzen

1/2 cup soy sauce

1/2 cup honey

1/2 cup olive oil

1/4 cup red wine vinegar

1/2 jalapeño pepper, finely chopped

2 tablespoons molasses

1 tablespoon hot-pepper sauce

1 tablespoon Worcestershire sauce

1/2 onion, minced

1/2 cup firmly packed brown sugar

3 garlic cloves, minced

1 tablespoon ground ginger

5 to 6 pounds beef short ribs, trimmed of excess fat

1 In a large pot, combine all of the ingredients except the short ribs, stirring well. Add the ribs and marinate in the refrigerator for at least 24 hours and up to 36 hours.

2 Preheat the oven to 300°F. Transfer the ribs and about half of the marinade to a deep roasting pan and cover the pan with aluminum foil, reserving the remaining marinade. Roast the ribs until the meat is very tender and falling off the bone, about 4 hours.

3 Meanwhile, transfer the reserved marinade to a saucepan and bring to a boil over medium-high heat. Cook until reduced by half to make a sauce, about 10 minutes. When the ribs are done, arrange on individual plates and spoon over the sauce. Serve immediately.

Cook's Tip: Chef Brent Wertz suggests serving these ribs with homemade french fries. You can use the recipe for Oven Fries on page 35.

Makes 8 servings

T-BONES with FENNEL and SALT

 Serve with an American-Style Amber Lager, such as Michelob Amber Bock

1 tablespoon fresh rosemary leaves

2 teaspoons fennel seed

1 tablespoon kosher salt

1/2 teaspoon whole black peppercorns

2 T-bone or Porterhouse steaks (each about 1 inch thick and 2 pounds), trimmed of excess fat

1 In a spice grinder or a coffee grinder reserved for that purpose, combine the rosemary, fennel seed, salt, and peppercorns and process until very finely ground. Rub the spice mixture over both sides of the steaks, cover loosely, and refrigerate overnight.

2 Remove the steaks from the refrigerator 1 hour before cooking.

3 Prepare a grill for cooking over high heat. First, oil the grill rack. If using a charcoal grill, prepare a solid bed of hot coals. If using a gas grill, preheat to high (you can hold your hand 1 to 2 inches above grill level only 2 to 3 seconds).

4 Lay the steaks on the grill rack. If using a gas grill, close the lid. Cook, turning once, until the meat is still pink in the center for medium-rare (cut to test), about 5 minutes on each side. Transfer the steaks to a serving platter or carving board, tent loosely with aluminum foil, and let stand for 5 minutes. Carve slices about 1 inch thick and serve.

Cook's Tip: T-bone and Porterhouse steaks both work beautifully with this aromatic rub. Letting the steaks warm up a bit before grilling helps ensure even cooking and also speeds the process, so watch carefully to avoid overcooking.

Makes 2 to 4 servings

PEPPER STEAKS with BALSAMIC ONIONS

Serve with an American-Style Amber Lager, such as Michelob Amber Bock

2 tablespoons butter

2 tablespoons olive oil

2 sweet onions (1^1/$_2$ pounds total) such as Walla Walla, Vidalia, or Maui, peeled and sliced lengthwise

1 teaspoon salt

^{1}/$_2$ teaspoon sugar

2 tablespoons balsamic vinegar

1 tablespoon fresh thyme leaves

4 boneless tender beef steaks (each 1 to 1^1/$_2$ inches thick and about 8 ounces), such as top loin (New York strip) or rib-eye

^{1}/$_4$ cup freshly cracked multicolored peppercorns (see Cook's Tip)

1 Preheat the oven to 375°F. In a large skillet, melt 1^1/$_2$ tablespoons of the butter with 1^1/$_2$ tablespoons of the olive oil over medium heat. Add the onions and stir in ^{1}/$_2$ teaspoon of the salt. Cover and cook, stirring occasionally, until the onions are softened, about 8 minutes. Uncover and sprinkle with the sugar. Raise the heat to medium-high and stir often until the onions begin to brown, 5 to 7 minutes. Add the vinegar and 1^1/$_2$ teaspoons of the thyme leaves. Continue to cook, stirring often, until the liquid is evaporated, 1 to 2 minutes longer.

2 Rinse the steaks and pat dry with paper towels. Sprinkle both sides lightly with the remaining ^{1}/$_2$ teaspoon salt, then coat with the cracked peppercorns.

3 In a large ovenproof skillet, melt the remaining ^{1}/$_2$ tablespoon butter with the remaining ^{1}/$_2$ tablespoon olive oil over medium-high heat (divide among two pans if there's not enough room for the steaks in one). Add the steaks and cook until well browned on the bottom, 4 to 5 minutes. Turn the steaks over and cook until beginning to brown on the other side, about 2 minutes.

4 Place the pan in the oven and bake until just pink in the center for medium-rare (cut to test), 7 to 8 minutes. (The steaks will continue cooking for a few minutes after you take them out of the oven.)

5 Transfer the steaks to individual plates. Spoon the onions over the top, sprinkle with the remaining 1^1/$_2$ teaspoons thyme leaves, and serve.

Cook's Tip: To crack the peppercorns, process them briefly in a spice or coffee grinder, or crush them with the flat side of a large knife or the bottom of a heavy pan.

Makes 4 servings

Super Bowl Frogs—At more than $2.5 million for a mere thirty seconds of airtime, the Super Bowl is one of the most expensive venues for advertisers, which is no doubt one of the main reasons why ads that run during the Super Bowl are often more exciting than the action down on the field. As one of the Super Bowl's biggest advertisers, Anheuser-Busch has run especially memorable ads, but one in particular consistently ranks in top-ten lists of best Super Bowl ads: the Budweiser Frogs, who made their Super Bowl debut in 1995. The ad was deceptively simple—three frogs, late at night, sitting on a trio of lily pads in front of a swamp-country bar. One burps "Bud," the second gurgles "Weis," the third slurs an "Er." The ad ends in a croaky crescendo of "Budweisers." To this day, the ad brings a smile to those who remember seeing it for the first time. It's a safe bet that fewer people remember the score (San Francisco 49, San Diego 26).

BEER-BRAISED SHRIMP

¹/₄ cup extra-light olive oil

10 garlic cloves, very coarsely chopped

1¹/₂ pounds (about 36) large shrimp, peeled and deveined

¹/₂ teaspoon cayenne pepper

Kosher salt and freshly ground black pepper

1 bottle (12 ounces) Budweiser

¹/₂ cup fresh lime juice

1 In a large heavy skillet over high heat, heat the olive oil and garlic until the garlic starts to caramelize, 1 to 2 minutes. Add the shrimp and season with the cayenne and the salt and black pepper to taste.

2 Pour in half of the beer and cook for 5 minutes. Turn the shrimp and add the lime juice and the remaining beer. Cook until the shrimp are firm and the flesh is white throughout. Serve immediately.

Makes 6 servings

BEER-BASTED GRILLED ANGUS STRIP

3 boneless Angus strip loin steaks (each about 3 inches thick and 1 pound), trimmed of all fat and silver skin

¹/₂ cup extra-light olive oil

¹/₂ cup pickling salt

2 tablespoons granulated garlic

1 tablespoon freshly ground black pepper

2 bottles (12 ounces each) Budweiser

1 Prepare a grill for cooking over indirect heat. First, oil the grill rack. If using a charcoal grill, light 50 to 60 briquettes and let burn until covered with ash, about 20 to 30 minutes, then mound them to one side. Place a drip pan on the side cleared of coals—this is the indirect heat area. Set the oiled grill rack in place. If using a gas grill, turn all burners to high and close the lid. When the temperature inside the grill reaches 350° to 400°F, lift the lid, turn off one of the burners, and lower the other burner(s) to medium. Place a drip pan under the turned-off burner—this is the indirect heat area. Set the oiled grill rack in place.

2 Brush the steaks with the olive oil and season with a generous amount of dry rub on all sides. When the coals are ready, lay the steaks on the grill rack directly over the heat. If using a gas grill, close the lid. Cook the steaks until a nice, dark caramelized color on the first side, 5 to 6 minutes. Repeat to brown the other 3 sides. Baste the steaks generously with the beer on all 4 sides. Place on the cooler side of the grill, close the lid, and cook for 10 to 12 minutes for medium-rare. Serve immediately.

Makes 6 servings

August A. Busch III prepares Beer-Braised Shrimp, one of his signature recipes, on an Evo grill. A grill pan or a large skillet deep enough to hold the braising liquid can also be used.

MUSHROOM-STUFFED FILET of BEEF

Serve with an English-Style Pale Ale, such as Michelob Pale Ale

3 tablespoons butter

2 shallots, finely chopped

1 small onion, finely chopped

4 garlic cloves, minced

2 cups thinly sliced shiitake mushroom caps (about 6 ounces)

2 cups chopped oyster mushrooms (about 6 ounces)

2 teaspoons chopped fresh oregano

1 teaspoon chopped fresh thyme

1½ teaspoons salt

⅓ cup Michelob Pale Ale

1 or 2 large slices country-style bread

1 beef tenderloin (3 pounds), trimmed of excess fat

2 teaspoons freshly ground black pepper

1 Preheat the oven to 450°F. Lightly oil a broiler pan. In a large skillet, melt the butter over medium-high heat. Add the shallots, onion, and garlic and sauté for 3 minutes. Add the mushrooms, oregano, thyme, and ½ teaspoon of the salt. Sauté until the liquid is evaporated and the mushrooms are darkened, about 5 minutes. Add the beer and cook until evaporated, about 2 minutes. Transfer the mixture to a large bowl.

2 In a food processor, pulse the bread until it forms coarse crumbs. Stir 1 cup of bread crumbs into the mushroom mixture. Set aside and let cool.

3 Rinse the beef tenderloin and pat dry with paper towels. Slice the beef lengthwise, cutting to, but not through, the other side. Open the tenderloin like a book, laying the beef flat. Slice each half lengthwise, cutting to, but not through, the other side. Lay a large sheet of wax paper over the beef. Using a rolling pin or the flat side of a meat mallet, pound the meat to an even thickness. Remove wax paper and spread the mushroom mixture down the center of the beef, leaving a ½-inch border. Roll up the beef, jelly-roll fashion, starting with the long side. Secure at 2-inch intervals with kitchen twine. Rub the beef with the remaining 1 teaspoon salt and the pepper and place on the broiler pan.

4 Roast until an instant-read thermometer registers 135°F, about 40 minutes. Transfer the beef to a carving board, tent loosely with aluminum foil, and let rest for 5 minutes, then slice and serve.

Makes 12 servings

Beer Steins—Lidded beer steins originated in the fourteenth century, when it was thought that flies were the culprits spreading Black Plague. Laws were passed mandating lids on beverage containers in restaurants and bars—these laws remained on the books for centuries, thus perpetuating the tradition of lidded beer steins. In 1894, Anheuser-Busch commissioned Villeroy & Boch to produce its first lidded stein. Since then, hundreds of steins have been created for collectors, in subjects ranging from Anheuser-Busch mascots to endangered species and sporting events.

GRILLED VEAL CHOPS with MUSTARD

Serve with an American-Style Light Amber Lager, such as Michelob Ultra Amber

1/4 cup coarse-grained Dijon mustard

2 tablespoons extra-virgin olive oil

2 teaspoons chopped fresh thyme

1 teaspoon salt

1/2 teaspoon freshly ground black pepper

4 veal rib chops (each about 1 1/2 inches thick and 8 ounces)

1 Prepare a grill for cooking over medium-high heat. First, oil the grill rack. If using a charcoal grill, prepare a solid bed of medium-hot coals. If using a gas grill, preheat to medium-high (you can hold your hand 1 to 2 inches above grill level only 3 to 4 seconds).

2 In a small bowl, stir together the mustard, olive oil, thyme, salt, and pepper. Spread the mustard mixture over both sides of the chops.

3 Lay the chops on the grill rack. If using a gas grill, close the lid. Cook, turning once, until an instant-read thermometer inserted in the thickest part of a chop registers 135°F and the meat is still slightly pink in the center for medium-rare (cut to test), about 8 minutes on each side. Let rest for 5 minutes, then serve.

Cook's Tip: You can find these chops in the supermarket, but make them for a special occasion since they're fairly pricey. You can also make this with thick pork chops.

Makes 4 servings

BEEF RIB ROAST with ROSEMARY

Serve with an American-Style Premium Lager, such as Busch

1 tablespoon salt

2 teaspoons freshly ground black pepper

1 shoulder-end bone-in beef rib roast with 4 ribs (about 8 pounds, with ribs left long)

8 large fresh rosemary sprigs

1 head garlic, separated into cloves, crushed and peeled

1 Preheat the oven to 450°F. In a small bowl, combine the salt and pepper. Using a sharp knife, cut a line down into the roast about 1/2 inch in front of the ribs to create a deep pocket. Sprinkle inside the pocket with about half of the salt mixture, then insert the rosemary sprigs and garlic cloves, allowing the rosemary to poke out. Tie the roast between the ribs with kitchen twine. Sprinkle the remaining salt mixture on the outside of the roast. Place in a large roasting pan with the ribs pointing up.

2 Roast for 15 minutes. Lower the oven temperature to 350°F and continue to roast until an instant-read thermometer inserted in the center of the meat registers 130°F for rare, 75 to 90 minutes, or 140°F for medium, about 2 hours. Transfer the roast to a carving board, tent loosely with aluminum foil, and let rest for 30 minutes. Cut the strings and remove the rosemary. Carve and serve.

Cook's Tip: You can ask your butcher to clean—or "french"—the ends of the ribs on your roast.

Makes 8 to 10 servings

HEARTY BEEF and TOMATO STEW

Serve with an English-Style Pale Ale, such as Michelob Pale Ale

2 pounds sirloin steak, trimmed and cut into
  1/2-inch cubes

3 tablespoons olive oil

1 onion, finely chopped

3 garlic cloves, minced

1 tablespoon tomato paste

1 1/2 cups beef stock

1 1/2 pounds red potatoes, cubed

2 large carrots, peeled and sliced

3/4 cup Michelob Pale Ale

2 teaspoons chopped fresh thyme

1 package (16 ounces) frozen pearl onions

1 can (28 ounces) crushed tomatoes, with their juices

1 fresh rosemary sprig

1 bay leaf

1 teaspoon salt

3/4 teaspoon freshly ground black pepper

1/2 cup chopped fresh flat-leaf parsley

1 Rinse the beef cubes and pat dry with paper towels. In a large Dutch oven, heat the olive oil over medium-high heat. Add the beef and cook, stirring frequently, until browned, about 5 minutes. Using a slotted spoon, transfer the beef to a bowl, reserving the drippings in the pan.

2 Add the onion and garlic to the pan and sauté until the onion begins to brown, about 2 minutes. Add the tomato paste and cook, stirring frequently, for 1 minute. Add the stock and bring to a boil. Return the beef to the pan. Add the potatoes, carrots, beer, thyme, pearl onions, tomatoes along with their juices, rosemary sprig, and bay leaf. Bring to a simmer, then cover, lower the heat to low, and cook, stirring occasionally, until the vegetables are tender, about 1 hour and 15 minutes. Discard the rosemary sprig and bay leaf. Stir in the salt and pepper. Remove from the heat. Sprinkle with the parsley and serve.

Cook's Tip: The ingredient list may look lengthy, but this recipe involves mostly measuring and adding ingredients to the pot to simmer. Serve with thick slices of crusty baguette.

Makes 8 servings

Reduce, Reuse, Recycle—As the world's largest brewer of beer, Anheuser-Busch is also the world's largest purchaser of aluminum for beer cans. This means that when Anheuser-Busch sets its sights on reducing the amount of aluminum used in its cans, the results can be staggering. In 1996, when the diameter of the company's can lids were reduced by a mere 1/8 inch, the savings topped 21 million pounds annually. When Anheuser-Busch decides to recycle, the numbers are equally impressive—the company's recycling division reclaims 1 1/4 cans for every one it fills with beer.

BEEF POT ROAST with GREMOLATA

Serve with a European-Style Pilsner, such as Grolsch

1 boneless cross-rib chuck roast (about 2½ pounds), trimmed of excess fat

1½ teaspoons salt

1 teaspoon freshly ground black pepper

2 tablespoons olive oil

1 large onion, chopped

1 cup beef stock

¾ cup Grolsch

¼ cup chopped drained oil-packed sun-dried tomatoes

¼ teaspoon red pepper flakes

4 fresh thyme sprigs

4 garlic cloves, crushed

2 bay leaves

3 large carrots, peeled and cut into 1-inch pieces

2 pounds baking potatoes, peeled and cut into 1-inch pieces

GREMOLATA

2 tablespoons chopped fresh flat-leaf parsley

1 teaspoon chopped fresh thyme

½ teaspoon grated lemon zest

1 garlic clove, minced

1 Rinse the roast and pat dry with paper towels. Sprinkle the roast evenly with the salt and pepper.

2 In a large nonstick skillet, heat 1 tablespoon olive oil over medium-high heat. Add the roast and cook, turning until browned on all sides, about 5 minutes. Transfer the roast to an electric slow-cooker.

3 In the skillet, heat the remaining olive oil over medium-high heat. Add the onion and sauté until tender, about 8 minutes. Add the stock, beer, sun-dried tomatoes, red pepper flakes, thyme sprigs, garlic, and bay leaves and bring to a simmer. Pour the stock mixture into the slow-cooker. Arrange the carrots and potatoes around the roast.

4 Cover the crock and cook on high heat for 2 hours. Lower the heat to low and cook for 4 hours longer. Remove and discard the bay leaves and thyme sprigs. Transfer the roast to a carving board and shred the meat with 2 forks.

5 To prepare the gremolata, in a small bowl, combine the parsley, thyme, lemon zest, and garlic, mixing well. Serve with the roast and the vegetable mixture.

Cook's Tip: To produce a successful slow-cooker pot roast, the classic recipe needs a flavor boost (here, from sun-dried tomatoes) and less liquid than oven or stove-top versions. A mixture of garlic, herbs, and lemon zest, gremolata is traditionally served in Italy with veal shanks.

Makes 6 servings

BEER-BRAISED BEEF with SALSA VERDE

Serve with a Dry Stout, such as Bare Knuckle Stout

SALSA VERDE

1 cup chopped fresh mint

²/₃ cup chopped fresh dill

¹/₃ cup chopped fresh flat-leaf parsley

¹/₄ cup finely chopped shallots

1 tablespoon chopped capers

3 tablespoons extra-virgin olive oil

¹/₂ teaspoon sea salt

¹/₄ teaspoon freshly ground black pepper

2 pounds boneless chuck roast, trimmed of excess fat and cut into 3-inch cubes

¹/₂ teaspoon sea salt

¹/₄ teaspoon freshly ground black pepper

5 teaspoons olive oil

1 large onion, sliced lengthwise

1 cup beef stock

1 can or bottle (12 ounces) dry stout

1 loaf Italian bread (1 pound), cut into 16 slices and toasted

1 Preheat the oven to 350°F. To prepare the salsa verde, in a small bowl, combine the mint, dill, parsley, shallots, capers, extra-virgin olive oil, salt, and pepper. Cover and refrigerate.

2 Rinse the beef cubes and pat dry with paper towels. Sprinkle the beef with the salt and pepper.

3 In a Dutch oven, heat 1 tablespoon of the olive oil over medium-high heat. Add the beef and cook, turning until browned on all sides, about 5 minutes. Transfer to a bowl and keep warm.

4 In the same pan, heat the remaining 2 teaspoons olive oil over medium-high heat. Add the onion, lower the heat to medium, and cook, stirring occasionally, until golden brown, about 12 minutes. Return the beef to the pan. Add the stock and beer and bring to a boil, then cover, lower the heat to low, and simmer until the meat is tender, about 1¹/₂ hours. Transfer the beef to a carving board and shred with 2 forks. Return the beef to the pan and stir well. Spoon ¹/₄ cup beef mixture over each toasted bread slice and top with salsa. Serve immediately.

Cook's Tip: You can prepare and refrigerate the salsa verde up to 2 weeks in advance of serving. It's good with chicken or fish, too, or simply atop grilled bread as an appetizer. Serve the beef and salsa over mashed potatoes instead of toasted bread, if you like.

Makes 8 servings

NEW ENGLAND–STYLE POT ROAST

 Serve with an American-Style Amber Lager, such as Michelob Amber Bock

3 tablespoons butter

3 large onions (about 1½ pounds total), sliced

1 beef rump roast (about 4 pounds), trimmed of excess fat

1½ teaspoons kosher salt

½ teaspoon freshly ground black pepper

1 tablespoon olive oil

1 cup beef stock

1 tablespoon fresh thyme leaves

1 bottle (12 ounces) Michelob Amber Bock

1 teaspoon all-purpose flour

MASHED POTATOES

4 cups milk

4 pounds baking potatoes, peeled and cubed

6 tablespoons butter

1 teaspoon poppy seeds (optional)

1 teaspoon kosher salt, or to taste

½ teaspoon freshly ground black pepper

Plymouth Rock—The decision of the Pilgrims to land at Plymouth Rock in the winter of 1620 may have been more a matter of practicality than a predisposition to New England's flinty climate. Apparently, the travelers were running out of beer, which was loaded on board ship in significant quantity because it could be kept for longer periods of time than perishable goods.

1 Preheat the oven to 300°F. In a large Dutch oven, melt the butter over medium-high heat. Add the onions and sauté until almost tender, about 12 minutes. Lower the heat to medium-low and cook, stirring frequently, until the onions are caramelized, about 40 minutes. Transfer the onions to a bowl.

2 Rinse the roast and pat dry with paper towels. Sprinkle the roast evenly with the salt and pepper. In the same pan, heat the olive oil over medium-high heat. Add the roast and cook, turning until browned on all sides, about 5 minutes. Add the onion mixture, stock, thyme, and beer and bring to a simmer. Remove from stove.

3 Cover and bake, turning the roast over halfway during cooking time, until tender, about 2 hours. Transfer the roast to a serving platter, cover, and keep warm.

4 Place the pan over medium-high heat on the stovetop. Add the flour, stirring with a whisk, and bring to a boil. Cook for 1 minute, stirring constantly. Remove from the heat and keep warm.

5 To prepare the mashed potatoes, pour the milk into a large saucepan, add the potatoes, and bring to a boil over high heat. Lower the heat to low and simmer until tender when pierced with a knife, about 15 minutes. Add the butter. Mash the potatoes, then stir in the poppy seeds, salt, and pepper. Serve with the roast and sauce.

Makes 8 servings

MUSHROOM, BARLEY, and BEEF SOUP

Serve with an American-Style Amber Lager, such as Michelob Amber Bock

½ cup dried porcini mushrooms (about ¼ ounce)

4 tablespoons olive oil

3½ cups sliced cremini mushrooms (about 8 ounces)

1 onion, chopped

1 carrot, peeled and finely chopped

1 small parsnip, finely chopped

½ cup finely chopped celery

2 garlic cloves, minced

12 ounces lean beef stew meat, cut into bite-size pieces

6 cups beef stock

½ teaspoon salt

¼ teaspoon freshly ground black pepper

2 fresh thyme sprigs

1 cup barley, preferably hulled

2 tablespoons chopped fresh flat-leaf parsley

1 Place the porcini mushrooms in a bowl and pour in 1 cup boiling water. Cover and let stand until tender, about 30 minutes. Drain in a colander set over a bowl, reserving the soaking liquid. Finely chop the porcini and set aside.

2 In a Dutch oven, heat 2 tablespoons of the olive oil over medium-high heat. Add the cremini mushrooms and onion and sauté until lightly browned, about 10 minutes. Transfer the onion mixture to a bowl.

3 In the same pan, heat 1 tablespoon of the olive oil over medium-high heat. Add the carrot, parsnip, celery, and garlic and sauté until lightly browned, about 4 minutes. Add the carrot mixture to the onion mixture in the bowl.

4 In the same pan, heat the remaining 1 tablespoon olive oil over medium-high heat. Add the beef and cook, turning until browned on all sides, about 3 minutes. Add 1 cup of the stock, scraping the pan bottom to loosen any browned bits. Return the onion mixture to the pan and add the remaining 5 cups stock, the chopped porcini, reserved soaking liquid, 2 cups water, salt, pepper, and thyme sprigs. Bring to a boil, then cover, lower the heat to medium-low, and simmer until the beef is just tender, about 1 hour.

5 Discard the thyme sprigs. Stir in the barley, re-cover the pan, and cook until the barley is tender to the bite, about 30 minutes. Uncover and cook for 15 minutes longer. Remove from the heat. Sprinkle with the parsley and serve.

Cook's Tip: Hulled barley has a rich, nutty flavor, though pearled barley would also work well in this soup.

Makes 6 servings

RANCH CHILI

Serve with an American-Style Premium Lager, such as Michelob

2 cans (14¹/₂ ounces each) beef stock, plus more if needed

6 to 8 dried New Mexico chiles (about 5 inches long and 1¹/₂ to 2 ounces total)

12 slices (12 ounces) bacon, chopped

4 pounds boneless beef chuck

Salt

2 large onions, chopped

¹/₄ cup minced garlic

1¹/₂ teaspoons ground cumin

1¹/₂ teaspoons dried oregano

2 cups (16 ounces) Michelob

4 fresh poblano chiles (10 ounces total)

1 Pour 1 can of the stock into a small saucepan and heat over medium heat just until simmering. Stem and seed the dried chiles, then rinse and cut into chunks. In a blender, pour the hot stock over the chiles and let stand for 10 minutes, then process to a smooth purée.

2 Meanwhile, in a large, heavy saucepan, cook the bacon over medium-high heat, stirring often, until browned, about 10 minutes. Using a slotted spoon, transfer to paper towels. Discard all but 2 tablespoons fat from the pan.

3 Rinse the beef and pat dry with paper towels. Cut the beef into 1¹/₂-inch chunks, trimming off any large lumps of fat. Sprinkle the beef lightly with salt. Working in batches, add the beef in a single layer to the pan and cook, turning until browned all over, 5 to 6 minutes per batch. Transfer the beef to a bowl.

4 Add the onion, garlic, cumin, and oregano to the pan and cook, stirring often, until the onion is limp and beginning to brown, 5 to 6 minutes. Return the beef and bacon to the pan. Add the chile purée, beer, and the remaining 1 can stock. Bring to a boil, scraping up any browned bits. Cover, lower the heat to low, and simmer, stirring occasionally, for 1 hour. Uncover and simmer, stirring occasionally, until the beef is very tender when pierced with a knife and the sauce is thickened, 1 to 1¹/₂ hours longer. (If the sauce gets too thick before the beef is done, add more stock as needed.)

5 While the beef mixture cooks, preheat the broiler. In a roasting pan, broil the poblano chiles 4 inches from the heating element, turning once, until charred all over, 5 to 7 minutes on each side. When cool enough to handle, peel, stem, seed, and coarsely chop. Stir into the chili during the last 30 minutes of cooking.

Cook's Tip: Top the chili with chopped onions and fresh cilantro. Serve with avocado, crumbled cheese, sour cream, and warm flour tortillas.

Makes 6 servings

King of Beers—If you are of a certain age, you probably associate the slogan "King of Beers" with the Budweiser ad campaign that began in the 1950s and continues to this day. But the roots of this slogan actually date to 1899, when Bud called itself the "King of Bottled Beers." Other memorable slogans include:

1911	The Old Reliable
1937	America's Social Companion
1940	Budweiser—A Beverage of Moderation
1956	Where There's Life…There's Bud
1967	Budweiser Is the Best Reason in the World to Drink Beer
1971	When You Say Budweiser, You've Said It All
1979	This Bud's For You

VEAL STEW with LEEKS and ALE

Serve with an English-Style Pale Ale, such as Michelob Pale Ale

½ ounce dried porcini mushrooms

3 tablespoons vegetable oil, or as needed

2 pounds veal shoulder, trimmed of excess fat and cut into 2-inch pieces

1 teaspoon salt

½ teaspoon freshly ground black pepper

½ cup all-purpose flour

3 tablespoons unsalted butter

3 garlic cloves, thinly sliced

2 leeks, white and tender green parts, chopped

4 carrots, peeled, 1 diced, 3 halved lengthwise and cut into 1-inch pieces

1 cup Michelob Pale Ale

½ cup chicken stock

6 sprigs fresh thyme

2 tablespoons chopped fresh flat-leaf parsley

Buttered egg noodles

1 In a glass measuring pitcher, combine the porcini and 1 cup water. Microwave on high for 1 minute. Cover and let stand for 10 minutes. Using a slotted spoon, lift out the porcini, pressing the excess liquid back into the pitcher, and transfer to a cutting board. Chop the porcini. Reserve the soaking liquid. Set both aside.

2 Preheat the oven to 325°F. In a large Dutch oven or heavy casserole (3- to 4-quart) with a lid, heat the oil over medium-high heat. Sprinkle the veal with the salt and pepper. Put the flour in a bowl. Dredge the veal in the flour, coating evenly. Working in batches, add the veal pieces to the hot oil and cook until browned on all sides, about 5 minutes total. Transfer the veal pieces to a plate as they are finished. Repeat with the remaining meat, adding more oil to the pan if needed.

3 Add the butter, garlic, leeks, and diced carrot to the same pot and sauté, scraping to loosen any browned bits on the bottom of the pot, until the leeks are tender, about 3 minutes. Add the reserved porcini soaking liquid (pour carefully to leave behind the sandy dregs), the mushrooms, beer, stock, and thyme sprigs. Return the meat and any accumulated juices on the plate to the pot and stir well. Bring to a simmer.

4 Cut a piece of parchment into a 12-inch square and crumple it up. Cover the braise with the parchment, pressing it directly onto the surface, and cover the pot with the lid. Slide the pot into the oven and cook for 1 hour. Stir in the carrot pieces and continue cooking until the meat is very tender, about 30 minutes longer. Remove the parchment and the thyme sprigs and discard. Taste and adjust the seasoning. Sprinkle with the parsley and serve with the noodles.

Cook's Tip: When shopping for veal stew meat, the best thing to do is buy a large chunk of veal shoulder and cut it yourself into 2-inch pieces. As with any braise, the flavor of this stew will only improve if made 1 or even 2 days in advance of serving. Reheat gently over medium-low heat.

Makes 4 servings

LAMB with YOGURT-MINT SAUCE

Serve with an American-Style Light Lager, such as Michelob Ultra

1 yellow onion, quartered

7 whole garlic cloves, peeled

2 tablespoons coarsely chopped rosemary

$1/2$ cup fresh lemon juice

$2^1/2$ teaspoons salt

$2/3$ cup olive oil

1 leg of lamb (4 to 5 pounds), boned and butterflied

YOGURT-MINT SAUCE

1 cup plain whole yogurt

1 garlic clove, minced

$2/3$ cup packed fresh mint leaves

1 teaspoon salt

1 teaspoon fresh lemon juice

$1/4$ teaspoon freshly ground black pepper

$1/8$ teaspoon cayenne pepper

1 red onion, thinly sliced

2 bunches radishes, trimmed

1 In a blender, combine the yellow onion, garlic cloves, rosemary, lemon juice, and salt. Process to a purée. With the blender running, slowly pour in the olive oil.

2 Rinse the lamb and pat dry with paper towels. Trim off any excess surface fat. Using a small, sharp knife, cut slits about 1 inch long and deep all over the lamb. Place in a large nonreactive baking dish and coat the lamb with the onion marinade, making sure the mixture gets into the slits. Cover and refrigerate, turning occasionally, for at least 2 hours or up to overnight.

3 To prepare the sauce, in a blender, combine $1/4$ cup of the yogurt, the garlic, mint, salt, lemon juice, black pepper, and cayenne. Process until smooth. Transfer to a serving bowl and stir in the remaining $3/4$ cup yogurt. Refrigerate until ready to serve.

4 Remove the lamb from the refrigerator and let come to room temperature about 1 hour before cooking. Reserve the marinade in the dish.

5 Prepare a grill for cooking over medium heat. First, oil the grill rack. If using a charcoal grill, prepare a solid bed of medium coals. If using a gas grill, preheat to high and close the lid, then open the lid and lower the heat to medium (you can hold your hand 1 to 2 inches above grill level only 4 to 5 seconds).

6 Spread the lamb flat on the grill rack. Close the grill lid. Cook the lamb, turning once and brushing with the marinade, until an instant-read thermometer inserted in the center of the thickest part registers 140°F, about 40 minutes. Discard the remaining marinade.

7 Transfer the lamb to a carving board or serving platter, tent loosely with aluminum foil, and let stand for 15 to 20 minutes. Slice the meat thinly. Garnish with the sliced red onion and radishes and serve with the yogurt-mint sauce.

Makes 8 servings

LAMB RIB CHOPS with COUSCOUS

Serve with an English-Style Pale Ale, such as Michelob Pale Ale

$^1/_3$ cup golden raisins

1 teaspoon kosher salt

$^3/_4$ cup couscous

$^1/_4$ teaspoon ground cumin

$^1/_4$ teaspoon ground coriander

$^1/_4$ teaspoon freshly ground black pepper

8 lamb rib chops (about 3 ounces each)

$^1/_4$ cup sliced almonds

$^1/_4$ cup chopped fresh flat-leaf parsley

1 Preheat the broiler. Line a rimmed baking sheet with aluminum foil.

2 In a saucepan, combine $1^1/_2$ cups water, the raisins, and $^1/_2$ teaspoon of the salt over high heat. Bring to a boil and add the couscous to the pan. Remove from the heat, cover, and let stand for 4 minutes. Fluff with a fork.

3 In a small bowl, combine the remaining $^1/_2$ teaspoon salt, the cumin, coriander, and pepper, stirring with a whisk. Rinse the lamb chops and pat dry with paper towels. Place on the prepared baking sheet and rub the spice mixture evenly over the lamb. Broil, turning once, until barely pink in the center (cut to test), about 4 minutes on each side.

4 In a small skillet, toast the almonds over medium heat, stirring constantly, until lightly toasted, about 3 minutes. Add the almonds and parsley to the couscous mixture, stirring well. Serve with the lamb.

Makes 4 servings

MOROCCAN LAMB CHOPS

Serve with a Porter, such as Michelob Porter

8 lamb loin chops (about 4 ounces each)

1 tablespoon olive oil

1 large onion, chopped

3 garlic cloves, minced or pressed

1 teaspoon ground cinnamon

1 teaspoon ground cumin

2 cups chicken stock

1 tablespoon tomato paste

1 cup dried apricots or pitted prunes, or a combination

1 can (15 ounces) garbanzo beans, drained and rinsed

1 tablespoon chopped fresh flat-leaf parsley

1 Rinse the lamb chops and pat dry with paper towels. In a large skillet, heat the olive oil over medium-high heat. When the oil is hot, add the lamb chops and cook, turning once, until browned on both sides, about 2 minutes on each side. Transfer the lamb chops to a plate.

2 Add the onion and garlic to the pan over medium heat. Cook, stirring often, until the onions are softened, about 4 minutes. Add the cinnamon and cumin, stirring until fragrant, about 1 minute. Stir in the stock, tomato paste, apricots, and garbanzos. Bring to a simmer, then return the lamb chops to the pan.

3 Cover and simmer, turning the chops once, until the apricots are plump and the chops are barely pink in the center (cut to test), 10 to 12 minutes.

4 Set 2 lamb chops on each of 4 plates or in shallow bowls. Spoon the bean mixture around the chops. Sprinkle with the parsley and serve.

Makes 4 servings

PALE ALE SHEPHERD'S PIE

Serve with an English-Style Pale Ale, such as Michelob Pale Ale

3 tablespoons olive oil, or as needed

3 pounds boneless lamb shoulder, cut into ¹/₂-inch cubes

Salt and freshly ground black pepper

1 onion, diced

1 carrot, peeled and diced

1 tablespoon chopped fresh rosemary

1 teaspoon fresh thyme

2 garlic cloves, minced

1 bottle (12 ounces) Michelob Pale Ale

2 cups fresh or thawed frozen corn kernels

6 cups mashed potatoes (page 206)

1 Preheat the oven to 350°F. In a large skillet, heat the olive oil over medium-high heat. Sprinkle the lamb with salt and pepper. Working in batches, add the lamb to the hot oil and cook until browned on all sides, about 5 minutes total. Transfer the lamb pieces to a plate as they are finished. Repeat with the remaining lamb, adding more oil to the pan if needed.

2 Add the onion, carrot, rosemary, thyme, and garlic to the pot and cook until the vegetables are softened, about 5 minutes. Add the beer and simmer until the juices thicken slightly, about 5 minutes. Return the lamb and any accumulated juices to the pot and stir to combine with the vegetables. Pour the contents of the skillet into a 12-by-10-by-3-inch baking dish. Sprinkle the corn over the lamb mixture, then spread the mashed potatoes evenly on top. Bake until the juices are bubbling and the potatoes are lightly browned, about 20 minutes. Serve hot.

Cook's Tip: For the best flavor, Chef Brent Wertz recommends using freshly made mashed potatoes in this dish.

Makes 8 servings

CHILE-LAMB STEW with SWEET SQUASH

Serve with a Honey-Flavored Specialty Beer, such as Michelob Honey Lager

8 garlic cloves, unpeeled

1 tablespoon vegetable or melted coconut oil, or as needed

1¹/₂ pounds boneless lamb, cut into 1-inch cubes

¹/₂ teaspoon salt, plus more to taste

¹/₂ teaspoon freshly ground black pepper

1 large white onion, chopped

2 poblano peppers, seeded and chopped

1 teaspoon dried oregano

¹/₄ teaspoon ground cumin

2 cups beef broth

1 butternut squash (about 2 pounds), peeled, seeded, and cut into 2-inch pieces

1 tablespoon honey

1 In a large heavy skillet, roast the garlic, turning occasionally, until soft and blackened in spots, about 15 minutes. Set aside to cool, then peel.

2 In the same skillet, heat the oil over high heat. Sprinkle the lamb with the salt and pepper. Working in batches, add the lamb to the hot oil and cook until browned on all sides, about 5 minutes total. Transfer the lamb to a plate as it is finished. Repeat with the remaining meat, adding more oil to the pan if needed.

3 Add the onion and peppers to the pan. Cook, stirring often, until the onion is golden and lightly browned, about 4 minutes. Stir in the roasted garlic, oregano, and cumin and return the meat to the pan. Add the broth and bring to a simmer. Cover and simmer over low heat for 45 minutes. Stir in the squash, cover partially, and simmer for about 15 minutes. Uncover and cook until the squash is tender, 15 to 20 minutes longer. Stir in the honey. Taste, adjust the seasoning with salt, and serve.

Makes 4 to 6 servings

VEGETABLES
MAIN COURSES & SIDE DISHES

MAIN COURSES

SIDE DISHES

Chef's Specialty

LEEK and CHANTERELLE TART

Serve with an American-Style Amber Lager, such as Michelob Amber Bock

CRUST

1 cup all-purpose flour

1/2 teaspoon salt

1/2 teaspoon freshly ground black pepper

7 tablespoons cold butter, cut into small pieces

FILLING

3 tablespoons butter

3 leeks, white and very light green parts only, halved, cleaned, and thinly sliced

1/2 teaspoon salt

1 pound chanterelle mushrooms, cut into 1-inch pieces

3 tablespoons heavy cream

2 teaspoons fresh thyme leaves

1/4 teaspoon freshly ground black pepper

1 cup shredded Gruyère cheese

1 To prepare the crust, in a bowl, combine the flour, salt, and pepper, stirring with a whisk. Cut in the butter with a pastry blender or 2 knives until the mixture resembles coarse meal but some larger, pea-size pieces remain. Drizzle in 3 tablespoons ice water while stirring quickly with a fork. (Or, in a food processor, combine the flour, salt, pepper, and butter, pulsing until a coarse, cornmeal-textured mixture forms, then drizzle in the ice water until the dough comes together.) Transfer the dough to a large piece of plastic wrap and use the wrap to press the dough into a disk 1 inch thick. Wrap tightly and refrigerate for at least 30 minutes or up to 2 days.

2 Preheat the oven to 375°F. Have ready a 9 1/2-inch tart pan with a removable rim.

3 Lightly flour a work surface. Using a rolling pin, gently roll out the chilled dough, making a quarter turn between each roll, to form a 12-inch round.

4 Transfer the dough round to the tart pan. Trim the dough edges flush with the rim. Line the dough with aluminum foil and weigh down with pie weights, dried beans, or uncooked rice.

5 Bake for 20 minutes. Remove the foil and weights and continue to bake until the crust is beginning to turn golden, about 10 minutes longer. Let cool to room temperature. Leave the oven on.

6 Meanwhile, prepare the filling: In a large frying pan, melt the butter over medium-high heat. Add the leeks and salt and cook, stirring, until the leeks are soft, about 3 minutes. Raise the heat to high and add the mushrooms. Cook, stirring constantly, until the mushrooms have given off their liquid, 5 to 10 minutes. Stir in the cream, thyme, and pepper, then remove from the heat and let cool to room temperature.

7 Scatter half of the cheese over the cooled tart crust. Spread the leek-mushroom mixture evenly on top and scatter the remaining cheese over the top.

8 Bake until the cheese is melted and golden, about 25 minutes. Let stand for 10 minutes before cutting. Serve warm or at room temperature.

Cook's Tip: The simple salt-and-pepper crust of this tart is worth making from scratch. If you do use a ready-made crust, pick one without sugar. You can substitute button or cremini mushrooms for the chanterelles.

Makes 4 servings

MOROCCAN VEGETABLE STEW

Serve with a Wheat Beer, such as Michelob Bavarian Style Wheat

2 tablespoons olive oil

3 garlic cloves, peeled and crushed with the flat side of a knife

1 teaspoon ground coriander

1 teaspoon ground cumin

1/2 teaspoon cayenne pepper

1/4 teaspoon ground cinnamon

5 cups vegetable or chicken stock

2 cups cauliflower florets

4 carrots (about 12 ounces total), peeled and cut into 1/2-inch lengths

3 zucchini, sliced 1/2 inch thick

1 eggplant, peeled and diced

1 onion, diced

2 cans (14 1/2 ounces each) stewed tomatoes

1 can (15 ounces) garbanzo beans, rinsed and drained

3/4 cup dried currants

1 cup chopped toasted almonds, plus more for serving

1/2 tablespoon kosher salt

1 cup plain yogurt, preferably Greek

2 tablespoons chopped fresh cilantro

1 In a small skillet, heat the olive oil over medium-low heat. Add the garlic, coriander, cumin, cayenne, and cinnamon. Cook, stirring often, until fragrant, 1 to 2 minutes, being careful not to scorch the garlic. Scrape the mixture into a slow-cooker (at least 5-quart capacity).

2 Add the stock, cauliflower, carrots, zucchini, eggplant, onion, tomatoes along with their juices, garbanzo beans, currants, almonds, and salt, stirring well to combine.

3 Cover the slow-cooker and cook on high until the vegetables are tender to the bite and the flavors are blended, 8 to 9 hours.

4 Ladle about 3 cups of the vegetable mixture into a blender or food processor and process until smooth. Return the purée to the slow-cooker and stir to blend. Ladle the stew into a tureen or individual bowls. Top each with a dollop of yogurt. Sprinkle with cilantro and toasted almonds and serve.

Makes 6 servings

A Can of Beer—In 1936, not long after Prohibition was repealed, the first can of Budweiser was sold. Unlike the two-piece aluminum cans of today, these early cans were made out of three pieces of tin-coated steel. They had flat tops and, until 1949, actually bore instructions on their sides showing customers how to use a church key to open them. Some of the first steel cans were lined with gold lacquer to keep the beer from reacting with the metal. Tab tops appeared on steel cans in 1962 and pull tabs made their Anheuser-Busch debut on aluminum cans in 1966. Today, more than half the company's beer is packaged in cans.

ORECCHIETTE with CORN and CHILES

Serve with an American-Style Light Amber Lager, such as Michelob Ultra Amber

2 poblano chiles

2 red bell peppers

2 ears sweet corn, husks and silks removed

8 ounces dried *orecchiette* pasta

2 tablespoons fresh lime juice

1 tablespoon extra-virgin olive oil

1 garlic clove, minced

1 teaspoon salt

$^1/_2$ teaspoon freshly ground black pepper

$^1/_2$ teaspoon ground cumin

2 cups grape tomatoes, halved

1 onion, finely chopped

1 avocado, pitted, peeled, and chopped

$^1/_4$ cup chopped fresh cilantro

$^3/_4$ cup (3 ounces) *queso fresco*

1 Preheat the broiler. Line a baking sheet with aluminum foil. Place the chiles, bell peppers, and corn on the baking sheet. Broil, turning as needed until the chiles and peppers are blackened on all sides and the corn is lightly browned, about 8 minutes. Transfer to a paper or plastic bag and close tightly. Let stand for 10 minutes, then peel, stem, and seed the chiles and peppers and coarsely chop. Cut the kernels from the ears of corn.

2 In a pot, bring 2 quarts salted water to a boil. Add the pasta and cook until al dente, 10 to 12 minutes. Drain.

3 Meanwhile, in a large bowl, combine the lime juice, olive oil, garlic, salt, pepper, and cumin, stirring with a whisk. Add the chiles, bell peppers, corn, cooked pasta, tomatoes, onion, avocado, and cilantro. Toss gently, then top with the cheese and serve.

Makes 4 servings

LEAFY GREENS with POLENTA

Serve with an English-Style Pale Ale, such as Michelob Pale Ale

3 tablespoons olive oil

8 to 12 Belgian endives, chopped (about 12 ounces)

4 cups chopped kale (about 4 ounces)

4 cups chopped turnip greens (about 4 ounces)

$^1/_3$ cup golden raisins

$^1/_4$ teaspoon salt

1 cup coarse-ground yellow cornmeal

$^1/_4$ teaspoon red pepper flakes

2 cups vegetable stock

1 cup milk

$^1/_2$ cup (2 ounces) freshly grated Parmesan cheese

1 garlic clove, thinly sliced

$^1/_4$ cup dried bread crumbs

4 teaspoons pine nuts, toasted

1 In a large skillet, heat 2 tablespoons of the olive oil over medium heat. Add the endive and cook, stirring until it begins to wilt, about 1 minute. Add the kale and turnip greens and cook for 2 minutes. Stir in the raisins and salt. Cover, lower the heat to low, and cook until all the greens are tender, about 6 minutes. Remove from the heat and keep warm.

2 In a saucepan, combine the cornmeal and red pepper flakes over medium-high heat. Gradually add the stock and milk, stirring with a whisk. Bring to a boil, cover, lower the heat to low, and simmer, stirring occasionally, for 10 minutes. Stir in $^1/_4$ cup of the Parmesan. Remove from the heat and keep warm.

3 Heat the remaining olive oil over medium heat. Add the garlic and cook until lightly browned. Stir in the bread crumbs and cook until golden brown. Remove from the heat and stir in the remaining $^1/_4$ cup Parmesan. Spoon the polenta into bowls. Top with the greens, sprinkle with the bread crumbs and nuts, and serve.

Makes 4 servings

ORZO with SUMMER VEGETABLES

Serve with an American-Style Premium Lager, such as Michelob Golden Draft

Salt

1 pound green beans, trimmed and cut into 2-inch lengths

8 ounces dried orzo pasta

3 ears sweet corn

½ cup white wine vinegar

½ cup extra-virgin olive oil

2 large shallots, minced

2 tablespoons Dijon mustard

2 tablespoons minced fresh tarragon or 2 teaspoons dried tarragon

Freshly ground black pepper

2 cups cherry tomatoes (about 12 ounces total), stemmed and halved

1 In a large saucepan over high heat, bring 2 quarts salted water to a boil. Add the green beans and cook just until barely tender to the bite, 3 to 5 minutes. Drain in a colander, then plunge the beans into a bowl of ice water to cool. Drain again and set aside.

2 In the same pan, bring 2 quarts salted water to a boil. Add the orzo and cook until barely al dente, about 8 minutes. Drain in a colander, then rinse with cold water, drain well, and set aside.

3 Over a large bowl, cut the kernels from the ears of corn. Scrape the remaining pulp from the cob using the dull side of the knife blade, then discard the cobs.

4 In a small bowl, combine the vinegar, olive oil, shallots, mustard, and tarragon, stirring with a whisk. Season to taste with salt and pepper.

5 In a large, wide serving bowl, mix the orzo with ½ cup of the dressing. Season to taste with salt and pepper. Spread level, then layer the corn kernels, green beans, and tomatoes over the orzo. Pour the remaining dressing into a container. Cover and refrigerate the dressing and salad until ready to serve.

6 Shortly before serving, pour three-fourths of the remaining dressing over the salad and mix gently to blend. Add the remaining dressing and season to taste with more salt and pepper. Serve immediately.

Cook's Tip: You can assemble this dish through step 5 up to a day ahead. For a shortcut, use 3 cups frozen corn kernels, thawed, instead of the fresh corn.

Makes 4 servings

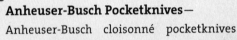

Anheuser-Busch Pocketknives— Anheuser-Busch cloisonné pocketknives were produced as gifts in the late 1800s when beer bottles had corks. These knives also featured tiny Stanhope lenses, which revealed miniature photos of Adolphus Busch. Thousands of these knives were given out over the years by company representatives or as promotional souvenirs at major events such as the St. Louis World's Fair in 1904.

PENNE with TRIPLE TOMATO SAUCE

Serve with an English-Style Pale Ale, such as Michelob Pale Ale

1 teaspoon olive oil

1/2 cup finely chopped onion

2 garlic cloves, minced

1/4 cup chopped drained oil-packed sun-dried tomatoes

4 plum tomatoes (about 1/2 pound total), chopped

1 can (14 1/2 ounces) diced tomatoes

1 teaspoon sugar

Salt and freshly ground black pepper

12 ounces dried penne pasta

1/2 cup (4 ounces) goat cheese

1/4 cup finely chopped fresh flat-leaf parsley

Fresh basil sprigs (optional)

1 In a large skillet, heat the olive oil over medium-high heat. Add the onion and sauté until tender, about 4 minutes. Add the garlic and sauté for 1 minute. Add the sun-dried tomatoes, plum tomatoes, diced tomatoes along with their juices, sugar, 1/4 teaspoon salt, and 1/4 teaspoon pepper. Lower the heat to medium and cook, stirring often, until the liquid is almost evaporated, about 20 minutes.

2 Meanwhile, in a large pot, bring 3 quarts salted water to a boil. Add the pasta and cook until al dente, 10 to 12 minutes. Drain and return the pasta to the pot. Stir in the tomato mixture, goat cheese, and parsley. Garnish with more freshly ground black pepper and basil sprigs, if desired, and serve.

Cook's Tip: Sun-dried, fresh, and canned tomatoes make this sauce rich in tomato flavor. You can use reserved oil from the sun-dried tomatoes instead of olive oil to sauté the onion.

Makes 4 servings

RIGATONI with GREEN OLIVE–ALMOND PESTO

Serve with a European-Style Pilsner, such as Kirin Ichiban

Salt

1 pound dried rigatoni pasta

1 1/4 cups (about 6 ounces) pitted manzanilla olives or other brine-cured green olives

1/2 cup sliced almonds, toasted

1/2 cup fresh flat-leaf parsley leaves

1 large garlic clove

1/4 teaspoon freshly ground black pepper

1 teaspoon white wine vinegar

1/2 cup (2 ounces) grated Asiago cheese

1 In a large pot, bring 4 quarts salted water to a boil. Add the pasta and cook until al dente, 12 to 14 minutes. Drain, reserving 6 tablespoons pasta water.

2 Meanwhile, in a food processor, combine the olives, almonds, parsley, garlic, and pepper. Pulse until coarsely chopped. With the machine on, add the vinegar and 2 tablespoons water through the food chute, processing until finely chopped.

3 In a large bowl, combine the cooked pasta, 4 tablespoons of the reserved pasta water, and the olive mixture, tossing well to coat the pasta. If needed, add the remaining 2 tablespoons pasta water to make the pasta mixture moist, tossing well to coat. Sprinkle with the cheese. Serve immediately.

Makes 4 servings

SPRING VEGETABLE MACARONI and CHEESE

Serve with an American-Style Premium Lager, such as Rolling Rock

1 bunch asparagus (about 12 ounces)

2 leeks

4¹/₂ tablespoons butter

Salt

12 ounces dried *orecchiette* pasta

³/₄ cup frozen petite peas

2 slices sourdough bread

3 tablespoons all-purpose flour

2 teaspoons fresh thyme leaves

3 cups whole milk

2 teaspoons grated lemon zest

1 tablespoon Dijon mustard

¹/₂ teaspoon freshly ground black pepper

6 ounces fresh goat cheese

1¹/₂ cups shredded Romano cheese

1 Preheat the oven to 400°F. Snap off the tough stem ends from the asparagus and discard, then cut the spears into ¹/₂-inch pieces. Cut the root ends and tough green tops from the leeks, then cut the leeks in half lengthwise. Rinse well under running water, then thinly slice crosswise.

2 In a saucepan, combine the asparagus, leeks, 1 tablespoon of the butter, and ¹/₂ teaspoon salt. Cook just until the asparagus is tender, about 7 minutes, then transfer to a bowl and set aside.

3 In a large saucepan, bring 3 quarts salted water to a boil. Add the pasta and cook until al dente, about 11 minutes, stirring in the peas at the end. Drain and return to the pan.

4 Meanwhile, tear the bread into chunks and combine in a food processor with ¹/₂ tablespoon butter. Process until crumbs form.

5 In a saucepan, melt the remaining 3 tablespoons butter over medium-high heat. Add the flour and thyme, stirring until smooth and bubbling, about 30 seconds. Slowly whisk in the milk and stir until boiling and thickened, 5 to 8 minutes. Add the lemon zest, mustard, pepper, and 1 teaspoon salt. Remove from the heat and add the goat cheese and 1 cup of the Romano cheese, stirring until smooth.

6 Pour the cheese sauce over the drained pasta and peas. Add the asparagus mixture and stir well. Scrape the pasta mixture into a 2¹/₂-quart baking dish and spread evenly. Sprinkle with the remaining ¹/₂ cup Romano and the bread crumbs.

7 Bake until the sauce is bubbling and the bread crumbs are browned, 15 to 20 minutes. Serve hot.

Makes 4 servings

Rolling Rock "33"—No one knows exactly why, but ever since the Tito family bought the Rolling Rock brewery in 1933 (the year Prohibition ended) with—legend has it—the winnings from a $33 bet on a horse whose number was 33, cans and bottles of Rolling Rock have featured the number 33 on their labels. Maybe it's the 33 streams that reportedly feed the reservoir that once supplied much of the beer's water, or the 33 steps that are said to span the distance from the brewmaster's office to the brewery floor . . .

GRILLED PORTOBELLO BURGERS

Serve with an English-Style Pale Ale, such as Michelob Pale Ale

2 tablespoons Worcestershire sauce

2 teaspoons honey mustard

2 garlic cloves, minced

1/4 teaspoon freshly ground black pepper

4 large portobello mushroom caps

1 red bell pepper, stemmed, seeded, and cut into 4 wedges

4 onion slices

8 sharp Cheddar cheese slices

Ketchup and mustard for serving

4 hamburger buns

4 Bibb lettuce leaves

8 sandwich-cut bread-and-butter pickles

1 Oil the grill rack. If using a charcoal grill, prepare a solid bed of medium-hot coals. If using a gas grill, preheat to high and close the lid, then open the lid and lower the heat to medium-high.

2 Meanwhile, in a small bowl, combine the Worcestershire sauce, mustard, garlic, and pepper, stirring with a whisk. Brush both sides of the mushroom caps with the Worcestershire mixture and set aside.

3 Lay the bell pepper wedges skin side down on the grill rack. Cook until blackened, about 10 minutes. Place in a plastic or paper bag and close tightly. Let stand for 10 minutes, then peel. Lay the onion slices and the mushroom caps top side down on the grill rack. Cook, turning once, until tender, 4 minutes on each side. Place 2 cheese slices on top of each mushroom cap; cover the grill and cook until the cheese melts, about 1 minute.

4 Spread ketchup and mustard on the top half of each hamburger bun. Place the mushroom caps on the bottom halves of the buns, top with the onion slices, peppers, lettuce leaves, and pickles. Serve immediately.

Makes 4 servings

REAL GRILLED CHEESE SANDWICHES

Serve with an American-Style Light Lager, such as Bud Light

8 slices rye bread

8 ounces Cheddar cheese, thinly sliced

1 firm, ripe tomato, cored and cut into thin slices

1 sweet onion, thinly sliced and separated into rings

About 2 tablespoons olive oil

1 Prepare a gas grill for cooking over medium heat. First, oil the grill rack. Preheat the burners to high and close the lid, then open the lid and lower the heat to medium (you can hold your hand 1 to 2 inches above grill level only 4 to 5 seconds).

2 For each sandwich, top 1 slice of bread with a thin layer of cheese slices, 2 tomato slices, a few rings of onion, and then more cheese. Top with a second slice of bread. Brush both sides of the sandwich lightly with olive oil, then push 2 or 3 toothpicks all the way through the sandwich to secure.

3 Lay the sandwiches on the grill rack and close the lid. Cook, turning to prevent the bread from scorching (remove the toothpicks when turning, if they catch on the grill), until the cheese is melted and the sandwiches are well browned on both sides with some darker grill marks in spots, 4 to 5 minutes on each side. Serve hot, while the cheese is still melted.

Makes 4 servings

SWISS CHARD and RICOTTA CALZONES

Serve with an English-Style Pale Ale, such as Michelob Pale Ale

Olive oil

1 sweet onion, such as Vidalia or Maui, cut into thin wedges

12 ounces Swiss chard, stemmed and leaves coarsely chopped

$1/8$ teaspoon ground nutmeg

Salt and freshly ground black pepper

1 pound purchased pizza dough, at room temperature

1 cup ricotta cheese

$2/3$ cup freshly grated Parmesan cheese

$1/3$ cup drained chopped oil-packed sun-dried tomatoes

$1/4$ cup pine nuts, toasted

$1/4$ teaspoon red pepper flakes (optional)

1 Preheat the oven to 450°F. In a large frying pan, heat 1 tablespoon olive oil over medium-high heat. Add the onion and cook, stirring often, until softened, about 4 minutes. Add the chard, sprinkle with the nutmeg, and season to taste with salt and pepper. Cook, stirring, until the chard is wilted, 3 to 5 minutes. Remove from the heat and set aside.

2 On a lightly floured surface, divide the pizza dough into 4 equal pieces. Using a lightly floured rolling pin or your hands, roll or stretch each piece into a 6-inch round. If the dough shrinks, let it rest for 5 minutes, then roll again.

3 In a small bowl, combine the ricotta, Parmesan, sun-dried tomatoes, pine nuts, and red pepper flakes (if using), mixing well. Season to taste with salt and pepper. Mound equal portions of the ricotta mixture in the center of the dough rounds. Top with the chard mixture.

4 Gently pull half of the dough over the filling to make a half-moon shape. Fold the bottom edge of dough over the top edge and pinch firmly to seal. Brush the tops lightly with more olive oil. Transfer to a large baking sheet.

5 Bake until golden brown, 20 to 25 minutes. Let cool for 5 minutes.

Cook's Tip: Savory, sweet, and just a little bit salty — a great main course for vegetarians and meat eaters alike. These calzones can be prepared through step 4, then wrapped individually in aluminum foil and kept in the freezer up to 1 month. Bake the frozen calzones at 375°F until browned and cooked through, 30 to 35 minutes.

Makes 4 servings

GARLICKY BROCCOLI RABE

Serve with an American-Style Light Lager, such as Michelob Golden Draft Light

2 pounds broccoli rabe, trimmed

1 tablespoon olive oil

2 large garlic cloves, thinly sliced

1/2 teaspoon salt

1/2 teaspoon freshly ground black pepper

1/4 teaspoon red pepper flakes

1 Fill a pot with water and bring to a boil over high heat. Add the broccoli rabe, bring the water back to a boil, and cook until crisp-tender, about 4 minutes. Drain the broccoli rabe, coarsely chop it, and set aside.

2 In a large skillet, heat the olive oil over medium heat. Add the garlic and cook, stirring constantly, for 2 minutes. Stir in the broccoli rabe, salt, pepper, and red pepper flakes. Cook until thoroughly heated, about 1 minute.

Cook's Tip: Boiling the broccoli rabe helps remove some of its bitterness. If you like it spicy hot, double the amount of red pepper flakes.

Makes 6 servings

ROASTED ASPARAGUS with LEMON

Serve with an English-Style Pale Ale, such as Michelob Pale Ale

1 1/2 pounds asparagus

2 teaspoons extra-virgin olive oil

Sea salt and freshly ground black pepper

2 teaspoons grated lemon zest

1 tablespoon lemon-flavored olive oil or plain olive oil

1 Preheat the oven to 400°F. Snap off the tough stem ends from the asparagus and discard. Spread the asparagus in a 10-by-15-inch baking pan. Drizzle with the extra-virgin olive oil, then shake the pan slightly to coat the asparagus. Sprinkle lightly with salt and pepper.

2 Roast the asparagus until crisp-tender to the bite, 9 to 10 minutes. Transfer to a platter. Sprinkle with the lemon zest and drizzle with the lemon-flavored olive oil. Serve warm or at room temperature.

Cook's Tip: Cooking time depends on the thickness of the asparagus spears.

Makes 6 servings

BRUSSELS SPROUTS with PARMESAN

Serve with an English-Style Pale Ale, such as Michelob Pale Ale

2 tablespoons olive oil

1 tablespoon sugar

1/2 teaspoon salt

2 pounds Brussels sprouts, trimmed and quartered

1/4 cup chopped fresh flat-leaf parsley

1 tablespoon butter, at room temperature

1 teaspoon freshly ground black pepper

3/4 teaspoon grated lemon zest

1/2 ounce shaved Parmesan cheese

1 Preheat the oven to 400°F. Lightly oil a rimmed baking sheet.

2 In a large bowl, combine the olive oil, sugar, and salt, stirring to dissolve the sugar. Add the Brussels sprouts and toss well. Arrange the Brussels sprouts in a single layer on the baking sheet.

3 Bake until the edges of the Brussels sprouts are lightly browned, about 20 minutes. Transfer to a serving bowl.

4 In a small bowl, combine the parsley, butter, pepper, and lemon zest, stirring well to blend. Add the butter mixture to the Brussels sprouts and toss well. Sprinkle with the Parmesan and serve.

Cook's Tip: Use good-quality Parmesan cheese for the most robust flavor.

Makes 6 servings

SPINACH with PINE NUTS and RAISINS

Serve with an American-Style Light Amber Lager, such as Michelob Ultra Amber

1/2 cup boiling water

1/3 cup golden raisins

2 packages (10 ounces each) fresh baby spinach

1 teaspoon olive oil

2 garlic cloves, minced

1/4 teaspoon salt

1/4 teaspoon freshly ground black pepper

4 teaspoons pine nuts, toasted

1 In a small bowl, pour the boiling water over the raisins. Let stand until the raisins are plump, about 15 minutes. Drain and set aside.

2 In a large Dutch oven, pour in 2 tablespoons water and add the spinach. Cook over medium-high heat, stirring frequently, just until the spinach wilts, about 3 minutes. Transfer the spinach to a bowl and set aside. Wipe out the pan with a paper towel.

3 Add the olive oil to the pan and heat over medium heat. Add the garlic and cook, stirring frequently, for 30 seconds. Add the spinach, raisins, salt, and pepper. Cook until thoroughly heated, about 1 minute. Stir in the pine nuts and serve.

Makes 4 servings

GRILLED VEGETABLES

Serve with an American-Style Light Amber Lager, such as Michelob Ultra Amber

MARINADE

³/₄ cup olive oil

³/₄ cup red wine vinegar

2 tablespoons peeled and minced fresh ginger

1 tablespoon minced garlic

1¹/₂ teaspoons salt

1 teaspoon *each* ground cinnamon, ground coriander, paprika, and sugar

¹/₂ teaspoon *each* ground cumin and freshly ground black pepper

¹/₄ teaspoon cayenne pepper

2 large bell peppers (red, orange, or yellow), halved, stemmed, and seeded

2 zucchini, trimmed and halved lengthwise

1 large eggplant, trimmed and thickly sliced

1 large sweet onion, thickly sliced

¹/₂ cup pine nuts, toasted

¹/₄ cup chopped fresh mint

Red wine vinegar

Salt and freshly ground black pepper

1 To prepare the marinade, in a small bowl, combine the ingredients, stirring with a whisk. If using a charcoal grill, prepare a solid bed of medium-hot coals. If using a gas grill, preheat to medium-high.

2 Brush both sides of the vegetables with the marinade. Reserve any remaining marinade. Lay the vegetables on the grill rack. Cook, turning once, until beginning to brown and just tender when pierced with a knife, about 10 minutes. Transfer to a large cutting board as each is done. Cut all the vegetables into 1-inch pieces and transfer to a serving bowl. Add the pine nuts, mint, and any remaining marinade. Toss gently to mix. Season to taste with vinegar, salt, and pepper.

Makes 6 servings

GRILLED CORN

Serve with an American-Style Premium Lager, such as Budweiser Select

CILANTRO-CHILE BUTTER

¹/₃ cup fresh cilantro leaves

1 teaspoon finely chopped serrano or jalapeño chile

1 large garlic clove, coarsely chopped

Pinch of salt

4 tablespoons unsalted butter, at room temperature

CHIVE BUTTER

3 tablespoons thinly sliced fresh chives

1 teaspoon grated lemon zest

1 teaspoon fresh lemon juice

Pinch of salt

4 tablespoons unsalted butter, at room temperature

4 ears sweet corn

1 To prepare the cilantro-chile butter, combine the cilantro, chile, garlic, and salt in a food processor and process until finely chopped, scraping down the sides of the work bowl as needed. Add the butter and process until the mixture is smooth and well blended. Transfer to a bowl.

2 To prepare the chive butter, combine the chives, lemon zest and juice, and salt in a food processor and process until finely chopped, scraping down the sides of the work bowl as needed. Add the butter and process until the mixture is smooth and well blended. Transfer to a bowl.

3 To cook the corn, pull the husks away from each ear and remove the silks. Wrap the husks back around the corn and soak in water to cover for 10 minutes.

4 If using a charcoal grill, prepare a solid bed of hot coals. If using a gas grill, preheat to high. Drain the corn and arrange on the grill rack. If using a gas grill, close the lid. Cook the corn in the husks for 10 minutes. Pull the husks back and grill, turning occasionally, until the kernels are lightly browned, about 5 minutes longer. Serve immediately with the flavored butters.

Makes 4 servings

GRILLED GREEN TOMATOES with SALSA

Serve with an American-Style Light Lager, such as Bud Light

6 unripe (green) tomatoes (about 3 pounds total)

1/4 cup extra-virgin olive oil

3 garlic cloves, minced

2 tablespoons chopped fresh marjoram or oregano

Salt and freshly ground black pepper

1 1/2 pounds ripe tomatoes (red, yellow, golden, green, or a combination; see Cook's Tip)

1 red onion, finely chopped

1/4 cup chopped red bell pepper

1/4 cup finely chopped fresh green or purple basil

1 1/2 tablespoons fresh lime juice

1/2 to 2 teaspoons chopped fresh jalapeño or habanero chile

1 Cut the unripe tomatoes crosswise into slices 1/2 inch thick, discarding the stem ends and bottoms. In a large bowl, combine the sliced tomatoes, olive oil, half of the garlic, and the marjoram, mixing gently to coat well. Season to taste with salt and pepper. Cover and refrigerate for at least 30 minutes or up to overnight.

2 Prepare a grill for cooking over medium-high heat. First, oil the grill rack. If using a charcoal grill, prepare a solid bed of medium-hot coals. If using a gas grill, preheat to high and close the lid, then open the lid and lower the heat to medium-high (you can hold your hand 1 to 2 inches above grill level only 3 to 4 seconds).

3 Meanwhile, core the ripe tomatoes and cut in half crosswise. Squeeze the tomato halves gently to remove the seeds. Chop the tomatoes. In a bowl, combine the chopped tomatoes, the remaining garlic, the onion, bell pepper, basil, lime juice, and chile. Season to taste with salt and pepper. Set aside.

4 Using a slotted spatula, lift the unripe tomatoes from the marinade and lay them on the grill rack. Cook, turning once, until nicely browned, 6 to 10 minutes. Arrange on a platter, spoon the ripe tomato salsa over the top, and serve.

Cook's Tip: Be sure to use sweet, ripe tomatoes for the salsa to offset the tartness of the green tomatoes. You can make the salsa up to 4 hours ahead, then cover and refrigerate. Bring to room temperature before serving.

Makes 6 servings

ROASTED FALL VEGETABLES

Serve with a Maerzen Beer, such as Michelob Marzen

3 yellow onions, peeled and cut into quarters, root ends intact

3 russet potatoes, cut lengthwise into slices 1/2 inch thick

3 turnips, peeled and cut into eighths

4 large carrots, peeled and cut into pieces 3 inches long (cut the thickest pieces into halves or quarters lengthwise)

3 large parsnips, peeled and cut into pieces 3 inches long (cut the thickest pieces into halves or quarters lengthwise)

4 red or golden beets, peeled and cut into quarters

10 to 20 garlic cloves, loose papery outer skins removed, inner skins intact

2 orange sweet potatoes, peeled and cut into pieces 3 inches long and 1 inch wide

3/4 cup extra-virgin olive oil

Coarse salt and freshly ground black pepper

7 rosemary sprigs

1 Preheat the oven to 400°F. In one or two large bowls, combine the onions, russet potatoes, turnips, carrots, parsnips, beets, and garlic. Put the sweet potatoes in a separate bowl. Drizzle the olive oil over all the vegetables and sprinkle with salt and pepper. Using your hands, toss gently to coat well. Spread half of the mixed vegetables, not yet including the sweet potatoes, in a single layer on two large baking sheets. Break up 3 of the rosemary sprigs and sprinkle over the vegetables.

2 Roast the mixed vegetables for 15 minutes, stirring gently with a metal spatula if they are sticking. Add half of the sweet potatoes to the pans. Continue to roast, stirring gently every 15 minutes if necessary and rotating the pans to ensure even browning, until the vegetables are browned and tender, 40 minutes to 1 1/4 hours. Transfer to a serving platter and set aside. Repeat with the remaining mixed vegetables, sweet potatoes, and 3 more of the rosemary sprigs.

3 Season the roasted vegetables to taste with salt and pepper. Garnish with the remaining rosemary sprig. Serve warm or at room temperature.

Cook's Tip: These roasted vegetables go well with just about any simply cooked meat. The vegetables need space around them on the baking sheet in order to brown, so you can roast them in batches if necessary.

Makes 8 servings

The yeast used today is a direct descendant of the original culture used by Adolphus Busch to brew the first batch of Budweiser in 1876. In the 1920s the company built its own yeast plant, and sold yeast for commercial purposes nationwide until 1990.

SCALLOPED VIDALIA ONIONS

Serve with a Honey-Flavored Specialty Beer, such as Michelob Honey Lager

4 pounds Vidalia or other sweet onions, trimmed and quartered

2 tablespoons olive oil

²/₃ cup chicken stock

1 tablespoon butter

2 tablespoons all-purpose flour

1 cup whole milk

¹/₄ cup (1 ounce) shredded Gruyère cheese

³/₄ teaspoon salt

¹/₄ teaspoon freshly ground black pepper

1 Preheat the oven to 400°F. Spread the onions in a 13-by-9-inch baking dish. Drizzle with the olive oil and toss to coat well.

2 Roast for 40 minutes, stirring halfway through the cooking time. Drizzle the chicken stock over the onions and stir to coat well. Roast for 40 minutes longer, stirring once.

3 Meanwhile, in a small saucepan, melt the butter over medium heat. Add the flour, stirring with a whisk until smooth. Gradually add the milk, stirring with the whisk until blended. Bring to a boil and cook, stirring constantly, for 1 minute. Remove from the heat and add the cheese, salt, and pepper, stirring until smooth. Pour the milk mixture over the onions, stirring to combine.

4 Continue to roast until the sauce is thick and beginning to brown on top, about 20 minutes longer. Remove from the oven and let stand for 10 minutes before serving.

Cook's Tip: This is a great side dish for red meat or poultry.

Makes 6 servings

BUTTERMILK OVEN-FRIED OKRA

Serve with an American-Style Premium Lager, such as Busch

Olive oil for baking sheet and for drizzling

1¹/₂ cups medium-ground yellow cornmeal

³/₄ teaspoon kosher salt

¹/₂ teaspoon freshly ground black pepper

Pinch of cayenne pepper

¹/₂ cup buttermilk

1 large egg, lightly beaten

1 pound fresh okra pods, trimmed and cut into slices ³/₄ inch thick

1 Preheat the oven to 450°F. Lightly oil a rimmed baking sheet.

2 In a shallow dish, combine the cornmeal, ¹/₂ teaspoon of the salt, the pepper, and cayenne, stirring with a whisk. Set aside.

3 In a large bowl, combine the buttermilk and egg, stirring with the whisk. Add the okra and toss to coat. Let stand for 3 minutes.

4 Dredge the okra in the cornmeal mixture. Arrange the okra in a single layer on the baking sheet. Drizzle with the olive oil.

5 Roast for 40 minutes, stirring once. Sprinkle with the remaining ¹/₄ teaspoon salt and serve.

Makes 6 servings

CHANTERELLE and POTATO SALAD

Serve with a Dry Stout, such as Bare Knuckle Stout

12 ounces fresh chanterelle mushrooms or 10 ounces shiitake mushrooms

6 ounces slab pancetta or thick-cut bacon, diced

3 pounds small Yukon gold potatoes, halved lengthwise

4 garlic cloves, minced

2 teaspoons fresh thyme leaves

1½ teaspoons kosher salt

¾ teaspoon freshly ground black pepper

2 tablespoons butter

1 shallot, minced

⅓ cup chicken stock

2 tablespoons chopped fresh tarragon

1 tablespoon snipped fresh chives

VINAIGRETTE

4 tablespoons good-quality white wine vinegar

⅔ cup vegetable oil

⅔ cup extra-virgin olive oil

1 shallot, chopped

½ teaspoon kosher salt

1 Preheat the oven to 375°F. Wipe the mushrooms with a damp cloth or scrape with a knife to remove any dirt. Trim off any dry, woody parts. Tear the mushrooms into 1-inch pieces and set aside.

2 In a large skillet, cook the pancetta over medium-high heat until crisp and browned, about 7 minutes. Using a slotted spoon, transfer the pancetta to paper towels, reserving the drippings in the pan.

3 In a large bowl, toss the potatoes with 3 tablespoons reserved pancetta drippings (see Cook's Tip), garlic, thyme, 1 teaspoon of the salt, and ½ teaspoon of the pepper. Divide the potatoes between two 13-by-9-inch baking dishes.

4 Bake, stirring every 10 minutes, until tender, well browned, and crisp, 25 to 35 minutes. Remove from the oven and keep warm.

5 Meanwhile, make the vinaigrette: Combine the ingredients in a blender and blend at medium speed until the mixture is pale yellow and emulsified.

6 In a large skillet, melt the butter over medium-high heat. Add the shallot and cook until soft, about 1 minute. Add the mushrooms and cook, stirring occasionally, until browned, 5 to 6 minutes. Add the stock, the remaining ½ teaspoon salt, and the remaining ¼ teaspoon pepper. Cook, scraping up the browned bits from the pan bottom, until the liquid evaporates, about 2 minutes.

7 In a large bowl, combine the potatoes, mushrooms, pancetta, tarragon, and chives. Drizzle with the vinaigrette and toss gently. Serve warm.

Cook's Tip: This recipe calls for small potatoes cut in half, but if your potatoes are longer than 2 inches, cut them into quarters. If you don't have enough pancetta drippings for the potatoes, add some olive oil.

Makes 8 servings

CREAMY CUMIN POTATO GRATIN

Serve with a Doppelbock, such as Brewmaster's Private Reserve

2 cups heavy cream

1¼ to 1¾ cups whole milk

2 tablespoons minced garlic

1½ teaspoons salt

½ teaspoon freshly ground black pepper

½ teaspoon ground cumin

2½ pounds Yukon gold potatoes

1 Preheat the oven to 375°F. In a saucepan, combine the cream, 1¼ cups of the milk, the garlic, salt, pepper, and cumin over medium-low heat. Simmer (don't let boil), stirring occasionally, for 5 minutes.

2 Meanwhile, peel the potatoes and thinly slice crosswise. Spread the sliced potatoes evenly in a shallow 2½-quart casserole or baking dish. Pour enough milk mixture over the potatoes to barely cover. If the potatoes aren't quite covered, add up to ½ cup more milk. Cover tightly with a lid or aluminum foil.

3 Bake the gratin for 30 minutes. Uncover and continue to bake until the potatoes are tender when pierced with a knife and the top is nicely browned, 30 to 40 minutes longer. Serve hot.

Cook's Tip: You can assemble this dish through step 3 up to a day ahead, then cover tightly with plastic wrap and refrigerate. Warm the gratin in the oven before serving.

Makes 6 servings

GARLIC SMASHED POTATO SALAD

Serve with a European-Style Pilsner, such as Grolsch

2 heads garlic

¼ cup extra-virgin olive oil

3 tablespoons Grolsch

Salt and freshly ground black pepper

2½ pounds Yukon gold potatoes, cut into 1-inch chunks

¼ cup snipped fresh chives

1 Preheat the oven to 400°F. Cut the garlic heads in half crosswise and wrap together tightly in one large piece of aluminum foil. Roast until the garlic is light golden brown and very soft when pressed (unwrap to test), 45 minutes to 1 hour. Remove the garlic from the foil and set aside to cool slightly.

2 While the garlic is roasting, place the potatoes in a large pot and add 4 quarts water. Cover and bring to a boil over high heat. Lower the heat to low and simmer until the potatoes are tender when pierced with a knife, about 20 minutes. Drain the potatoes and return them to the pot.

3 When the garlic is cool enough to handle, squeeze the cloves from their skins into a small bowl. Add the olive oil, beer, 1½ teaspoons salt, and ½ teaspoon pepper. Mash the garlic with a fork until the mixture is smooth.

4 Add the garlic mixture and chives to the potatoes and stir gently until well combined but still chunky. Taste and adjust the seasoning. Let cool completely, then cover tightly with plastic wrap and refrigerate for up to 1 day. Serve cold.

Makes 6 servings

WARM POTATO SALAD

Serve with an English-Style Pale Ale, such as Michelob Pale Ale

3 pounds red potatoes, halved lengthwise

1/2 cup finely chopped red onion

1/4 cup *each* thinly sliced green onions, chopped celery, finely chopped sweet pickles, and chopped fresh flat-leaf parsley

2 tablespoons Michelob Pale Ale

2 tablespoons cider vinegar

DRESSING

1/4 cup olive oil

3/4 cup finely chopped yellow onion

3/4 cup Michelob Pale Ale

1/4 cup cider vinegar

1 teaspoon sugar

3/4 teaspoon salt

1/8 teaspoon freshly ground black pepper

2 tablespoons Dijon mustard

1 Place the potatoes in a large saucepan and add water to cover. Bring to a boil over high heat, then lower the heat and simmer until tender, about 20 minutes. Drain and let cool. Cut the potatoes into slices 1/4 inch thick. In a large bowl, combine the potatoes, red and green onions, celery, pickles, parsley, beer, and vinegar. Toss gently.

2 To prepare the dressing, in a small skillet, heat 2 tablespoons of the olive oil over medium-high heat. Add the yellow onion and sauté until tender, about 3 minutes. Add the beer, vinegar, sugar, salt, and pepper, stirring well. Bring to a boil and cook until reduced to 1/2 cup, about 6 minutes. In a food processor, combine the yellow onion mixture and mustard. With the processor on, slowly pour the remaining 2 tablespoons olive oil through the food chute, processing until smooth. Pour the dressing over the potato mixture, toss gently, and serve.

Makes 6 servings

FINGERLING POTATOES with SMOKED TROUT

Serve with an American-Style Light Amber Lager, such as Michelob Ultra Amber

2 tablespoons large capers, rinsed and drained

2 pounds fingerling potatoes (2 inches wide), halved lengthwise

8 ounces smoked trout

1/3 cup olive oil

1/4 cup fresh lemon juice

1/2 teaspoon freshly ground black pepper

1 small Granny Smith apple, thinly sliced

1 tablespoon chopped fresh dill

Sour cream (optional)

1 If using salt-cured capers, put them in a small bowl, cover with water, and let soak for 10 minutes. Rinse and pat completely dry. (For brine-packed capers, rinse and pat dry.)

2 Fill a large saucepan half full with water and bring to a boil over high heat. Add the potatoes and cook, uncovered, until tender, about 15 minutes. Drain and set aside. Meanwhile, pull off and discard the skin from the trout. Break the fish into bite-size pieces.

3 Heat a small saucepan over medium-high heat. When hot, add the olive oil. When the oil is hot, add the capers. Cook, stirring once, until the capers open and are light brown and crisp, about 1 minute. Pour into a fine-mesh sieve set over a glass measuring cup. Spread the capers on paper towels to drain. Reserve the oil.

4 In a large serving bowl, combine the reserved caper oil, lemon juice, and pepper, stirring with a whisk. Add the potatoes, trout, apple, and dill and mix gently to coat well. Sprinkle the fried capers over the top. Serve with sour cream, if you like.

Makes 4 servings

BAKED POTATOES with CARAMELIZED ONIONS

 Serve with a Porter, such as Michelob Porter

6 baking potatoes (about 3 pounds total)

3 tablespoons butter

4 onions, thinly sliced

4 garlic cloves, minced

2 teaspoons finely chopped fresh rosemary

1/4 teaspoon salt

1/2 teaspoon freshly ground black pepper

3/4 cup (3 ounces) shredded Gruyère cheese

1 Preheat the oven to 375°F. Pierce the potatoes in several places with a fork. Place the potatoes on a baking sheet or directly on the oven rack. Bake until tender when pierced with a knife, about 1 hour. Let cool slightly.

2 In a large skillet, melt the butter over medium heat. Add the onions and garlic and cook until browned, about 20 minutes. Stir in the rosemary, salt, and pepper.

3 Preheat the broiler. Split the baked potatoes lengthwise, cutting to, but not through, the other side. Spoon about 1/3 cup onion mixture into each potato. Sprinkle each with 2 tablespoons cheese. Broil until the cheese is lightly browned, about 3 minutes. Serve hot.

Makes 6 servings

BAKED POTATOES with GORGONZOLA

 Serve with a Dry Stout, such as Bare Knuckle Stout

6 large Yukon gold potatoes (about 3 pounds total)

1/2 cup sour cream

1/4 cup (1 ounce) crumbled Gorgonzola cheese

3 ounces pancetta, finely diced

2 garlic cloves, minced

3 tablespoons finely snipped fresh chives

1 Preheat the oven to 375°F. Pierce the potatoes in several places with a fork. Place the potatoes on a baking sheet or directly on the oven rack. Bake until tender when pierced with a knife, about 1 hour. Let cool slightly.

2 In a small bowl, combine the sour cream and cheese, partially mashing with a fork.

3 Heat a small skillet over medium heat. When the pan is hot, add the pancetta and cook for 2 minutes. Add the garlic and cook for 1 minute. Remove from the heat.

4 Split the potatoes lengthwise, cutting to, but not through, the other side. Spoon 2 tablespoons cheese mixture into each potato. Top each with a heaping tablespoon pancetta mixture and a sprinkling of chives, and serve immediately.

Makes 6 servings

GRILLED SPICY SWEET-POTATO PACKETS

Serve with an American-Style Amber Lager, such as Michelob Amber Bock

2 sweet potatoes, peeled, halved lengthwise, and cut into half-moons ¼ inch thick

1 large red onion, peeled, halved, and cut into wedges ⅓ inch thick

⅓ cup olive oil

2 tablespoons ketchup

2 teaspoons chopped fresh thyme

2 teaspoons chili powder

2 teaspoons salt

1 teaspoon freshly ground black pepper

1 lime, cut into 6 wedges

1 Prepare a grill for cooking over indirect heat. First, oil the grill rack. If using a charcoal grill, light 50 to 60 briquettes and let burn until covered with ash, about 20 to 30 minutes, then mound them to one side. Place a drip pan on the side cleared of coals—this is the indirect heat area. Set the oiled grill rack in place. If using a gas grill, turn all the burners to high and close the lid. When the temperature inside the grill reaches 350° to 400°F, lift the lid and turn off one of the burners. Place a drip pan under the turned-off burner—this is the indirect heat area. Set the oiled grill rack in place.

2 Meanwhile, in a large bowl, combine the sweet potato slices, onion wedges, olive oil, ketchup, thyme, chili powder, salt, and pepper. Toss gently to coat well.

3 Lay out six 12-by-14-inch sheets of heavy-duty aluminum foil (see Cook's Tip) on the counter, shiny side down. Distribute the potato mixture evenly among the sheets, mounding it in the center of each sheet. Fold the top edge of foil down over the potato mixture. Crimp all the edges together to form a tight seal.

4 Lay the foil packets on the grill rack, overlapping slightly if needed, and close the lid. Cook until the potatoes are tender when pierced with a knife, 25 to 30 minutes. (If cooking with the Smoke-Roasted Chicken —see Cook's Tip—add to grill during the last 30 minutes of cooking.) Remove the packets from the grill and let cool for 10 minutes. Serve with the lime wedges.

Cook's Tip: Be sure to use heavy-duty aluminum foil for your packets, as regular foil may tear on the grill. These potatoes are delicious with Smoke-Roasted Chicken, page 110.

Makes 6 servings

ZESTY BEAN SALAD

Serve with an American-Style Premium Lager, such as Michelob

2 ears sweet corn

3 tablespoons olive oil

1 pound green beans, trimmed, cut into 1-inch pieces

1 small red bell pepper, stemmed, seeded, and diced

$1/2$ red onion, minced

1 tablespoon minced seeded jalapeño chile

1 can (16 ounces) cannellini (white kidney) beans or other white beans, rinsed and drained

1 can (15 ounces) black beans, rinsed and drained

$1/4$ cup chopped fresh cilantro

$1/4$ cup fresh lime juice

$1/4$ cup red wine vinegar

$1/4$ teaspoon hot sauce

3 garlic cloves, minced

2 teaspoons ground cumin

1 teaspoon chili powder

$1/2$ teaspoon salt

Pinch of cayenne pepper

2 tomatoes, seeded and diced

1 avocado, pitted, peeled, and diced

1 Over a small bowl, cut the kernels from the ears of corn. Scrape the remaining pulp from the cobs using the dull side of the knife blade, then discard the cobs. In a large skillet, heat 2 tablespoons of the olive oil over medium-high heat. Add the corn and green beans and sauté until lightly browned, about 3 minutes. Transfer the bean mixture to a bowl. Add the bell pepper, onion, chile, cannellini, black beans, and cilantro. Toss well.

2 In a small bowl, combine the lime juice, vinegar, the remaining 1 tablespoon olive oil, the hot sauce, garlic, cumin, chili powder, salt, and cayenne. Add the lime juice mixture to the bean mixture and toss well. Cover and refrigerate for 30 minutes. Gently stir in the tomatoes and avocado and serve.

Makes 8 servings

ALE-BAKED BEANS

Serve with an American-Style Amber Lager, such as Michelob Amber Bock

4 cans (16 ounces each) pinto beans, rinsed and drained

$1^3/4$ cups chicken stock

1 yellow onion, quartered

2 bay leaves

2 bacon slices, chopped

2 yellow onions, chopped

3 garlic cloves, minced

2 teaspoons chili powder

$3/4$ cup ketchup

$1/3$ cup firmly packed brown sugar

3 tablespoons Dijon mustard

2 tablespoons Worcestershire sauce

$1/4$ teaspoon freshly ground black pepper

1 bottle (12 ounces) Michelob Amber Bock

1 Preheat the oven to 300°F. Oil a 13-by-9-inch baking dish. In a large saucepan, pour in 2 cups water and add the beans, stock, quartered onion, and bay leaves. Bring to a boil over high heat, then lower the heat and simmer for 15 minutes. Pour into a sieve set over a large bowl. Set the beans aside, discarding the onion and bay leaves. Reserve the cooking liquid.

2 In a large skillet, cook the bacon over medium heat until crisp, about 6 minutes. Transfer the bacon to paper towels to drain, reserving 1 tablespoon drippings in the pan. Add the chopped onions to the pan and cook, stirring frequently, until golden brown, about 10 minutes. Add the garlic and chili powder and cook, for 1 minute. Add the ketchup, brown sugar, mustard, Worcestershire sauce, pepper, beer, and $1/2$ cup reserved bean liquid. Bring to a boil. Add the beans and bacon, then lower heat to low and simmer until slightly thickened, about 10 minutes. Transfer the bean mixture to the prepared baking dish. Bake until thickened, 45 minutes, and serve.

Makes 8 servings

BARLEY with BELL PEPPERS and MAERZEN

Serve with a Maerzen Beer, such as Michelob Marzen

2 cups pearled barley

8 cups chicken stock

1 bottle (12 ounces) Michelob Marzen

1 onion, chopped

1 red bell pepper, stemmed, seeded, and chopped

1 yellow bell pepper, stemmed, seeded, and chopped

1 green bell pepper, stemmed, seeded, and chopped

¼ cup finely chopped shallots

5 garlic cloves, finely chopped

1 teaspoon kosher salt

2 cups freshly grated Parmesan cheese

1 In a large saucepan, combine the barley, 4 cups of the stock, the beer, onion, bell peppers, shallots, garlic, and salt over medium-high heat. Bring to a boil and cook, stirring often, for 20 minutes. Add 2 cups more stock and cook for 20 minutes longer, stirring often. Add the remaining 2 cups stock and cook until the barley is tender, about 20 minutes longer. Add the cheese and stir to mix well. Serve hot.

Cook's Tip: Chef Sam Niemann serves this flavorful side dish with roast beef.

Makes 8 to 10 servings

LEMONY COUSCOUS with MINT and FETA

Serve with a Wheat Beer, such as Michelob Bavarian Style Wheat

1 tablespoon extra-virgin olive oil

1 large garlic clove, minced

1 teaspoon salt

1 box (10 ounces) whole-wheat couscous

2 cups grape or cherry tomatoes, halved

1½ cups diced English cucumber

⅓ cup chopped green onions, white and tender green parts

⅓ cup fresh lemon juice

2 tablespoons chopped fresh mint

1 tablespoon chopped fresh dill

4 ounces crumbled feta cheese

1 Fill a saucepan with 2 cups water and add the olive oil, garlic, and salt. Bring to a boil over high heat. Gradually stir in the couscous and remove from the heat. Cover and let stand for 5 minutes. Fluff with a fork and let cool.

2 In a large bowl, combine the couscous, tomatoes, cucumber, green onions, lemon juice, mint, and dill, tossing well. Scatter the feta cheese over the top.

Cook's Tip: You can substitute regular couscous for the whole wheat. This dish is delicious served alongside grilled lamb.

Makes 6 servings

DESSERTS

Chef's Specialty

GRILL-BAKED APPLE CRISP

Serve with an American-Style Amber Lager, such as Michelob Amber Bock

½ cup (1 stick) unsalted butter

10 apples (about 5 pounds total), preferably a mixture of Granny Smith and Golden Delicious

2 cups all-purpose flour

1 cup sugar

2 teaspoons ground cinnamon

2 teaspoons baking powder

¾ teaspoon salt

2 large eggs

Vanilla ice cream (optional)

1 Prepare a grill for cooking over indirect heat. First oil the grill rack. If using a charcoal grill, light 50 to 60 briquettes and let burn until covered with ash, about 20 to 30 minutes, then mound them to one side. Place a drip pan on the side cleared of coals—this is the indirect heat area. Set the oiled grill rack in place. If using a gas grill, turn all the burners to high and close the lid. When the temperature inside the grill reaches 350° to 400°F, lift the lid, turn off one of the burners, and lower the other burner(s) to medium. Place a drip pan under the turned-off burner—this is the indirect heat area. Set the oiled grill rack in place.

2 In a small saucepan, melt the butter over low heat. Set aside.

3 Peel, core, and cut the apples into slices ⅓ inch thick. Spread the apples in an even layer in a 13-by-9-inch baking pan (see Cook's Tip).

4 In a large bowl, combine the flour, sugar, cinnamon, baking powder, and salt, stirring with a fork. Add the eggs and mix with the fork until crumbly (the mixture will resemble streusel). Spread the topping evenly over the apples. Drizzle with the melted butter.

5 Place the baking pan over the indirect heat area on the grill and close the lid. Cook until the topping is browned and the apples are bubbling, 40 to 45 minutes. Serve warm with vanilla ice cream, if desired.

Cook's Tip: For easy cleanup, use a disposable aluminum pan or a foil-lined metal baking pan to bake this crisp on the grill.

Makes 8 to 10 servings

Anheuser-Busch Ice Cream—Prohibition was an enormously difficult time for the nation's beer brewers. Leveraging its refrigeration assets, Anheuser-Busch stayed afloat, in part, by producing ice cream at plants in New Orleans, Oklahoma City, and New York City. At the height of production, in 1926, sales topped one million gallons. By 1932, however, focus had returned to frosty beverages, and the frozen confections were abandoned.

APPLE BARS with DATES and PECANS

Serve with a Wheat Beer, such as Michelob Bavarian Style Wheat

2 cups all-purpose flour, plus 1 teaspoon

1 teaspoon baking soda

1 teaspoon baking powder

$1/2$ teaspoon ground cinnamon

$1/4$ teaspoon salt

2 cups sugar

7 tablespoons unsalted butter, at room temperature

1 large egg

2 large egg whites

$1/4$ cup applesauce

1 teaspoon vanilla extract

1 cup chopped pitted dates

2 large Granny Smith apples, peeled, cored, and chopped

$1/2$ teaspoon fresh lemon juice

$2/3$ cup chopped pecans

1 Preheat the oven to 325°F. Lightly butter a 13-by-9-inch baking dish. In a large bowl, combine the 2 cups flour, baking soda, baking powder, cinnamon, and salt, stirring with a whisk. Set aside.

2 In another large bowl, combine the sugar and butter, beating with an electric mixer until light and fluffy, about 2 minutes. Add the egg and the egg whites one at a time, beating well after each addition. Stir in the applesauce and vanilla. Gradually add the flour mixture to the sugar mixture, stirring just until combined. Toss the dates with the 1 teaspoon flour. Toss the apples with the lemon juice. Add the dates, apples, and nuts to the flour mixture, stirring just until combined. Spoon the batter into the prepared baking dish.

3 Bake until a toothpick inserted in the center comes out clean, about 1 hour and 5 minutes. Let cool completely on a wire rack, then cut into 16 pieces.

Makes 16 bars

BAKED BANANAS with TROPICAL FLAVORS

Serve with a Wheat Beer, such as Michelob Bavarian Style Wheat

4 small bananas, halved lengthwise and thinly sliced

4 tablespoons unsalted butter, chopped

4 tablespoons unsweetened shredded coconut

2 tablespoons brown sugar

4 tablespoons chopped roasted and salted macadamia nuts or peanuts

4 tablespoons mini semisweet chocolate chips

Vanilla ice cream

1 Prepare a grill for cooking over medium-high heat or preheat the oven to 400°F. If grilling, first, oil the grill rack. If using a charcoal grill, prepare a solid bed of medium-hot coals. If using a gas grill, preheat to high and close the lid, then open the lid and lower the heat to medium-high (you can hold your hand 1 to 2 inches above grill level only 3 to 4 seconds).

2 Cut out four 12-inch squares of aluminum foil, if grilling, or parchment paper, if baking in the oven. Divide the bananas among the squares and sprinkle with the butter, coconut, brown sugar, and nuts. Fold up to seal. Lay the packets on the grill rack directly over the heat or place them on a baking sheet. Grill or bake until the bananas are soft and bubbling (open one packet with the tip of a knife to peek), 10 to 12 minutes.

3 Remove from the grill or oven. Transfer packets to serving dishes, open carefully, and sprinkle with the chocolate chips. Top each with a scoop of ice cream and serve immediately.

Makes 4 servings

PEACH-BLACKBERRY CLAFOUTI

 Serve with a Porter, such as Michelob Porter

2 tablespoons unsalted butter

2 large peaches, pitted and cut into ^{1}/$_2$-inch wedges, peeled if desired

1^1/$_2$ cups blackberries or marionberries

^{1}/$_2$ cup granulated sugar

1 tablespoon fresh lemon juice

4 ounces almond paste

^{1}/$_2$ cup whole milk

^{1}/$_4$ cup heavy cream

3 large eggs

Pinch of salt

^{1}/$_4$ cup all-purpose flour

Confectioners' sugar

1 Preheat the oven to 400°F. Butter a 9-inch deep-dish glass pie plate or baking dish. In a large skillet over medium-high heat, melt the butter. Add the peaches, blackberries, and ^{1}/$_4$ cup of the granulated sugar. Cook, stirring often, until the fruit starts to release its juices, 2 to 3 minutes. Stir in the lemon juice, then pour the fruit into the bottom of the prepared dish, spreading evenly.

2 In a blender or food processor, combine the remaining ^{1}/$_4$ cup granulated sugar and the almond paste and process until smooth. With the motor running, pour in the milk and heavy cream. Add the eggs and salt and process until smooth.

3 Put the flour in a large bowl and slowly whisk the almond paste mixture into the flour until smooth. Pour the batter over the fruit. Bake until golden brown, about 40 minutes. Transfer to a wire rack and let cool for about 10 minutes. Serve warm, dusted with the confectioners' sugar.

Cook's Tip: Clafouti is a rustic French dessert that is a combination custard, cake, and pudding all in one.

Makes 6 servings

MELON and BERRIES in CHILE-LIME SYRUP

Serve with an American-Style Light Lager, such as Michelob Ultra

1 cup sugar

1 serrano or jalapeño chile, cut in half lengthwise

Zest and juice of ^{1}/$_2$ lime

^{1}/$_2$ honeydew melon (about 1^1/$_2$ pounds), seeded and cut into 1-inch chunks

2 cups strawberries, hulled and quartered

1 In a small saucepan, combine 1^1/$_2$ cups water, the sugar, and the chile over high heat. Bring to a boil, stirring until the sugar dissolves. Stir in the lime zest and juice and remove from the heat.

2 In a large bowl, combine the melon and strawberries and toss gently to mix. Strain the chile-lime syrup through a fine-mesh sieve into the bowl and toss gently to coat. Refrigerate until well chilled, at least 2 hours and up to 6 hours. Serve cold.

Cook's Tip: This fruit dessert has a sugar syrup that's lightly spiked with fresh chile. It's not spicy at all with the chile pepper cut in half, but adds a warm flavor to the fruit. If you'd like it spicier, just chop the pepper coarsely before adding it.

Makes 4 servings

PEAR-CARDAMOM UPSIDE-DOWN CAKE

Serve with a Wheat Beer, such as Michelob Bavarian Style Wheat

2 tablespoons unsalted butter, plus 4 tablespoons at room temperature

¹/₄ cup firmly packed brown sugar

¹/₄ teaspoon ground cardamom

2 Bartlett or Anjou pears, peeled, cored, and each cut into 12 wedges

1¹/₂ cups all-purpose flour

2 teaspoons baking powder

¹/₄ teaspoon ground cardamom

¹/₈ teaspoon salt

³/₄ cup granulated sugar

2 large eggs

³/₄ cup milk

1 teaspoon vanilla extract

1 Preheat the oven to 350°F. Lightly butter a 9-inch round cake pan.

2 In a small skillet, melt the 2 tablespoons butter over medium heat. Add the brown sugar and cardamom. Cook, stirring constantly, until the sugar dissolves, about 3 minutes. Pour the sugar mixture into the prepared cake pan. Arrange the pears in an overlapping circle over the sugar mixture. Set aside.

3 In a large bowl, sift together the flour, baking powder, cardamom, and salt, stirring well with a whisk.

4 In another large bowl, combine the granulated sugar and 4 tablespoons butter, beating with an electric mixer set on medium speed until well blended. Add the eggs and beat until blended. Add the flour mixture to the egg mixture alternately with the milk, beginning and ending with the flour mixture. Stir in the vanilla. Spoon the batter into the center of the cake pan and gently spread the batter to cover the pears evenly.

5 Bake until a toothpick inserted in the center comes out clean, about 50 minutes. Let cool in the pan on a wire rack for 10 minutes, then run a knife around the edge. Place a serving plate upside down on top of the pan and invert onto the plate. Let stand for 2 minutes before removing the pan. Cut into wedges and serve warm.

Cook's Tip: An ideal spice for sweet, juicy pears, cardamom has a pronounced, slightly spicy flavor similar to ginger. This cake is best served warm.

Makes 8 servings

RASPBERRY CHEESECAKE

Serve with an American-Style Light Lager, such as Michelob Light

CRUST

1 cup graham cracker crumbs

3 tablespoons sugar

3 tablespoons unsalted butter, melted

FILLING

1 cup seedless raspberry preserves

5 packages (8 ounces each) cream cheese, at room temperature

1 cup sugar

3 tablespoons all-purpose flour

1 tablespoon vanilla extract

1 cup sour cream

4 large eggs

2 cups fresh raspberries

1 Preheat the oven to 325°F. Butter the bottom and sides of a 9-inch springform pan.

2 To prepare the crust, in a bowl, combine the graham cracker crumbs, sugar, and melted butter, stirring well. Press the mixture firmly into the bottom of the prepared pan. Bake until dry, about 10 minutes. Remove from the oven and leave the oven on.

3 To prepare the filling, in a small saucepan over low heat, stir the raspberry preserves until melted. Remove from the heat and set aside. In a large bowl, with an electric mixer set on medium speed, beat together the cream cheese, sugar, flour, and vanilla until well blended. Add the sour cream and beat until well blended. Add the eggs one at a time, beating in each one just until blended.

4 Pour the filling into the crust. Pour the melted raspberry preserves slowly over the filling and use a wooden skewer to swirl it into a pretty pattern.

5 Bake until the center is set, about 1 hour and 15 minutes. Transfer to a wire rack and let cool. Run a knife around the rim of the pan to loosen the cheesecake, then remove the sides of the pan. Refrigerate for at least 5 hours or up to overnight.

6 Cut into wedges and serve cold with the fresh raspberries alongside.

Cook's Tip: This is one of Chef Sam Niemann's signature desserts.

Makes 8 servings

PINEAPPLE-CARROT CAKE

 Serve with an American-Style Amber Lager, such as Michelob Amber Bock

1 cup walnut halves

½ cup (1 stick) unsalted butter, at room temperature

1 cup granulated sugar

½ cup firmly packed brown sugar

4 large eggs

½ cup coconut oil, melted, or vegetable oil

2 cups pastry flour

2 teaspoons baking soda

1½ teaspoons ground cinnamon

1 teaspoon ground ginger

½ teaspoon salt

1 cup fresh or well-drained canned pineapple chunks, coarsely chopped

1 cup large-flake unsweetened coconut (see Cook's Tip)

3 cups peeled and grated carrots (about 4 large)

Confectioners' sugar

1 Preheat the oven to 325°F. Spread the walnuts in a single layer on a small baking sheet. Bake until lightly browned and fragrant, 8 to 10 minutes. Transfer to a plate and let cool, then coarsely chop. Set aside.

2 Butter the bottom and sides of a 10-inch spring-form pan. Line the bottom with a circle of parchment paper, then dust the sides with flour. Tap out the excess.

3 In a large bowl, with an electric mixer set on medium-high speed, beat together the butter, granulated sugar, and brown sugar until light and fluffy. Add the eggs, one at a time, beating well after each addition. Beat until thick and light, about 2 minutes. Add the oil in a thin, steady stream and beat until blended.

4 In a bowl, whisk together the flour, baking soda, cinnamon, ginger, and salt. Slowly add the flour mixture to the butter mixture, beating on low speed just until blended. Stir in the walnuts, pineapple, coconut, and carrots. Scrape the batter into the prepared pan.

5 Bake until a toothpick inserted in the center of the cake comes out dry, 75 to 90 minutes. Transfer to a wire rack and let cool. When cool, remove from the pan, peel off the parchment, and place on a cake plate. Dust with the confectioners' sugar and serve.

Cook's Tip: This is one of those dense, moist cakes that actually improves in flavor as it stands. It keeps very well for a few days, well wrapped. This recipe calls for large-flake dried coconut, not the more usual small flakes; you can find it in the bulk section of well-stocked supermarkets or in natural-food stores.

Makes 12 servings

Beer for Breakfast—Well into the seventeenth century, it's believed, most Europeans drank a glass of beer at breakfast. It wasn't until the following century that a caffeinated beverage, tea, took over.

LEMON POLENTA CAKE

Serve with a Wheat Beer, such as Michelob Bavarian Style Wheat

1¼ cups all-purpose flour

1 cup sugar

½ cup yellow cornmeal

½ teaspoon baking soda

¼ teaspoon salt

⅔ cup buttermilk

¼ cup extra-virgin olive oil

2 large eggs

2 teaspoons grated lemon zest

1 cup unsweetened apple juice

½ cup golden raisins

½ cup fresh cranberries

2 pears, peeled, cored, and finely chopped (1¾ cups)

2 teaspoons fresh lemon juice

1 Preheat the oven to 350°F. Butter an 8-inch round cake pan, line the bottom with parchment paper, and butter the paper. In a large bowl, combine the dry ingredients, stirring well. Make a well in the center of the mixture. In another bowl, combine the buttermilk, olive oil, eggs, and lemon zest. Add the buttermilk mixture to the flour mixture, stirring until moist. Pour the batter into the prepared pan.

2 Bake until a toothpick inserted in the center comes out clean, about 40 minutes. Let cool in the pan for 10 minutes, then remove from the pan and let cool completely.

3 In a saucepan, combine the apple juice and raisins over medium-high heat and bring to a boil. Lower the heat to medium and cook until reduced to ⅔ cup, about 5 minutes. Add the cranberries and cook until they pop. Add the pears and cook until tender. Remove from the heat and stir in the lemon juice. Cut the cake into wedges and serve with the warm compote.

Makes 8 servings

GINGERBREAD CAKE

Serve with a Dry Stout, such as Bare Knuckle Stout

1 cup dry stout

1 cup dark molasses (not blackstrap)

1 teaspoon baking soda

2½ cups all-purpose flour

2 tablespoons ground ginger

2 teaspoons ground cinnamon

1 teaspoon ground allspice

½ teaspoon salt

1½ cups finely chopped crystallized ginger

1½ cups unsalted butter, melted and cooled

1 cup firmly packed dark brown sugar

2 large eggs, lightly beaten

1½ tablespoons grated lemon zest

Confectioners' sugar for dusting

1 cup heavy cream

2 tablespoons granulated sugar

1 Preheat the oven to 325°F. Butter two 8-inch square glass baking dishes. In a deep saucepan, combine the stout and dark molasses over medium-high heat and bring to a boil. Remove from the heat and whisk in the baking soda (it will foam up). Set aside and let cool.

2 In a bowl, combine the flour, ginger, cinnamon, allspice, and salt. In a bowl, combine 1 cup of the crystallized ginger, the melted butter, and brown sugar. Stir in the eggs and lemon zest. Stir in the flour mixture in four additions alternating with the stout mixture. Pour the batter into the baking dishes, dividing evenly. Bake until a toothpick inserted in the centers comes out clean, 30 to 40 minutes. Let cool completely, dust the tops with confectioners' sugar, and cut each into 6 squares.

3 In a bowl, combine the cream and granulated sugar, beating until soft peaks form. Stir in all but 1 teaspoon of the remaining crystallized ginger. Serve the cream with the cake, sprinkled with the last bit of ginger.

Makes 12 servings

WALNUT-CARAMEL TART

 Serve with a Porter, such as Michelob Porter

³/₄ cup (1¹/₂ sticks) unsalted butter, at room temperature

¹/₄ cup firmly packed brown sugar

1 large egg yolk

¹/₂ teaspoon vanilla extract

1¹/₂ cups all-purpose flour

³/₄ teaspoon salt

2³/₄ cups walnut halves

1³/₄ cups granulated sugar

2 tablespoons light corn syrup

¹/₂ cup crème fraîche or heavy cream

1 Preheat the oven to 350°F. Have ready a 9-inch fluted tart pan with removable rim.

2 In a bowl, combine ¹/₂ cup of the butter and the brown sugar, beating with an electric mixer set on medium speed until smooth. Beat in the egg yolk and vanilla. Add the flour and ¹/₄ teaspoon of the salt and beat until the mixture forms a ball.

3 Press the dough evenly over the bottom and up the sides to the rim of the tart pan. Freeze until firm, about 15 minutes.

4 Meanwhile, spread the walnuts in a large baking pan. Bake until lightly golden under the skins (break one to test), about 8 minutes. Remove from the oven and let cool. Leave oven set at 350°F. When the walnuts are cool enough to handle, chop 2 cups and set aside; reserve the remaining walnut halves for garnish.

5 Bake the chilled tart shell until golden, 16 to 18 minutes. Let cool on a wire rack.

6 Meanwhile, in a large saucepan, combine the granulated sugar, corn syrup, and ¹/₄ cup water over medium heat. Stir until the sugar is dissolved, then raise the heat to high and boil, swirling occasionally, until the mixture is a deep golden brown, 10 to 15 minutes. Remove from the heat and stir in the crème fraîche, the remaining ¹/₄ cup butter, and the remaining ¹/₂ teaspoon salt (the mixture will foam). Stir until smooth.

7 Spread the chopped walnuts in the tart shell, then pour in the hot caramel and spread evenly. Garnish the edge of the tart with the reserved walnut halves. Let the tart cool completely until the caramel is firm enough to slice, at least 4 hours, or refrigerate for up to 2 days (bring to room temperature before serving). Cut into thin wedges and serve.

Cook's Tip: A press-in crust makes this tart a snap to prepare.

Makes 12 servings

FALLEN CHOCOLATE CAKE with CHERRIES

Serve with a Chocolate-Flavored Specialty Beer, such as Michelob Celebrate Chocolate

1/2 cup shelled pistachios

1 1/4 cups sugar

4 ounces bittersweet chocolate, coarsely chopped

Pinch of salt

1/2 cup unsweetened cocoa powder

3 large eggs

1/2 teaspoon vanilla extract

1/8 teaspoon almond extract

4 large egg whites

2 cups fresh cherries

1 Preheat the oven to 350°F. Butter a 9-inch round springform pan.

2 Place the pistachios in a food processor and process until finely ground. Sprinkle the ground pistachios over the bottom of the springform pan.

3 In a saucepan over high heat, combine 1 cup of the sugar and 1/4 cup water and bring to a boil. Remove from the heat and stir in the chocolate and salt until the chocolate is melted. Add the cocoa powder, stirring until well blended. Beat in the whole eggs, one at a time, stirring well after each addition. Stir in the vanilla and almond extracts.

4 Beat the egg whites with an electric mixer set on high speed until foamy. Gradually add the remaining 1/4 cup sugar, 1 tablespoon at a time, beating until stiff peaks form. Gently stir one-fourth of the egg white mixture into the chocolate mixture and gently fold in the remaining egg white mixture. Spoon the mixture into the prepared pan. Bake until a toothpick inserted in the center comes out nearly clean, about 25 minutes. Transfer to a wire rack and let cool. Run a knife around the edge of the cake to loosen it, then remove the sides of the pan. Serve with the fresh cherries.

Cook's Tip: To achieve the cake's fudgy texture, be sure to pull it from the oven when the toothpick comes out nearly clean.

Makes 8 servings

MIXED BERRY SHORTCAKES

Serve with a Wheat Beer, such as Michelob Bavarian Style Wheat

SHORTCAKES

1¹/₂ cups all-purpose flour, plus more for dusting

¹/₄ cup sugar, plus 1 teaspoon

1 tablespoon baking powder

¹/₄ teaspoon salt

6 tablespoons unsalted butter, cut into chunks

³/₄ cup heavy cream

FILLING

4 cups mixed berries, large berries cut into bite-size pieces

3 tablespoons sugar

³/₄ cup heavy cream

¹/₂ teaspoon vanilla extract

1 To make the shortcakes, preheat the oven to 375°F. In a bowl, combine the 1¹/₂ cups flour, the ¹/₄ cup sugar, the baking powder, and the salt. Add the butter and cut into the flour mixture using a pastry blender, 2 knives, or your fingers until fine crumbs form. Add the cream and stir with a fork just until a soft dough comes together.

2 On a lightly floured work surface, knead the dough just until smooth, 3 or 4 turns. Dust the surface with more flour and roll the dough out into a 4-by-8-inch rectangle. With a floured knife or fluted cutter, cut into 6 equal rectangles. Space the rectangles 2 inches apart on a large baking sheet. Sprinkle evenly with the 1 teaspoon sugar.

3 Bake until the shortcakes are a deep, golden brown, 20 to 25 minutes. Let cool on the baking sheet for at least 15 minutes.

4 While the shortcakes are baking, in a bowl, gently toss the berries with 2 tablespoons of the sugar for the filling. In another bowl, with an electric mixer set on medium-high speed, beat together the cream, the remaining 1 tablespoon sugar, and the vanilla until soft peaks form. Cover and refrigerate.

5 With a serrated knife, split the shortcakes in half horizontally. Place the bottoms, cut side up, on individual plates. Mound the berries and whipped cream on the bottoms. Set the tops, cut side down, on the fruit and cream and serve immediately.

Cook's Tip: You can prepare these shortcakes through step 3 up to 1 day in advance of serving. Let them cool completely, then store in an airtight container at room temperature. Use a colorful mix of berries here.

Makes 6 servings

OAT BLONDIES with CARAMEL SAUCE

 Serve with a Porter, such as Michelob Porter

1¹⁄₂ cups all-purpose flour

¹⁄₂ cup quick-cooking oats

1 teaspoon baking powder

¹⁄₄ teaspoon salt

1 cup firmly packed brown sugar

¹⁄₃ cup unsalted butter, at room temperature

3 large eggs, lightly beaten

¹⁄₃ cup mini semisweet chocolate chips

1 teaspoon vanilla extract

CARAMEL SAUCE

¹⁄₂ cup butter

1 cup sugar

¹⁄₂ cup heavy cream

2 teaspoons vanilla extract

1 Preheat the oven to 350°F. Lightly butter a 9-inch square baking pan. In a bowl, combine the flour, oats, baking powder, and salt, stirring with a whisk.

2 In another bowl, combine the brown sugar and butter, beating with a mixer at medium speed until well blended. Add the eggs and beat well. Add the flour mixture and beat just until combined. Stir in the chocolate chips and vanilla. Spoon the batter into the prepared pan. Bake until a toothpick inserted in the center comes out clean, about 25 minutes. Let cool on a wire rack.

3 To prepare the sauce, in a small, heavy saucepan, melt the butter and sugar over medium heat, stirring constantly. Add the cream. Bring to a boil, then cook for 1 minute or until slightly thickened, stirring constantly. Stir in the vanilla. Pour the mixture into a bowl and refrigerate for 1 hour. Drizzle the caramel sauce over the cooled blondies, then cut into 16 squares.

Makes 16 squares

TRIPLE-CHOCOLATE BROWNIES

Serve with a Chocolate-Flavored Specialty Beer, such as Michelob Celebrate Chocolate

3 ounces bittersweet chocolate, chopped

¹⁄₂ cup (1 stick) unsalted butter

1 cup firmly packed light brown sugar

1 teaspoon vanilla extract

2 large eggs, lightly beaten

¹⁄₂ cup all-purpose flour

¹⁄₄ cup unsweetened cocoa powder (not Dutch-processed)

¹⁄₂ teaspoon salt

1 cup semisweet chocolate chips

1 Preheat the oven to 350°F. Lightly butter an 8-inch square baking pan.

2 In the top of a double boiler or in a large heatproof bowl set over a pan of barely simmering water (but not touching it), melt the bittersweet chocolate and butter, stirring until smooth. Stir in the brown sugar and vanilla. Remove the bowl or pan from over the water and whisk in the eggs. Add the flour, cocoa, and salt, mixing until smooth. Stir in the chocolate chips. Pour the batter into the prepared baking pan.

3 Bake until a toothpick inserted in the center comes out with moist crumbs sticking to it, 20 to 25 minutes. Transfer to a wire rack and let cool, then cut into 16 squares.

Cook's Tip: If you like super-chocolaty, fudgy brownies, these are for you.

Makes 16 squares

BLACK-and-WHITE COOKIES

 Serve with a Honey-Flavored Specialty Beer, such as Michelob Honey Lager

12 ounces bittersweet or semisweet chocolate, chopped

³/₄ cup (1¹/₂ sticks) unsalted butter, cut into chunks

1¹/₂ cups sugar

3 large eggs

2 teaspoons vanilla extract

2¹/₄ cups all-purpose flour

1¹/₂ teaspoons baking powder

¹/₂ teaspoon baking soda

¹/₂ teaspoon salt

8 to 10 ounces coarsely chopped white chocolate or 2 cups white chocolate chips

1 Preheat the oven to 325°F. Lightly butter one or two 15-by-12-inch baking sheets or line with parchment paper.

2 In a large heatproof bowl set over a pan of barely simmering water (but not touching it), melt the bittersweet chocolate and butter, stirring until smooth, about 5 minutes. Remove the bowl from over the water and whisk in the sugar, eggs, and vanilla.

3 In another bowl, combine the flour, baking powder, baking soda, and salt, stirring with a whisk. Add the flour mixture to the chocolate mixture and stir until well blended. Stir in the white chocolate. Cover and refrigerate until firm, at least 1 hour.

4 Shape the chilled dough into 2-inch balls and place about 3 inches apart on the prepared baking sheet(s). Bake until the cookies are set at the edges but still soft in the center, 12 to 15 minutes. (If baking more than one pan at a time, switch pan positions halfway through baking.) Let cool for 5 minutes on the pans, then transfer to wire racks and let cool completely.

Makes about 28 cookies

TUSCAN ALMOND BISCOTTI

Serve with a Porter, such as Michelob Porter

1³/₄ cups all-purpose flour

1 cup sugar

1 teaspoon baking powder

¹/₄ teaspoon salt

1 cup whole almonds, toasted

2 large eggs

¹/₂ teaspoon almond extract

1 Preheat the oven to 375°F. Lightly butter a baking sheet.

2 In a large bowl, combine the flour, sugar, baking powder, and salt, stirring with a whisk. Place the almonds in a food processor and pulse 10 times. Stir the nuts into the flour mixture.

3 In a small bowl, combine the eggs and almond extract, stirring well with a whisk. Add the egg mixture to the flour mixture, stirring just until blended (the dough will be crumbly).

4 Turn the dough out onto a lightly floured surface and knead lightly 7 or 8 times. Divide the dough into 2 equal portions. Shape each portion into a log 6 inches long. Place the logs 6 inches apart on the prepared baking sheet and pat to 1 inch thick.

5 Bake until lightly browned, about 25 minutes. Let cool for 5 minutes on a wire rack. Leave the oven set at 375°F.

6 Cut each log crosswise into 12 slices ¹/₂ inch thick. Lay the slices on the baking sheet. Bake for 14 minutes longer (the cookies will be slightly soft in the center but will harden as they cool). Remove from the baking sheet and let cool completely on the wire rack.

Makes 24 biscotti

READER'S RESOURCE

Anheuser-Busch brews a wide variety of beers, from hoppy, fresh American-style premium lagers to rich, malty ales. The company also imports and distributes a number of other popular brands from around the world. While most of these beers are available all year around, a handful are seasonal specialties.

AMERICAN-STYLE PREMIUM LAGER

BUDWEISER

Introduced in 1876, Budweiser has fresh and subtle fruit notes, a delicate malt sweetness, and balanced bitterness for a clean, "snappy" finish. It is a medium-bodied, flavorful, crisp, and pure beer with blended layers of premium American and European hop aromas.

MICHELOB

Introduced in 1896, Michelob is a malty and full-bodied lager with an elegant European hop profile. It is brewed traditionally for full, distinctive, and classic character.

BUDWEISER SELECT

Introduced in 2005, Budweiser Select is a distinctive and sophisticated full-flavored beer with fine hop aroma, bold caramel malt flavor, and a refreshingly clean finish.

MICHELOB GOLDEN DRAFT

Introduced in 1991, Michelob Golden Draft offers light fruit and malt aromas, which complement its medium-body, slightly sweet taste, and exceptionally smooth finish.

BUSCH

Introduced in 1955, Busch offers a refreshingly smooth taste with a pleasant hop aroma and a smooth, slightly sweet finish.

ROLLING ROCK

Introduced in 1939 and acquired by Anheuser-Busch in 2006, Rolling Rock is a balanced and medium-light bodied lager with a unique and flavorful malt character that lends to its distinctive taste and subtle hop finish.

BUD LIGHT

Introduced in 1982, Bud Light is a light-bodied brew with a fresh, clean, and subtle hop aroma, delicate malt sweetness, and crisp finish for ultimate refreshment.

BUSCH LIGHT

Introduced in 1989, Busch Light offers light, balanced flavor with fewer calories than the original Busch lager. It has a pleasant hop aroma and a smooth, slightly sweet finish.

MICHELOB GOLDEN DRAFT LIGHT

Introduced in 1991, Michelob Golden Draft Light offers light fruit and malt aromas, which complement its medium-body, slightly sweet taste, and exceptionally smooth finish.

MICHELOB LIGHT

Introduced in 1978, Michelob Light is a full-flavored and rich-tasting light lager offering a malty sweetness and aromatic hop profile with surprisingly low calories and carbohydrate content. It is brewed traditionally for full, distinctive, and classic character.

MICHELOB ULTRA

Introduced in 2002, Michelob Ultra has subtle fruit and citrus aromas that complement its light-body and smooth, refreshing taste.

EUROPEAN-STYLE PILSNER

GROLSCH

Introduced in 1615 and imported by Anheuser-Busch since 2006, Grolsch offers a smooth, crisp and full-bodied classic European lager taste.

HARBIN

Introduced in 2006, Harbin Lager offers a complex floral and fruity hop aroma from the use of the unique "Qindao Dahua" aroma hop variety grown in China's remote Northwestern Regions. This distinctive hop character is layered on a balanced and round malty body and has a crisp finish.

KIRIN ICHIBAN

Introduced in 1990, Kirin Ichiban has a smooth, full-bodied, and refreshing taste.

EUROPEAN-STYLE PILSNER continued

TIGER

Introduced in 1932 and imported by Anheuser-Busch since 2006, Tiger is a smooth, full-flavored beer with classic hop character and malty body.

WHEAT BEER

MICHELOB BAVARIAN STYLE WHEAT

Introduced in 1997, Michelob Bavarian Style Wheat is an unfiltered wheat beer that is lightly hopped and fermented using a unique yeast strain to create characteristic banana and clove aromas.

AMERICAN-STYLE AMBER LAGER

MICHELOB AMBER BOCK

Introduced in 1995, Michelob Amber Bock is a rich, full-bodied beer with mild caramel malt undertones, subtle spice, and citrus-like European hop aromas. It is deep amber in color and has a roasted, malty taste that finishes clean.

AMERICAN-STYLE LIGHT AMBER LAGER

MICHELOB ULTRA AMBER

Introduced in 2006, Michelob Ultra Amber features a beautifully rich, deep amber color with a complex, malty, full-flavored taste that is also low in calories and carbohydrates.

ENGLISH-STYLE PALE ALE

MICHELOB PALE ALE

Introduced in 1997, Michelob Pale Ale is a classic English-style pale ale brewed with noble aroma hop varieties grown in the Northwestern United States and Europe and two-row and caramel barley malts. This beer is dark gold in color and has a spicy, hoppy character.

MAERZEN AND OKTOBERFEST

MICHELOB MARZEN

Introduced in 1997, Michelob Marzen is a German-style Marzen brewed according to a traditional German recipe. Two-row and Munich barley malts are used to create a rich, full-bodied beer with an amber color and malty aroma.

DOPPELBOCK

BREWMASTER'S PRIVATE RESERVE

Introduced in 2005, Brewmaster's Private Reserve is a smooth, all-malt lager with a distinctive honey color and robust taste. Based on the tradition of collecting the richest part of the brew from the brew kettles, this rich, flavorful reserve, available seasonally, is prized for its unusual smoothness despite its robust alcohol content (8.5% alcohol by volume).

SPECIALTY BEER

MICHELOB CELEBRATE CHOCOLATE

Introduced in 2006, Michelob Celebrate Chocolate is brewed with caramel and roasted malts and matured on cocoa beans. This robust beer (8.5% alcohol by volume) has a deep, dark chocolate color and aroma and is available seasonally.

MICHELOB HONEY LAGER

Introduced in 1997, Michelob Honey Lager is brewed using the finest two-row and caramel barley malts, a blend of aromatic European imported hops, and a touch of natural wildflower honey to enhance the naturally round, malty, and slightly sweet flavor of the beer.

PORTER

MICHELOB PORTER

Introduced in 1997, Michelob Porter is brewed using the finest aroma hop varieties grown in the Northwestern United States and two-row, caramel, and chocolate barley malts, giving it an aroma of coffee and a hint of chocolate. It is dark brown in color with ruby-red highlights.

DRY STOUT

BARE KNUCKLE STOUT

Introduced in 2004, Bare Knuckle Stout has a smooth Irish character with rich taste, a creamy head, and exceptional drinkability. Full notes of coffee and chocolate with roasted malt are balanced with robust hopping for a full-flavored and satisfying stout.

INDEX

RECIPES BY TYPE OF BEER

American-Style Premium Lager
Beechwood-Smoked St. Louis Strip, 189
Beef Rib Roast with Rosemary, 198
Beer-Basted Grilled Angus Strip, 194
Beer-Braised Shrimp, 194
Bratwurst with Caramelized Onions, 170
Buttermilk Oven-Fried Okra, 249
Cajun Jambalaya with Wild Rice, 126
Carrot, Feta, and Black Olive Salad, 56
Cheesy Pigs-in-a-Blanket, 40
Chicken Fried Steak with Cream Gravy, 186
Corn and Tomato Salad, 55
Cornmeal-Crusted Catfish, 81
Creamy Lager and Jalapeño Soup, 51
Deviled Chicken Wings, 105
Gorgonzola Burgers, 177
Grilled Chicken with Chipotle-Lime Butter, 102
Grilled Corn, 242
Grilled Lobster with Beer Butter, 89
Grilled Snapper Packets, 78
Grilled Trout with Bacon and Spinach, 66
Lemon-Garlic Shrimp Skewers, 82
Mesquite-Grilled Chicken, 109
Orzo with Summer Vegetables, 229
Pasta with Scallops, Tomatoes, and Capers, 86
Pork Chops with Carolina Rub, 165
Ranch Chili, 210
Salmon with Cream and Fresh Chives, 70
Smoke-Roasted Chicken, 110
Spanish-Style Shrimp with Garlic, 39
Spicy Pork Ribs, 166
Spring Vegetable Macaroni and Cheese, 233
Turkey Meatball Subs, 146
Upland Game Chili, 142
Zesty Bean Salad, 261

American-Style Light Lager
Garlic-Poblano Guacamole, 47
Garlic-Stuffed Mushrooms, 44
Garlicky Broccoli Rabe, 238
Grilled Green Tomatoes with Salsa, 245
Lamb with Yogurt-Mint Sauce, 214
Light Swedish Meatballs, 134
Marinated Cucumber Salad, 55
Melon and Berries in Chile-Lime Syrup, 270
Mussels and Clams with Green Curry, 85
Oven-Fried Chicken, 106
Pork Skewers with Moroccan Spices, 161
Raspberry Cheesecake, 274
Real Grilled Cheese Sandwiches, 234

Roasted Red Peppers with Garlic, 44
Salmon with Picholine Olives, 73
Seared Chicken with Tomatillo Salsa, 105
Spicy Shrimp Cakes with Corn Salsa, 28
Steak Tacos with Green Salsa, 181
Tuna Ceviche with Cumin and Chile, 35

European-Style Pilsner
Baja-Style Fried Fish Tacos, 69
Beef Pot Roast with Gremolata, 202
Braised Pork with Lemon and Sage, 153
Chicken Divan, 117
Chicken with Sesame Noodles, 118
Classic Cioppino, 89
Cuban Pork with Pineapple, 162
Game Hens with Tapenade, 138
Garlic Smashed Potato Salad, 253
Ginger Beef Mini Skewers, 40
Hoisin Pork and Snow Pea Stir-Fry, 154
Hot-and-Sour Asian Beef Salad, 174
Lemongrass Roasted Chicken, 106
Melon, Serrano, and Arugula Salad, 59
Mussels and Oven Fries, 35
Parmesan-Breaded Turkey Cutlets, 145
Pork Pot Stickers, 43
Rigatoni with Green Olive–Almond Pesto, 230
Spicy Rice Noodles with Chicken, 122
Striped Bass with Lemongrass, 77
Teriyaki Chicken Wings, 39
Thai Satay with Pineapple Relish, 94
Vietnamese Skewers with Dipping Sauce, 173

Wheat Beer
Apple Bars with Dates and Pecans, 269
Baked Bananas with Tropical Flavors, 269
Chicken Stew with Olives and Lemon, 133
Green Chile Chicken Stew, 129
Lemon Polenta Cake, 278
Lemony Couscous with Mint and Feta, 262
Mixed Berry Shortcakes, 285
Moroccan Vegetable Stew, 225
Orange-Olive Chicken Scaloppine, 98
Pear and Cranberry Stuffed Pork Roast, 157
Pear-Cardamom Upside-Down Cake, 273
Roast Chicken with Wild Rice Stuffing, 113
Roasted Beet and Citrus Salad, 60
Sausage and Cabbage Soup, 52
Seared Salmon with Almonds and Orange, 70
Shrimp Wraps with Lime Dipping Sauce, 31

Spice-Rubbed Pork with Tomatoes, 161
Swordfish with Sicilian Flavors, 81

American-Style Amber Lager

Ale-Baked Beans, 261
Bistec Argentino al Chimichurri, 182
Chicken Skewers with Onion and Bay, 94
Chicken with Amber Lager and Honey, 109
Corn Pancakes with Smoked Salmon, 32
Crisp Roast Duck, 141
Green Bean and Hazelnut Salad, 60
Grill-Baked Apple Crisp, 266
Grilled Amber Duck, 141
Grilled Spicy Sweet-Potato Packets, 258
Grilled Tuna Niçoise, 65
Leek and Chanterelle Tart, 222
Mushroom, Barley, and Beef Soup, 209
New England–Style Pot Roast, 206
Pasta with Sausage and Broccoli Rabe, 121
Pepper Steaks with Balsamic Onions, 193
Pineapple-Carrot Cake, 277
Pork Chops with Country Gravy, 165
Pork Loin Braised with Cabbage, 154
T-Bones with Fennel and Salt, 190
Warm Artichoke and Amber Bock Dip, 47

American-Style Light Amber Lager

Chicken and Potato Soup with Dumplings, 125
Chicken Stew with Saffron, 130
Fingerling Potatoes with Smoked Trout, 254
Grilled Veal Chops with Mustard, 198
Grilled Vegetables, 242
Orecchiette with Corn and Chiles, 226
Pulled Chicken Sandwiches, 137
Roasted Red Pepper and Tomato Soup, 52
Spinach with Pine Nuts and Raisins, 241

English-Style Pale Ale

Brussels Sprouts with Parmesan, 241
Chicken Stew with Mushrooms and Ale, 130
Chile Verde, 150
Escarole and White Bean Soup, 51
Grilled Game Hens with Herbs, 138
Grilled Portobello Burgers, 234
Hearty Beef and Tomato Stew, 201
Lamb Rib Chops with Couscous, 217
Leafy Greens with Polenta, 226
Lemon Sole with Lemon-Caper Sauce, 77
Moroccan-Style Beef Kebabs, 173
Mushroom-Stuffed Filet of Beef, 197
Northwest Waldorf Salad, 59
Pale Ale Shepherd's Pie, 218
Penne with Triple Tomato Sauce, 230
Quesadilla with Cranberry Chutney, 142

Roadhouse Steaks with Ancho Chile Rub, 186
Roast Chicken with Balsamic Glaze, 114
Roasted Asparagus with Lemon, 238
Seared Snapper Provençale, 78
Shrimp Garam Masala, 85
Slow-Cooker Chicken Paprikash, 134
Spicy Shredded Beef Sandwiches, 178
Swiss Chard and Ricotta Calzones, 237
Turkey Sausage with White Beans, 146
The Ultimate Bacon, Lettuce, and Tomato, 170
Veal Stew with Leeks and Ale, 213
Warm Potato Salad, 254

Maerzen and Oktoberfest

Barley with Bell Peppers and Maerzen, 262
Maerzen-Braised Short Ribs, 190
Roasted Fall Vegetables, 246
Sausage and Potato Skillet, 178

Doppelbock

Creamy Cumin Potato Gratin, 253
Flank Steak with Chermoula, 185
Grilled Salmon with Chermoula Sauce, 74
Spiced Chicken Kebabs, 97

Specialty Beer

Black-and-White Cookies, 289
Chile-Lamb Stew with Sweet Squash, 218
Fallen Chocolate Cake with Cherries, 282
Scalloped Vidalia Onions, 249
Triple-Chocolate Brownies, 286
Warm Spinach Salad with Apples and Bacon, 56

Porter

Baked Polenta with Sausage and Tomato, 169
Baked Potatoes with Caramelized Onions, 257
Moroccan Lamb Chops, 217
Mushroom-Potato Soup with Paprika, 48
Oat Blondies with Caramel Sauce, 286
Peach-Blackberry Clafouti, 270
Pork Medallions with Porcini Sauce, 158
Scallops with Black Bean Sauce, 86
Spicy Chicken with Sweet Peppers, 101
Tuscan Almond Biscotti, 289
Walnut-Caramel Tart, 281

Dry Stout

Baked Potatoes with Gorgonzola, 257
Beer-Braised Beef with Salsa Verde, 205
Chanterelle and Potato Salad, 250
Étoufée with Sausage and Shrimp, 90
Gingerbread Cake, 278
Oysters on the Half Shell, 36

Sunset

Vice President, Editorial Director: Bob Doyle

Director of Sales: Brad Moses

Marketing Manager: Linda Barker

Editor: Val Cipollone

Designer: Catherine Jacobes

Assistant editor: Carrie Dodson Davis

Contributing writers: Jean Galton, Ben Marks,
and Kate Washington

Copyeditors and proofreaders: Desne Ahlers,
Carrie Bradley, and Denise Griffiths

Indexer: Ken DellaPenta

Food stylist: George Dolese

Assistant food stylist: Elisabet Nederlanden

Prop stylist: Emma Star Jensen

Prepress coordinator: Danielle Johnson

Production specialist: Linda M. Bouchard

First edition.
First Printing, October 2007.
10 9 8 7 6 5 4 3 2

ISBN-13: 978-0-376-02048-2
ISBN-10: 0-376-02048-2
Library of Congress Control Number: 2007925940.

Printed in the United States of America.

For additional copies of *The Anheuser-Busch Cookbook—
Great Food, Great Beer* or any other Sunset book, visit us
at www.sunsetbooks.com or call 1-800-526-5111.

ACKNOWLEDGMENTS

We would like to thank the following people at Anheuser-
Busch for their generous assistance in producing this
book: Matt Stroble, Mary Steibel, Mike Amad, Dan
LaRocca, and George Reisch.

Key Consultants
Brent Wertz, CEC, AAC, joined Anheuser-Busch's Kingsmill
Resort & Spa in 2002 and has since attracted an enthu-
siastic following for his innovative beer-pairing menus.
An honors graduate of The Culinary Institute of America,
Executive Chef Wertz contributed recipes for several of
his signature dishes to this book.

Tracy Lauer has spent the past eight years in the archives
of Anheuser-Busch, where she currently serves as Senior
Manager and Curator of Collections. Her department
gives home to an extraordinary collection of historical
photographs, beer industry memorabilia, artifacts and
images—a small sampling of which appears throughout
these pages.

Sam Niemann has been a working chef since 1985 and
an Executive Chef with Anheuser-Busch since 1993. Sam-
plings of his inventive recipes for crowd pleasers such
as Warm Artichoke Dip and Mesquite-Grilled Chicken are
showcased in every chapter of this book. Along with Brent
Wertz, Sam fine-tuned the beer pairing recommendations
that accompany every recipe.

Be sure to visit herestobeer.com